LEVEL 1

문제로 마스터하는 중학영문법

문제로 마스터하는 중학영문법 LEVEL 1

지은이 NE능률 영어교육연구소

연구원 신유승 노지희 박서경 이강혁

영문 교열 Patrick Ferraro Nathaniel Galletta August Niederhaus MyAn Thi Le

디자인 안훈정 오솔길

맥편집 이정임

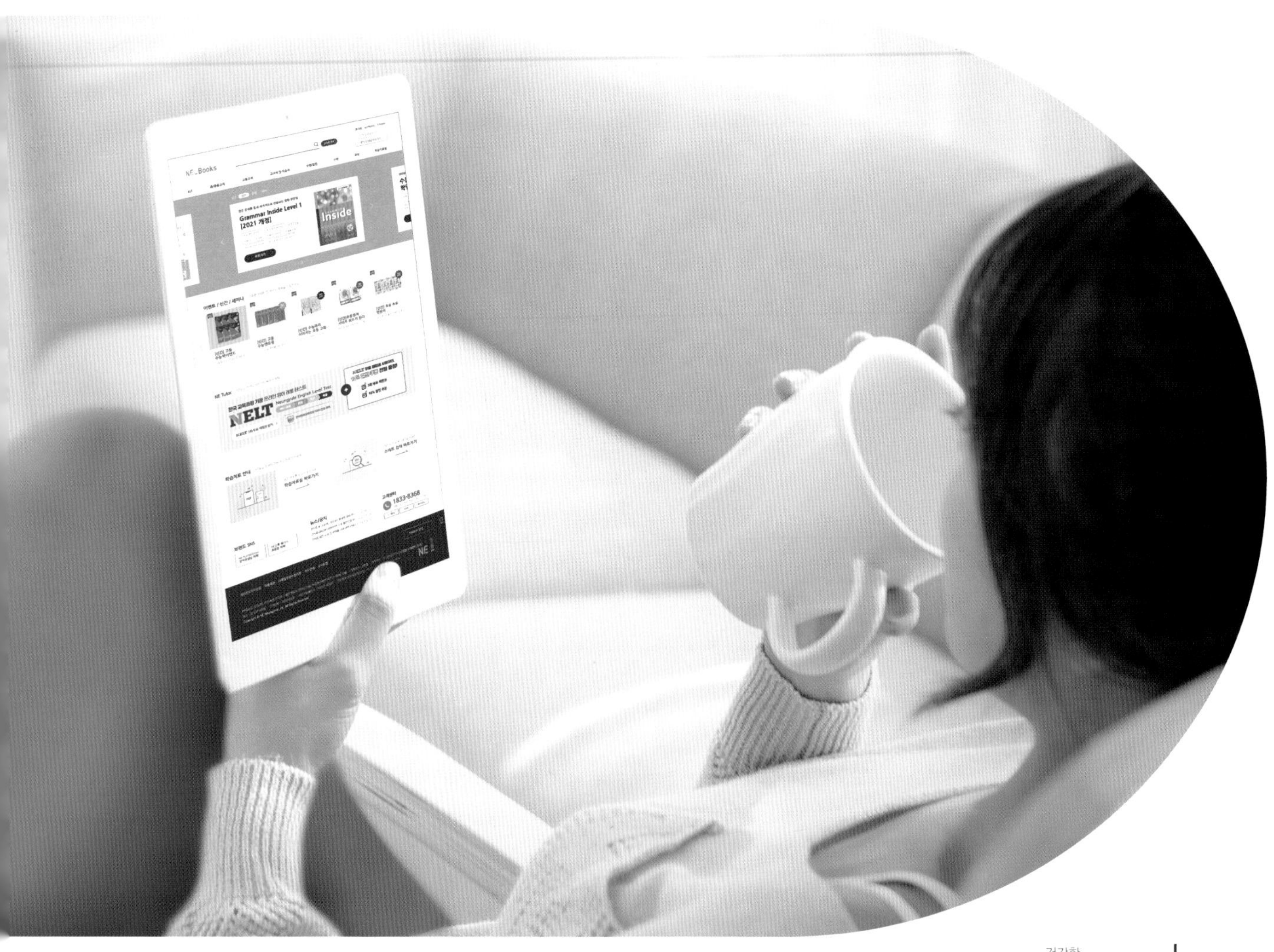

Start where you are.
Use what you have.
Do what you can.

당신이 있는 곳에서 시작하라.
당신이 가진 것을 사용하라.
당신이 할 수 있는 것을 하라.

- Arthur Ashe

Structure & Features

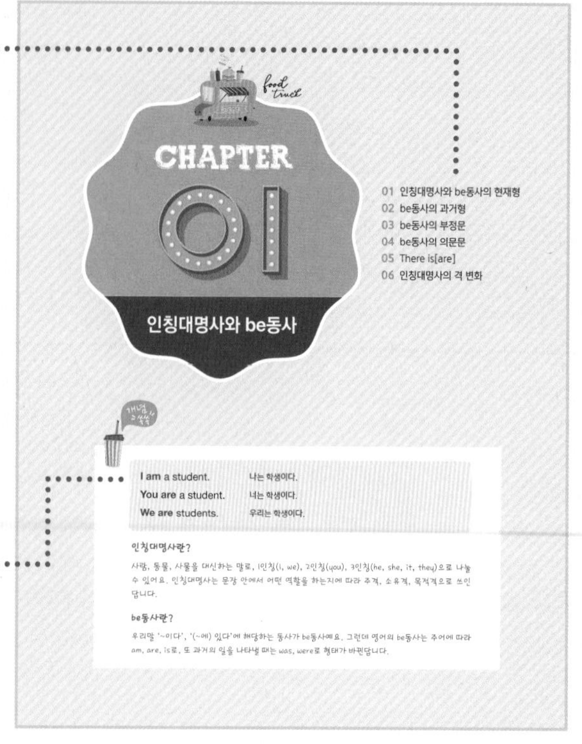

1 자세하게 나뉜 문법 POINT

문법 항목을 세분화하여 그에 따른 각각의 POINT를 제시하였습니다. 각 POINT를 차례대로 학습하면 큰 문법 항목을 보다 쉽게 이해할 수 있습니다.

2 개념 쏙쏙

각 Chapter에서 배울 문법 내용을 한눈에 보기 쉽게 정리하였습니다.

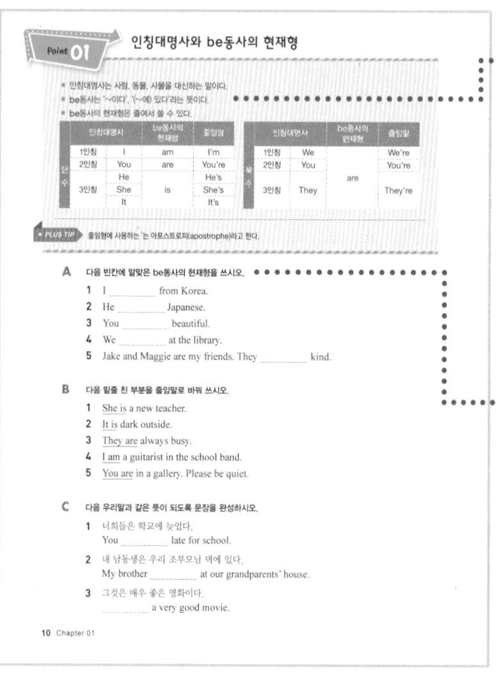

3 핵심만 담은 문법 설명

문법 설명에서 군더더기를 걷어내고, 중학교 과정에서 꼭 배워야 하는 핵심 문법 내용만을 체계적으로 제시하였습니다. <PLUS TIP>과 <내신만점 TIP>을 통해 알아두면 좋은 문법 사항과 기출 포인트를 익힐 수 있습니다.

4 문법 항목별로 주관식 위주의 문제 다수 수록

세분화된 문법 항목별로 많은 수의 주관식 문제를 수록하였습니다. 스스로 써 보는 문제를 많이 풀어 보면서 확실하게 문법에 대한 이해를 점검하고 작문 실력을 향상시킬 수 있으며, 나아가 중학 영문법을 마스터하게 될 것입니다.

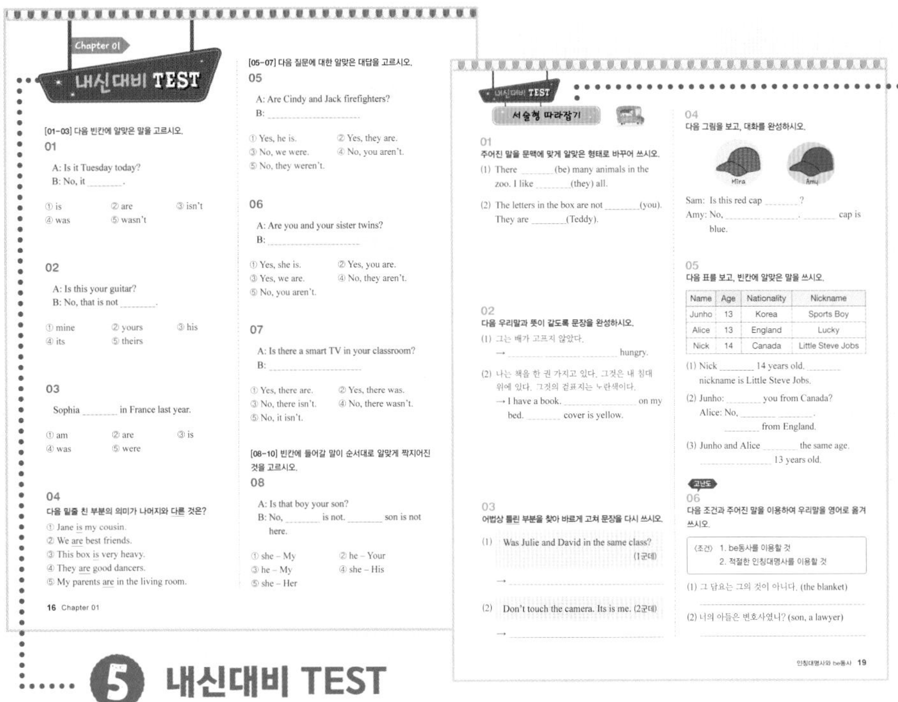

Chapter 01

내신대비 TEST

[01~03] 다음 빈칸에 알맞은 말을 고르시오.

01

A: Is it Tuesday today?
B: No, it ________.

① is ② are ③ isn't ④ was ⑤ wasn't

02

A: Is this your guitar?
B: No, that is not ________.

① mine ② yours ③ his ④ its ⑤ theirs

03

Sophia ________ in France last year.

① am ② are ③ is ④ was ⑤ were

04

다음 밑줄 친 부분의 의미가 나머지와 다른 것은?

① Jane is my cousin.
② We are best friends.
③ This box is very heavy.
④ They are good dancers.
⑤ My parents are in the living room.

[05~07] 다음 질문에 대한 알맞은 대답을 고르시오.

05

A: Are Cindy and Jack firefighters?
B: ________________

① Yes, he is. ② Yes, they are. ③ No, we were. ④ No, you aren't. ⑤ No, they weren't.

06

A: Are you and your sister twins?
B: ________________

① Yes, she is. ② Yes, you are. ③ Yes, we are. ④ No, they aren't. ⑤ No, you aren't.

07

A: Is there a smart TV in your classroom?
B: ________________

① Yes, there are. ② Yes, there was. ③ No, there isn't. ④ No, there wasn't. ⑤ No, it isn't.

[08~10] 빈칸에 들어갈 말이 순서대로 알맞게 짝지어진 것을 고르시오.

08

A: Is that boy your son?
B: No, ________ is not. ________ son is not here.

① she – My ② he – Your ③ he – My ④ she – His ⑤ she – Her

16 Chapter 01

내신대비 TEST

서술형 따라잡기

01

주어진 말을 문맥에 맞게 알맞은 형태로 바꾸어 쓰시오.

(1) There ________(be) many animals in the zoo. I like ________(they) all.

(2) The letters in the box are not ________(you). They are ________(Teddy).

02

다음 우리말과 뜻이 같도록 문장을 완성하시오.

(1) 그는 배가 고프지 않았다.
→ ________________ hungry.

(2) 나는 책을 한 권 가지고 있다. 그것은 내 침대 위에 있다. 그것의 겉표지는 노란색이다.
→ I have a book. ________ on my bed. ________ cover is yellow.

03

어법상 틀린 부분을 찾아 바르게 고쳐 문장을 다시 쓰시오.

(1) Was Julie and David in the same class? (1군데)
→ ________________

(2) Don't touch the camera. Its is me. (2군데)
→ ________________

04

다음 그림을 보고, 대화를 완성하시오.

Sam: Is this red cap ________?
Amy: No, ________. ________ cap is blue.

05

다음 표를 보고, 빈칸에 알맞은 말을 쓰시오.

Name	Age	Nationality	Nickname
Junho	13	Korea	Sports Boy
Alice	13	England	Lucky
Nick	14	Canada	Little Steve Jobs

(1) Nick ________ 14 years old. ________ nickname is Little Steve Jobs.

(2) Junho: ________ you from Canada?
Alice: No, ________. ________ from England.

(3) Junho and Alice ________ the same age. ________ 13 years old.

고난도

06

다음 조건과 주어진 말을 이용하여 우리말을 영어로 옮겨 쓰시오.

〈조건〉 1. be동사를 이용할 것
2. 적절한 인칭대명사를 이용할 것

(1) 그 담요는 그의 것이 아니다. (the blanket)

(2) 너의 아들은 변호사였니? (son, a lawyer)

인칭대명사와 be동사 19

6 서술형 따라잡기

다양한 유형의 서술형 문제들을 통해 응용력과 문제 해결력을 높이고, 실제 서술형 평가를 효과적으로 준비할 수 있습니다.

5 내신대비 TEST

통합적인 문제들을 제시하여 해당 Chapter의 학습 내용을 빠짐없이 확인할 수 있게 하였습니다. 최신 기출 유형 문제들이 포함되어 있어 어려워진 학교 시험에도 완벽하게 대비할 수 있습니다.

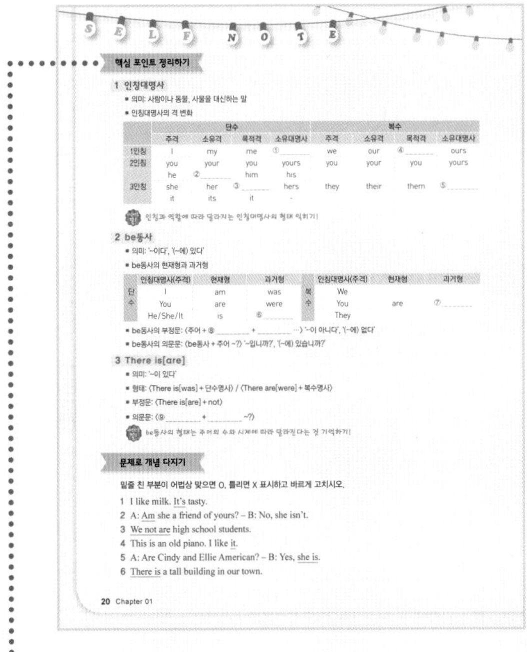

SELF NOTE

핵심 포인트 정리하기

1 인칭대명사

- 의미: 사람이나 동물, 사물을 대신하는 말
- 인칭대명사의 격 변화

	단수				복수			
	주격	소유격	목적격	소유대명사	주격	소유격	목적격	소유대명사
1인칭	I	my	me	① ______	we	our	④ ______	ours
2인칭	you	your	you	yours	you	your	you	yours
3인칭	he	② ______	him	his	they	their	them	⑤ ______
	she	her	③ ______	hers				
	it	its	it	-				

인칭과 격형에 따라 달라지는 인칭대명사의 형태 익히기!

2 be동사

- 의미: '~이다', '(~에) 있다'
- be동사의 현재형과 과거형

인칭대명사(주격)	현재형	과거형	인칭대명사(주격)	현재형	과거형
단수 I	am	was	복수 We		
You	are	were	You	are	⑦ ______
He/She/It	is	⑥ ______	They		

- be동사의 부정문: (주어 + ⑧ ______ + ______ ~) '~이 아니다', '(~에) 없다'
- be동사의 의문문: (be동사 + 주어 ~?) '~입니까?', '(~에) 있습니까?'

3 There is[are]

- 의미: '~이 있다'
- 형태: (There is[was] + 단수명사) / (There are[were] + 복수명사)
- 부정문: (There is[are] + not)
- 의문문: (⑨ ______ + ______ ~?)

be동사의 형태는 주어의 수와 시제에 따라 달라진다는 것 기억하기!

문제로 개념 다지기

밑줄 친 부분이 어법상 맞으면 O, 틀리면 X 표시하고 바르게 고치시오.

1 I like milk. It's tasty.
2 A: Am she a friend of yours? – B: No, she isn't.
3 We not are high school students.
4 This is an old piano. I like it.
5 A: Are Cindy and Ellie American? – B: Yes, she is.
6 There is a tall building in our town.

20 Chapter 01

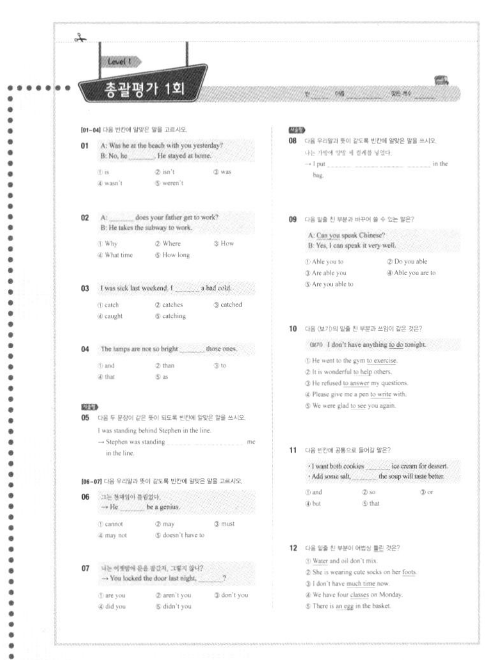

Level 1

총괄평가 1회

[01~04] 다음 빈칸에 알맞은 말을 고르시오.

01 A: Was he at the beach with you yesterday?
B: No, he ________. He stayed at home.

① is ② isn't ③ was ④ wasn't ⑤ weren't

02 A: ________ does your father get to work?
B: He takes the subway to work.

① Why ② Where ③ How ④ What time ⑤ How long

03 I was sick last weekend. I ________ a bad cold.

① catch ② catches ③ catched ④ caught ⑤ catching

04 The lamps are not so bright ________ those ones.

① and ② than ③ to ④ that ⑤ as

05 다음 두 문장이 같은 뜻이 되도록 빈칸에 알맞은 말을 쓰시오.

I was standing behind Stephen in the line.
→ Stephen was standing ________ me in the line.

[06~07] 다음 우리말과 뜻이 같도록 빈칸에 알맞은 말을 고르시오.

06 그는 천재임이 틀림없다.
→ He ________ be a genius.

① cannot ② may ③ must ④ may not ⑤ doesn't have to

07 너는 어젯밤에 문을 잠갔지, 그렇지 않니?
→ You locked the door last night, ________?

① are you ② aren't you ③ don't you ④ did you ⑤ didn't you

08 다음 우리말과 뜻이 같도록 빈칸에 알맞은 말을 쓰시오.

→ I put ________ in the bag.

09 다음 밑줄 친 부분과 바꾸어 쓸 수 있는 말은?

A: Can you speak Chinese?
B: Yes, I can speak it very well.

① Able you to ② Do you able ③ Are able you ④ Able you are to ⑤ Are you able to

10 다음 〈보기〉의 밑줄 친 부분과 쓰임이 같은 것은?

〈보기〉 I don't have anything to do tonight.

① He went to the gym to exercise.
② It is wonderful to help others.
③ He refused to answer my questions.
④ Please give me a pen to write with.
⑤ We were glad to see you again.

11 다음 빈칸에 공통으로 들어갈 말은?

• I want both cookies ________ ice cream for dessert.
• Add some salt, ________ the soup will taste better.

① and ② so ③ or ④ but ⑤ that

12 다음 밑줄 친 부분이 어법상 틀린 것은?

① Water and oil don't mix.
② She is wearing cute socks on her foots.
③ I don't have much time now.
④ We have four classes on Monday.
⑤ There is an egg in the basket.

7 SELF NOTE

각 Chapter에서 배운 문법 사항을 스스로 정리하고, <이것만은 꼭!>을 참고하여 확인 문제를 풀어보면서 문법 실력을 탄탄하게 다질 수 있습니다.

8 총괄평가

3회분의 총괄평가를 별도 제공하였습니다. 총괄평가를 통해 내신 대비에 필요한 실전 감각을 기를 수 있습니다.

Contents

Contents

food truck
BURGER
CHAPTER
01
인칭대명사와 be동사

I am a student. 나는 학생이다.
You are a student. 너는 학생이다.
We are students. 우리는 학생이다.

인칭대명사란?

사람, 동물, 사물을 대신하는 말로, 1인칭(I, we), 2인칭(you), 3인칭(he, she, it, they)으로 나눌 수 있어요. 인칭대명사는 문장 안에서 어떤 역할을 하는지에 따라 주격, 소유격, 목적격으로 쓰인답니다.

be동사란?

우리말 '~이다', '(~에) 있다'에 해당하는 동사가 be동사예요. 그런데 영어의 be동사는 주어에 따라 am, are, is로, 또 과거의 일을 나타낼 때는 was, were로 형태가 바뀐답니다.

Point 01 인칭대명사와 be동사의 현재형

- 인칭대명사는 사람, 동물, 사물을 대신하는 말이다.
- be동사는 '~이다', '(~에) 있다'라는 뜻이다.
- be동사의 현재형은 줄여서 쓸 수 있다.

	인칭대명사		be동사의 현재형	줄임말
단수	1인칭	I	am	I'm
	2인칭	You	are	You're
	3인칭	He	is	He's
		She		She's
		It		It's

	인칭대명사		be동사의 현재형	줄임말
복수	1인칭	We	are	We're
	2인칭	You		You're
	3인칭	They		They're

★ PLUS TIP 줄임형에 사용하는 '는 아포스트로피(apostrophe)라고 한다.

A 다음 빈칸에 알맞은 be동사의 현재형을 쓰시오.

1 I __________ from Korea.
2 He __________ Japanese.
3 You __________ beautiful.
4 We __________ at the library.
5 Jake and Maggie are my friends. They __________ kind.

B 다음 밑줄 친 부분을 줄임말로 바꿔 쓰시오.

1 She is a new teacher.
2 It is dark outside.
3 They are always busy.
4 I am a guitarist in the school band.
5 You are in a gallery. Please be quiet.

C 다음 우리말과 같은 뜻이 되도록 문장을 완성하시오.

1 너희들은 학교에 늦었다.
You __________ late for school.

2 내 남동생은 우리 조부모님 댁에 있다.
My brother __________ at our grandparents' house.

3 그것은 매우 좋은 영화이다.
__________ a very good movie.

Point 02 be동사의 과거형

<table>
<tr><th></th><th>be동사의 현재형</th><th>be동사의 과거형</th><th></th><th>be동사의 현재형</th><th>be동사의 과거형</th></tr>
<tr><td rowspan="5">단수</td><td>I am</td><td>I was</td><td rowspan="5">복수</td><td>We are</td><td>We were</td></tr>
<tr><td>You are</td><td>You were</td><td>You are</td><td>You were</td></tr>
<tr><td>He is</td><td>He was</td><td rowspan="3">They are</td><td rowspan="3">They were</td></tr>
<tr><td>She is</td><td>She was</td></tr>
<tr><td>It is</td><td>It was</td></tr>
</table>

A 다음 빈칸에 알맞은 be동사의 과거형을 쓰시오.

1 I __________ tired yesterday.
2 It __________ very cold last week.
3 You __________ at the movie theater last night.
4 We __________ happy at Troy's birthday party.
5 The singer __________ popular all around the world.

B 다음 ( ) 안에서 알맞은 말을 고르시오.

1 My parents (are / were) home now.
2 You (are / were) great on the stage yesterday.
3 Nancy (is / was) my classmate last year.
4 He (is / was) in Hong Kong right now.
5 They (are / were) elementary school students last year.

C 다음 우리말과 같은 뜻이 되도록 문장을 완성하시오.

1 오늘은 날씨가 맑다.
It __________ sunny today.

2 Jennie는 지금 체육관에 있다.
Jennie __________ at the gym now.

3 그 학생들은 매우 용감했다.
The students __________ very brave.

4 너는 작년에 운이 좋았다.
__________ __________ lucky last year.

5 그는 오늘 아침 시청 앞에 있었다.
__________ __________ in front of City Hall this morning.

be동사의 부정문

■ be동사의 부정문은 '~이 아니다', '(~에) 없다'라는 뜻이다.

주어+be동사+not	〈주어+be동사〉의 줄임말	〈be동사+not〉의 줄임말
I **am not**	I'**m** **not**	-
You **are not**	You'**re** **not**	You **aren't**
He She **is not** It	He'**s** She'**s** **not** It'**s**	He She **isn't** It
We You **are not** They	We'**re** You'**re** **not** They'**re**	We You **aren't** They

★ PLUS TIP be동사 과거형의 부정형은 was not[wasn't] 또는 were not[weren't]이다.
She **was not[wasn't]** tired. / We **were not[weren't]** there.

A 다음 밑줄 친 부분을 줄임말로 바꿔 쓰시오.

1 He is not an actor.
2 You are not alone.
3 They were not there at that time.
4 She was not thirteen years old.
5 It is not my fault.
6 We are not busy now.

B 다음 문장을 부정문으로 바꿔 쓰시오.

1 We are in the same class.
→ ______________________

2 I am a baseball player.
→ ______________________

3 My mother is in the office.
→ ______________________

4 Mark was with his girlfriend.
→ ______________________

5 Some people are afraid of ghosts.
→ ______________________

6 They were in New York last month.
→ ______________________

Point 04

be동사의 의문문

■ be동사의 의문문은 '~입니까?', '(~에) 있습니까?'라는 뜻이다.

be동사+주어 ~?			긍정 대답			부정 대답		
Am	**I**	**~?**	Yes,	you	are.	No,	you	aren't.
Are	**you**	**~?**	Yes,	I	am.	No,	I'm	not.
Is	**he she it**	**~?**	Yes,	he she it	is.	No,	he she it	isn't.
Are	**we you they**	**~?**	Yes,	you we they	are.	No,	you we they	aren't.

★ PLUS TIP be동사 과거형의 의문문은 was 또는 were를 이용해서 만든다.
Was he in the park? / **Were** they late?

A 다음 문장을 의문문으로 바꾸어 쓰시오.

1 She was in the hospital.
→ ______________________

2 John is at the museum.
→ ______________________

3 It is very interesting.
→ ______________________

4 You were a police officer.
→ ______________________

5 They are cheerleaders for our team.
→ ______________________

B 다음 빈칸에 알맞은 말을 넣어 대화를 완성하시오.

1 A: ________ ________ a student at this school?
B: No, I'm not.

2 A: Is your mother still sick?
B: Yes, ________ ________.

3 A: ________ ________ ready for the show?
B: No, he wasn't.

4 A: Were you and your friend at the supermarket yesterday?
B: Yes, ________ ________.

There is[are]

- There is[are]는 '~이 있다'라는 의미를 나타내며, 이때 there에는 아무 뜻이 없다.
- 〈There is+단수명사〉, 〈There are+복수명사〉의 형태로 쓴다.
  There is an apple in the basket. / **There are apples** in the basket.
- 부정문은 〈There is[are]+not〉, 의문문은 〈Is[Are]+there ~?〉의 형태로 쓴다.
  There is not[isn't] a student in the playground.
  Is there a ball in the box? — Yes, there is. / No, there isn't.
- 과거형은 〈There+was[were]〉의 형태로 쓴다.
  There was a pencil on the desk. / **There were** lions at the zoo.

There is[are] 구문에서는 be동사 뒤에 오는 명사를 주어로 본다는 것을 기억하자.
There is **a cat** on the sofa. 한 마리의 고양이가 소파 위에 있다.

A 다음 ( ) 안에서 알맞은 말을 고르시오.

1 There (is / are) famous singers on the stage.
2 There (was / were) a tree in the park.
3 (There were not / There not were) any caps in the shop.
4 A: (Is / Are) there a box in the room? – B: Yes, (there is / is there).

B 다음 문장을 지시대로 바꾸어 쓰시오.

1 There is a book in my bag. (부정문)
→ ______________________________

2 There is a big sport event. (과거형)
→ ______________________________

3 There are hamburgers on the table. (의문문)
→ ______________________________

C 다음 우리말과 같은 뜻이 되도록 ( ) 안의 말을 배열하여 문장을 완성하시오.

1 그녀의 지갑에는 동전이 하나도 없다. (in her purse, there, any coins, aren't)
____

2 그의 방에 컴퓨터가 있니? (there, in his room, is, a computer)
____

3 지붕 위에 두 마리의 새가 있었다. (two birds, were, on the roof, there)
____

Point 06 인칭대명사의 격 변화 – 주격/소유격/목적격/소유대명사

- 주격은 문장에서 주어 역할을 하는 말로 '~은[~는/~이/~가]'이라는 뜻이다.
- 소유격은 명사 앞에 쓰여 소유 관계를 나타내는 말로 '~의'라는 뜻이다.
- 목적격은 문장에서 목적어 역할을 하는 말로 '~을[를]'이라는 뜻이다.
- 소유대명사는 '~의 것'이라는 뜻으로 〈소유격+명사〉를 대신한다.

	주격	소유격	목적격	소유대명사
단수	I	my	me	mine
	you	your	you	yours
	he	his	him	his
	she	her	her	hers
	it	its	it	-

	주격	소유격	목적격	소유대명사
복수	we	our	us	ours
	you	your	you	yours
	they	their	them	theirs

★ PLUS TIP 사람의 이름을 나타내는 고유명사의 소유격과 소유대명사는 고유명사에 's를 붙여서 쓴다.
Tom – Tom**'s** (Tom의, Tom의 것) / Betty – Betty**'s** (Betty의, Betty의 것)

A 다음 밑줄 친 부분을 어법에 맞게 고쳐 쓰시오.

1 I like he hair style.
2 My parents love she.
3 Green is I favorite color.
4 Its is Roald Dahl's novel.
5 We photos are always fantastic.
6 Please take his to the hospital.
7 The bookcases are them.

B 다음 우리말과 같은 뜻이 되도록 문장을 완성하시오.

1 그들의 부모님은 나에게 매우 친절하시다.
__________ parents are very kind to __________.

2 내 머리카락은 검은색이고, 그녀의 것은 붉은색이다.
__________ hair is black, and __________ is red.

3 그녀는 Laura의 이메일 주소를 안다.
__________ knows __________ email address.

4 이 장화들은 나의 것이다. 나는 그것들을 좋아한다.
These rain boots are __________. I like __________.

5 이 케이크는 너를 위한 것이다. 그것은 너의 것이다.
This cake is for __________. It is __________.

[01-03] 다음 빈칸에 알맞은 말을 고르시오.

01

A: Is it Tuesday today?
B: No, it ________.

① is ② are ③ isn't
④ was ⑤ wasn't

02

A: Is this your guitar?
B: No, that is not ________.

① mine ② yours ③ his
④ its ⑤ theirs

03

Sophia ________ in France last year.

① am ② are ③ is
④ was ⑤ were

04

다음 밑줄 친 부분의 의미가 나머지와 다른 것은?

① Jane is my cousin.
② We are best friends.
③ This box is very heavy.
④ They are good dancers.
⑤ My parents are in the living room.

[05-07] 다음 질문에 대한 알맞은 대답을 고르시오.

05

A: Are Cindy and Jack firefighters?
B: ____________________

① Yes, he is. ② Yes, they are.
③ No, we were. ④ No, you aren't.
⑤ No, they weren't.

06

A: Are you and your sister twins?
B: ____________________

① Yes, she is. ② Yes, you are.
③ Yes, we are. ④ No, they aren't.
⑤ No, you aren't.

07

A: Is there a smart TV in your classroom?
B: ____________________

① Yes, there are. ② Yes, there was.
③ No, there isn't. ④ No, there wasn't.
⑤ No, it isn't.

[08-10] 빈칸에 들어갈 말이 순서대로 알맞게 짝지어진 것을 고르시오.

08

A: Is that boy your son?
B: No, ________ is not. ________ son is not here.

① she – My ② he – Your
③ he – My ④ she – His
⑤ she – Her

09

A: Is this Mark's cell phone?
B: No, it _______. It's not _______.

① is – hers ② are – yours
③ isn't – his ④ aren't – his
⑤ isn't – theirs

10

There _______ cookies on the table. They are for _______.

① are – you ② are – your
③ is – yours ④ was – you
⑤ were – your

11

다음 대화 중 자연스럽지 않은 것은?

① A: Am I right?
B: Yes, you are.
② A: Are you his fans?
B: Yes, we are.
③ A: Is Anna free today?
B: No, she isn't.
④ A: Are they your classmates?
B: Yes, they are.
⑤ A: Is Mr. Andrew in the teachers' room?
B: Yes, he was.

[12-13] 다음 우리말을 영어로 바르게 옮긴 것을 고르시오.

12

그 가방들은 우리의 것이 아니었다.

① Those bags were not us.
② Those bags not were our.
③ Those bags was not yours.
④ Those bags were not ours.
⑤ Those bags were not yours.

13

그녀의 정원에는 소나무 한 그루가 있다.

① There are a pine tree in her garden.
② There is a pine tree in her garden.
③ There is a pine tree in his garden.
④ There is a pine tree in our garden.
⑤ There are a pine tree in hers garden.

[14-15] 다음 중 어법상 틀린 것을 고르시오.

14

① They weren't from Taiwan.
② Lincoln wasn't a musician.
③ She wasn't absent from school.
④ You wasn't at the museum.
⑤ We weren't busy at that time.

15

① The baseball glove is Harry's.
② The books on the desk are their.
③ Were you in Italy last year?
④ Is the girl a new student?
⑤ Your birthday present is in my bag.

[16-17] 다음 밑줄 친 부분의 쓰임이 나머지와 다른 것을 고르시오.

16

① I meet her every day.
② Ms. Kim loves her job.
③ We know her very well.
④ I teach English to her.
⑤ George misses her a lot.

17

① Cooking is one of his hobbies.
② John told me about his future dream.
③ He sang a song for his parents.
④ The socks under the chair are his.
⑤ He is happy with his new shoes.

18

다음 빈칸에 공통으로 들어갈 말은?

• A: ________ Ms. Wolf?
B: Yes, I am.
• A: ________ ready to go?
B: No, we aren't. Please wait.

① Am I
② Are you
③ Is she
④ Are we
⑤ Are they

기출응용

19

(A), (B), (C)의 괄호 안에서 알맞은 것끼리 바르게 짝지어진 것은?

(A) [Was / Were] you late for the movie?
(B) Mr. Kim helps [their / them] all the time.
(C) Jason and his cousin [is / are] at the park now.

	(A)		(B)		(C)
①	Was	……	their	……	are
②	Was	……	them	……	are
③	Were	……	them	……	are
④	Were	……	them	……	is
⑤	Were	……	their	……	is

고난도

20

다음 중 어법상 옳은 것끼리 짝지어진 것은?

(a) You aren't rude at all.
(b) Those hairpins are hers.
(c) Dan and I am good friends.
(d) Was he popular in yours country?
(e) Were you sad at the news?

① (a), (b), (c)
② (a), (b), (e)
③ (b), (c), (e)
④ (b), (d), (e)
⑤ (c), (d), (e)

서술형 따라잡기

01
주어진 말을 문맥에 맞게 알맞은 형태로 바꾸어 쓰시오.

(1) There ________(be) many animals in the zoo. I like ________(they) all.

(2) The letters in the box are not ________(you). They are ________(Teddy).

02
다음 우리말과 뜻이 같도록 문장을 완성하시오.

(1) 그는 배가 고프지 않았다.
→ ________ ________ ________ hungry.

(2) 나는 책을 한 권 가지고 있다. 그것은 내 침대 위에 있다. 그것의 겉표지는 노란색이다.
→ I have a book. ________ ________ on my bed. ________ cover is yellow.

03
어법상 틀린 부분을 찾아 바르게 고쳐 문장을 다시 쓰시오.

(1) Was Julie and David in the same class? (1군데)

→ ________________________

(2) Don't touch the camera. Its is me. (2군데)

→ ________________________

04
다음 그림을 보고, 대화를 완성하시오.

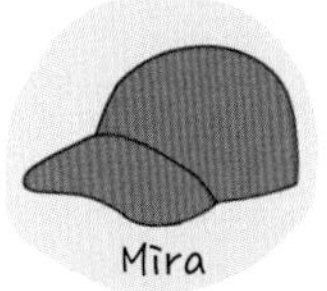

Sam: Is this red cap ________?
Amy: No, ________ ________. ________ cap is blue.

05
다음 표를 보고, 빈칸에 알맞은 말을 쓰시오.

Name	Age	Nationality	Nickname
Junho	13	Korea	Sports Boy
Alice	13	England	Lucky
Nick	14	Canada	Little Steve Jobs

(1) Nick ________ 14 years old. ________ nickname is Little Steve Jobs.

(2) Junho: ________ you from Canada?
Alice: No, ________ ________.
________ from England.

(3) Junho and Alice ________ the same age. ________ ________ 13 years old.

고난도
06
다음 조건과 주어진 말을 이용하여 우리말을 영어로 옮겨 쓰시오.

〈조건〉 1. be동사를 이용할 것
2. 적절한 인칭대명사를 이용할 것

(1) 그 담요는 그의 것이 아니다. (the blanket)
____

(2) 너의 아들은 변호사였니? (son, a lawyer)
____

S E L F N O T E

핵심 포인트 정리하기

1 인칭대명사

■ 의미: 사람이나 동물, 사물을 대신하는 말

■ 인칭대명사의 격 변화

	단수				복수			
	주격	소유격	목적격	소유대명사	주격	소유격	목적격	소유대명사
1인칭	I	my	me	① ______	we	our	④ ______	ours
2인칭	you	your	you	yours	you	your	you	yours
3인칭	he	② ______	him	his	they	their	them	⑤ ______
	she	her	③ ______	hers				
	it	its	it	-				

인칭과 역할에 따라 달라지는 인칭대명사의 형태 익히기!

2 be동사

■ 의미: '~이다', '(~에) 있다'

■ be동사의 현재형과 과거형

	인칭대명사(주격)	현재형	과거형		인칭대명사(주격)	현재형	과거형
단수	I	am	was	복수	We	are	⑦ ______
	You	are	were		You		
	He/She/It	is	⑥ ______		They		

■ be동사의 부정문: 〈주어 + ⑧ ______ + ______ …〉 '~이 아니다', '(~에) 없다'

■ be동사의 의문문: 〈be동사 + 주어 ~?〉 '~입니까?', '(~에) 있습니까?'

3 There is[are]

■ 의미: '~이 있다'

■ 형태: 〈There is[was] + 단수명사〉 / 〈There are[were] + 복수명사〉

■ 부정문: 〈There is[are] + not〉

■ 의문문: 〈⑨ ______ + ______ ~?〉

be동사의 형태는 주어의 수와 시제에 따라 달라진다는 것 기억하기!

문제로 개념 다지기

밑줄 친 부분이 어법상 맞으면 O, 틀리면 X 표시하고 바르게 고치시오.

1 I like milk. It's tasty.

2 A: Am she a friend of yours? – B: No, she isn't.

3 We not are high school students.

4 This is an old piano. I like it.

5 A: Are Cindy and Ellie American? – B: Yes, she is.

6 There is a tall building in our town.

She **bakes** cakes. 그녀는 케이크를 굽는다.
She **baked** cakes. 그녀는 케이크를 구웠다.

일반동사란?

주어의 동작이나 상태를 나타내는 일반동사는 주어의 인칭과 수에 따라 형태가 바뀐답니다. 일반동사의 현재형은 주어가 3인칭 단수일 때만 <동사원형+-(e)s>의 형태로 쓰고, 그 외에는 모두 동사원형으로 씁니다. 일반동사의 과거형은 대부분 <동사원형+-(e)d>의 형태로 쓴다는 것을 기억해 두세요.

Point 01 일반동사의 현재형 I – 1인칭/2인칭 주어

- 일반동사는 be동사와 조동사를 제외한 모든 동사로 주어의 동작이나 상태를 나타낸다.
- 주어가 1인칭이나 2인칭이고 현재시제인 경우 수에 관계없이 일반동사의 원형(동사원형)을 그대로 사용한다.

  I **drink** milk every morning. (주어가 1인칭 단수)
  We **wear** school uniforms. (주어가 1인칭 복수)
  You **like** English novels. (주어가 2인칭 단수)
  Mia and you **know** the schedule. (주어가 2인칭 복수)

A 다음 우리말과 같은 뜻이 되도록 〈보기〉에서 알맞은 말을 골라 빈칸에 적절한 형태로 써넣으시오.

〈보기〉 make practice speak watch work

1 나는 내 아들과 쿠키를 만든다.
I __________ cookies with my son.

2 내 여동생과 나는 일본어를 한다.
My sister and I __________ Japanese.

3 나는 주말에 코미디 영화를 본다.
I __________ comedy movies on weekends.

4 우리는 방과 후에 축구를 연습한다.
We __________ soccer after school.

5 너희들은 식당에서 아르바이트를 한다.
You __________ part-time at a restaurant.

B 다음 우리말과 같은 뜻이 되도록 ( ) 안의 말을 배열하여 문장을 완성하시오.

1 나는 네 조언이 필요하다. (your, need, I, advice)

____

2 우리는 크리스마스에 행복하다. (feel, we, on Christmas, happy)

____

3 Julia와 너는 서로 좋아한다. (Julia, you, each other, like, and)

____

4 나는 오늘 저녁에 계획이 있다. (this evening, I, plans, have)

____

Point 02 일반동사의 현재형 II – 3인칭 주어

- 주어가 3인칭 단수이고 현재시제인 경우 동사원형에 -s 또는 -es를 붙인다.
  He **knows** a lot of funny stories. (know+s)
  She **teaches** science. (teach+es)
  It **grows** fast. (grow+s)
- 주어가 3인칭 복수이고 현재시제인 경우 일반동사의 원형을 그대로 사용한다.
  My brothers **play** tennis every day. / They **eat** cereal with milk.

A 다음 밑줄 친 부분을 어법에 맞게 고쳐 쓰시오. (단, 현재형으로 쓸 것)

1 My cat eat too much.
2 She like K-pop music.
3 My friends calls me "Dr. No."
4 Kate walk to school every morning.
5 He get up at seven o'clock in the morning.
6 Mr. Johnson work late every Thursday.
7 They always drinks Coke with hamburgers.

B 다음 우리말과 같은 뜻이 되도록 ( ) 안의 말을 이용하여 문장을 완성하시오.

1 그는 오늘 슬퍼 보인다. (look)
He __________ sad today.

2 이 수업은 2시 30분에 시작한다. (begin)
This class __________ at 2:30.

3 그녀는 초콜릿이 좀 필요하다. (need)
She __________ some chocolate.

4 이 카페는 11시에 문을 닫는다. (close)
This café __________ at eleven o'clock.

5 Benny와 Joon은 일요일마다 자전거를 탄다. (ride)
Benny and Joon __________ bicycles on Sundays.

6 Olivia는 매년 나에게 카드를 보낸다. (send)
Olivia __________ a card to me every year.

7 그들은 한 달에 한 번 등산한다. (climb)
They __________ a mountain once a month.

Point 03 일반동사의 3인칭 단수형 만드는 방법

■ 주어가 3인칭 단수일 때 일반동사의 현재형은 주로 〈동사원형+-(e)s〉이다.

대부분의 동사	동사원형+**-s**	eat**s**, meet**s**, buy**s**, like**s**, read**s**, want**s**
〈-o, -s, -ch, -sh, -x〉로 끝나는 동사	동사원형+**-es**	go**es**, pass**es**, catch**es**, wash**es**, fix**es**
〈자음+y〉로 끝나는 동사	**y**를 **i**로 바꾸고+**-es**	cry → cr**ies**, study → stud**ies**, try → tr**ies**
have	**has**	

A 다음 밑줄 친 부분을 어법에 맞게 고쳐 쓰시오. (단, 현재형으로 쓸 것)

1 Time fly.
2 Mr. Miller teach math.
3 James have a guitar.
4 Bill want a new jacket.
5 Mary cry when she is hungry.
6 He do his homework at night.
7 She use honey instead of sugar.
8 Joy play badminton once a week.
9 Ross wash the dishes after meals.
10 My mother read magazines in the morning.

B 다음 우리말과 같은 뜻이 되도록 〈보기〉에서 알맞은 말을 골라 빈칸에 적절한 형태로 써넣으시오.

〈보기〉 envy enjoy make run go

1 그녀는 매주 일요일 교회에 간다.
She __________ to church on Sundays.

2 Smith 씨는 도전을 즐긴다.
Mrs. Smith __________ a challenge.

3 이 버스는 15분마다 운행한다.
This bus __________ every 15 minutes.

4 Sophia는 그녀의 가장 친한 친구를 부러워한다.
Sophia __________ her best friend.

5 할머니께서는 우리에게 자주 애플파이를 만들어 주신다.
My grandmother often __________ apple pies for us.

Point 04 일반동사의 과거형 I – 규칙 변화

■ 일반동사의 과거형은 주로 〈동사원형+-(e)d〉이다.

대부분의 동사	동사+-ed	want → want**ed**, learn → learn**ed**
〈자음+e〉로 끝나는 동사	동사+-d	like → like**d**, move → move**d**
〈자음+y〉로 끝나는 동사	y를 i로 바꾸고+-ed	study → stud**ied**, try → tr**ied**
〈단모음+단자음〉으로 끝나는 동사	자음을 한 번 더 쓰고+-ed	stop → stop**ped**, drop → drop**ped** plan → plan**ned**

A 다음 밑줄 친 부분을 어법에 맞게 고쳐 쓰시오.

1 Julia study very hard last week.
2 I work at a bank last year.
3 A police officer stop me last night.
4 Mr. Ban arrive in Seoul yesterday.
5 He ask her a lot of questions last time.
6 They visit their grandparents last winter.
7 My best friend move to Jeju two years ago.

B 다음 우리말과 같은 뜻이 되도록 ( ) 안의 말을 이용하여 문장을 완성하시오.

1 그는 유리컵을 떨어뜨렸다. (drop)
He __________ the glass.

2 그녀는 지난달에 가게를 열었다. (open)
She __________ a shop last month.

3 William은 그의 친구들을 믿었다. (trust)
William __________ his friends.

4 Ben은 나에게 그의 그림을 보여주었다. (show)
Ben __________ me his drawings.

5 Susan은 인도로 여행하는 것을 계획했다. (plan)
Susan __________ a trip to India.

6 Janet은 그 시험에서 최선을 다했다. (try)
Janet __________ her best on the test.

7 나는 온종일 그 호텔에 머물렀다. (stay)
I __________ in the hotel all day long.

Point 05 일반동사의 과거형 II – 불규칙 변화 1

■ 일반동사의 과거형 중 -(e)d가 붙지 않고 형태가 불규칙하게 바뀌는 것이 있다.

go → went	eat → ate	find → found	build → built
get → got	keep → kept	give → gave	catch → caught
buy → bought	come → came	have → had	feel → felt
send → sent	do → did	meet → met	hear → heard
sit → sat	run → ran	think → thought	see → saw
say → said	leave → left	lose → lost	spend → spent

I **got** up late yesterday. / She **bought** noodles and mushrooms.

A ( ) 안의 말을 빈칸에 적절한 형태로 써넣으시오.

1 I __________ Tom and Nicole yesterday. (meet)

2 Rachel __________ home late last night. (come)

3 Monica's cat died. Jack __________ sorry for her at that time. (feel)

4 He __________ a ten-dollar bill in his pocket this morning. (find)

5 I __________ to Myeong-dong yesterday. (go)

6 His dog __________ too much yesterday. It is sick now. (eat)

7 Ewan __________ flowers to Jenny last weekend. (give)

8 She visited me, but she __________ nothing. (say)

9 We were at the museum. We __________ an actress there. (see)

B 다음 우리말과 같은 뜻이 되도록 〈보기〉에서 알맞은 말을 골라 빈칸에 적절한 형태로 써넣으시오.

〈보기〉 build catch leave hear think

1 Peter는 감기에 걸렸다.
Peter __________ a cold.

2 그들은 그 소식을 들었다.
They __________ the news.

3 Miranda는 그 문제에 대해 생각해 보았다.
Miranda __________ about the problem.

4 우리 할아버지께서 이 집을 지으셨다.
My grandfather __________ this house.

5 그들의 친구들은 아침 일찍 떠났다.
Their friends __________ early in the morning.

Point 06

일반동사의 과거형 III – 불규칙 변화 2

■ 과거형과 현재형이 같은 형태인 일반동사도 있다. (put, cut, set, hurt, shut, hit, cost 등)

I always **put** my bag on my chair. (현재형)

I **put** my bag on my chair last night. (과거형)

★ PLUS TIP

read는 현재형과 과거형의 형태는 같지만 발음이 다르다.
read[ri:d](현재형) – read[red](과거형)

A 다음 밑줄 친 부분을 어법에 맞게 고쳐 쓰시오.

1 I make a big mistake yesterday.

2 Diana lose her wallet last week.

3 I have a headache early this morning.

4 I sing a song at the festival yesterday.

5 My brother and I carry many books yesterday.

6 The show was great. I enjoy it very much.

7 He went to the mall. He spend a lot of money.

8 She buy a present. She send it to him last month.

B 다음 우리말과 같은 뜻이 되도록 ( ) 안의 말을 이용하여 문장을 완성하시오.

1 Betty는 등을 다쳤다. (hurt)
Betty __________ her back.

2 그들은 오랫동안 산책을 했다. (take)
They __________ a long walk.

3 그녀는 선물상자에 몇 개의 쿠키들을 넣었다. (put)
She __________ some cookies in the gift box.

4 Jamie는 문을 닫았다. (shut)
Jamie __________ the door.

5 그는 망치로 자신의 손가락을 쳤다. (hit)
He __________ his finger with the hammer.

6 Jimmy는 사과를 반으로 잘랐다. (cut)
Jimmy __________ the apple in half.

7 그 콘서트 티켓은 25달러였다. (cost)
The concert ticket __________ 25 dollars.

8 Steve는 지난 겨울 방학에 많은 책을 읽었다. (read)
Steve __________ many books last winter vacation.

Point 07 일반동사의 부정문 I – don't / doesn't

■ 현재시제인 경우, 동사원형 앞에 don't나 doesn't를 써서 부정문을 만든다.

주어	부정문
I / You / We / They	주어+**don't**+동사원형
He / She / It	주어+**doesn't**+동사원형

I **don't** play soccer. / You **don't** need my help. / They **don't** like sweets.
He **doesn't** know the truth. / She **doesn't** wear glasses. / It **doesn't** smell good.

★ PLUS TIP don't[doesn't]는 do not[does not]의 줄임말로, 줄임말이 더 자주 사용된다.
부정의 의미를 강조할 때는 do not[does not]의 형태를 쓰기도 한다.

A 다음 ( ) 안에서 알맞은 말을 고르시오.

1 I (don't / doesn't) eat chocolate cake.
2 It (don't / doesn't) sound interesting.
3 He (doesn't keep / don't keep) a diary.
4 My father (doesn't gets / doesn't get) enough sleep every day.
5 Miki and James (don't know / doesn't know) him very well.

B 다음 문장을 부정문으로 바꾸어 쓰시오. (단, 줄임말로 쓸 것)

1 Alex has a car.
→ ______________________

2 I practice the violin in the morning.
→ ______________________

3 My dog looks healthy.
→ ______________________

4 Nick and Lily have lunch together at school.
→ ______________________

C 다음 우리말과 같은 뜻이 되도록 ( ) 안의 말을 이용하여 문장을 완성하시오.

1 내 컴퓨터는 작동하지 않는다. (work)
My computer ________ ________.

2 그들은 패스트푸드점에 가지 않는다. (go)
They ________ ________ to fast-food restaurants.

3 그녀는 옷에 많은 돈을 쓰지 않는다. (spend)
She ________ ________ much money on clothes.

Point 08 일반동사의 부정문 II – didn't

- 과거시제인 경우, 주어의 인칭과 수에 관계없이 동사원형 앞에 didn't를 써서 부정문을 만든다.
  I **didn't** call you last night.
  He **didn't** eat dinner yesterday.
  They **didn't** watch the show last Saturday.

A 다음 문장을 부정문으로 바꾸어 쓰시오. (단, 줄임말로 쓸 것)

1 I turned off the light.
→ ____________________

2 Susie passed the exam.
→ ____________________

3 They understood the questions.
→ ____________________

4 You wanted a tablet PC for a gift.
→ ____________________

5 Jake told me about the rumor.
→ ____________________

6 We bought a birthday cake for Judy.
→ ____________________

B 다음 우리말과 같은 뜻이 되도록 ( ) 안의 말을 이용하여 문장을 완성하시오.

1 나는 어제 Tim을 만나지 않았다. (meet)
______ ______ ______ Tim yesterday.

2 그들은 잘 시간이 없었다. (have)
______ ______ ______ time to sleep.

3 Ross는 그녀에게 이메일을 쓰지 않았다. (write)
______ ______ ______ an email to her.

4 그는 나를 보았지만 나에게 인사하지 않았다. (see, say)
______ ______ me, but ______ ______ ______ hello to me.

5 Sophia는 미끄럼틀에서 떨어졌지만 울지 않았다. (fall, cry)
______ ______ off the slide, but ______ ______ ______.

Point 09 일반동사의 의문문 I – Do/Does

■ 현재시제인 경우, 주어 앞에 Do나 Does를 쓰고 주어 뒤에 동사원형을 써서 의문문을 만든다.

주어	의문문	긍정 대답	부정 대답
I / You / We / They	**Do**+주어+동사원형 ~?	Yes, 주어+do.	No, 주어+don't.
He / She / It	**Does**+주어+동사원형 ~?	Yes, 주어+does.	No, 주어+doesn't.

Do they play rock music? – **Yes, they do.** / **No, they don't.**
Does he read soccer magazines? – **Yes, he does.** / **No, he doesn't.**

A 다음 문장을 의문문으로 바꾸어 쓰시오.

1 I look smart. → ______________________

2 He eats garlic. → ______________________

3 You live in Beijing. → ______________________

4 They study French. → ______________________

5 Kate has three brothers. → ______________________

6 We take a test every month. → ______________________

B 다음 우리말과 같은 뜻이 되도록 ( ) 안의 말을 이용하여 문장을 완성하시오.

1 Andy는 인도 음식을 좋아하니? (love)
_______ _______ _______ Indian food?

2 당신은 고양이를 좋아합니까? (like)
_______ _______ _______ cats?

3 그들이 네 주소를 알고 있니? (know)
_______ _______ _______ your address?

4 그녀는 자동차가 있나요? (have)
_______ _______ _______ a car?

5 A: 이 버스는 시청으로 가나요? (go)
_______ _______ _______ _______ to City Hall?
B: 네, 가요.
Yes, _______ _______.

6 A: 너는 학교에 걸어서 오니? (walk)
_______ _______ _______ to school?
B: 아니, 그렇지 않아.
No, _______ _______.

Point 10

일반동사의 의문문 II – Did

- 과거시제인 경우, 주어의 인칭과 수에 관계없이 〈Did+주어+동사원형 ~?〉의 형태로 의문문을 만든다.
  A: **Did you meet** Tim yesterday?
  B: **Yes, I did.** / **No, I didn't.**

★ 내신만점 TIP 일반동사의 부정문과 의문문에서는 주어의 인칭과 시제에 따라 do/does/did를 쓰고, 뒤에 동사원형을 쓴다는 것을 기억하자.

A 다음 문장을 의문문으로 바꾸어 쓰시오.

1 He caught the ball. → ______________________

2 Lily lost her passport. → ______________________

3 You went to the museum. → ______________________

4 They helped the old man. → ______________________

5 Your classmates came here. → ______________________

B 다음 ( ) 안에서 알맞은 말을 고르시오.

1 (Do / Did) you enjoy your trip last weekend?

2 (Does / Do) Lisa have a pet snake?

3 (Do / Does) your sisters learn yoga these days?

4 (Does / Did) he go to bed before 10 last night?

5 (Do / Does) we have enough time?

C 다음 우리말과 같은 뜻이 되도록 ( ) 안의 말을 이용하여 문장을 완성하시오.

1 그는 부산으로 떠났나요? (leave)
  ________ ________ ________ for Busan?

2 A: 너는 Damon과 재미있게 놀았니? (have)
  ________ ________ ________ fun with Damon?
  B: 응, 그랬어. 우린 정말 재미있게 놀았어. (have)
  Yes, ________ ________. We ________ great fun.

3 A: Ben과 Kelly가 제 선물을 좋아했나요? (like)
  ________ Ben and Kelly ________ my present?
  B: 네, 좋아했어요. 그들은 당신에게 고마워했어요. (thank)
  Yes, ________ ________. They ________ you.

[01-03] 다음 빈칸에 알맞은 말을 고르시오.

01

_______ drives a taxi.

① I ② You ③ She
④ We ⑤ They

02

_______ don't drink coffee.

① He ② It
③ My mother ④ Mr. Kim
⑤ They

03

_______ you play computer games?

① Is ② Are ③ Does
④ Do ⑤ Were

[04-06] 다음 질문에 대한 알맞은 대답을 고르시오.

04

A: Did she watch TV last night?
B: _______________

① Yes, she does. ② Yes, she did.
③ No, she don't. ④ No, she doesn't.
⑤ No, she wasn't.

05

A: Does Matt run fast?
B: _______________

① Yes, he does. ② Yes, he is.
③ No, he isn't. ④ No, he didn't.
⑤ No, he does.

06

A: Do you listen to the radio?
B: _______________ It is interesting.

① Yes, I am. ② Yes, I do.
③ Yes, you do. ④ No, I don't.
⑤ No, you don't.

[07-08] 다음 밑줄 친 부분이 어법상 틀린 것을 고르시오.

07

① She didn't buy chocolate.
② They didn't go on a picnic.
③ Joe doesn't cross the road.
④ We don't sells cheese and butter.
⑤ Barry doesn't like strawberry jam.

08

① I have my own blog.
② Jane caught the train.
③ She asked me a question.
④ He usually finish his work at five.
⑤ They tried bungee jumping yesterday.

[09-10] 다음 빈칸에 공통으로 들어갈 말을 고르시오.

09

- _______ Frank live in New York?
- She _______ not want to meet him again.

① Is[is] ② Are[are]
③ Was[was] ④ Do[do]
⑤ Does[does]

10

- I was there yesterday, but I _______ stay for long.
- A: Did they swim at the lake?
  B: No, they _______.

① didn't ② weren't
③ wasn't ④ don't
⑤ aren't

11

다음 우리말을 영어로 바르게 옮긴 것은?

그는 충고를 원하지 않는다.

① He wants not advice.
② He don't want advice.
③ He didn't want advice.
④ He doesn't want advice.
⑤ He doesn't wants advice.

기출응용

12

다음 밑줄 친 부분을 바르게 고친 것을 모두 고르면? (2개)

Yesterday, we ① <u>look</u> for a cake at the bakery. We ② <u>buy</u> one. It ③ <u>cost</u> 25 dollars and I ④ <u>pay</u> for it. We ⑤ <u>give</u> it to my friend Kelly.

① lookd ② bought ③ costed
④ payed ⑤ gave

[13-14] 빈칸에 들어갈 말이 순서대로 알맞게 짝지어진 것을 고르시오.

13

A: Does Julie study English hard?
B: Yes, she _______. She _______ it almost every day.

① do – study ② do – studies
③ does – study ④ does – studies
⑤ did – studies

14

A: _______ they _______ the window?
B: No, they didn't.

① Do – break ② Do – broke
③ Did – break ④ Did – broke
⑤ Does – break

[15-16] 다음 중 어법상 틀린 것을 고르시오.

15

① Did you talk to Tim?
② Does Cindy get up early?
③ Does your baby sleep well?
④ Did David call you last night?
⑤ Does your parents like Italian food?

16

① He looks very nice.
② I tried my best at that time.
③ She keeped her photos in the drawer.
④ Minho read comic books yesterday.
⑤ They sent a letter to their grandparents.

17

다음 밑줄 친 부분의 쓰임이 나머지와 다른 것은?

① Does he like Linda?
② My mom does not buy flowers.
③ This watch does not work.
④ He does not watch the news.
⑤ She does her homework after school.

고난도

18

빈칸에 들어갈 말이 나머지와 다른 것은?

① We ________ not take the same class last year.
② He ________ not go there yesterday.
③ ________ you go on a vacation last week?
④ ________ Amy take a shower an hour ago?
⑤ I ________ not know his name, but I know his brother's name.

기출응용

19

다음 중 어법상 옳은 문장의 개수는?

(a) Do he speak Korean?
(b) We doesn't like rock music.
(c) James went to the library with his friend.
(d) Emily didn't make noise in the classroom.

① 0개 ② 1개 ③ 2개 ④ 3개 ⑤ 4개

20

다음 문장을 지시대로 바르게 바꾸지 않은 것은?

① She really likes the singer. (과거형)
→ She really liked the singer.
② He finished the report. (부정문)
→ He didn't finish the report.
③ Tim and Sarah worry about the final test. (과거형)
→ Tim and Sarah worryed about the final test.
④ They clean their office every day. (부정문)
→ They don't clean their office every day.
⑤ You and your sister had a great dinner. (의문문)
→ Did you and your sister have a great dinner?

서술형 따라잡기

01
주어진 말을 이용하여 우리말과 뜻이 같도록 문장을 완성하시오.

(1) 그는 Cindy와 함께 그 영화를 보지 않았다. (watch the movie)
→ He ____________________ with Cindy.

(2) 매일 아침, Julie는 그녀의 개와 함께 산책한다. (take a walk)
→ Every morning, Julie ________________ with her dog.

02
다음 문장을 지시대로 바꾸어 쓰시오.

(1) Sharon and Brad eat meat.
→ ____________________________ (의문문)
→ ____________________________ (부정문)

(2) Joseph hit 20 home runs last season.
→ ____________________________ (의문문)
→ ____________________________ (부정문)

03
다음 그림을 보고, 주어진 표현을 이용하여 문장을 완성하시오.

yesterday

last weekend

(study at the library)

(1) I ____________________________ yesterday.

(2) I ____________________________ last weekend.

04
주어진 말을 이용하여 대화를 완성하시오.

A: ________ ________ ________ at home? (cook)
B: No, he doesn't.

05
다음 Suji의 일정표를 보고, Suji가 지난주에 한 일과 하지 않은 일을 영어로 쓰시오.

요일	해야 할 일	실천 여부
Mon.	visit my grandmother	X
Wed.	eat pizza with my friends	O
Fri.	do my homework	O

(1) Suji ________ ________ ________ ________ on Monday.

(2) Suji ________ ________ ________ ________ ________ on Wednesday.

(3) Suji ________ ________ ________ on Friday.

고난도

06
다음 대화를 읽고, 어법상 틀린 부분을 모두 찾아 바르게 고쳐 쓰시오. (2군데)

A: Is this your pet?
B: Yes, this is my pet, Coco. My father bring him home a month ago.
A: He is so cute.
B: Yes, he is. He likes playing with me. But he don't like taking baths.

S E L F N O T E

핵심 포인트 정리하기

1 일반동사

- 주어의 동작이나 상태를 나타내는 동사

2 일반동사의 현재형

- 1인칭 · 2인칭 단수 · 복수 주어, 3인칭 복수 주어 → 〈동사원형〉
- 3인칭 단수 주어 → 〈동사원형 + ① ________ 나 ________〉

3 일반동사의 과거형

- 규칙 변화 → 〈동사원형 + ② ________ 나 ________〉
- 불규칙 변화

일반동사의 3인칭 단수 현재형과 과거형의 불규칙 변화에 유의할 것!

4 일반동사의 부정문

- 현재시제 → 〈③ ________ 나 ________ + 동사원형〉
- 과거시제 → 〈④ ________ + 동사원형〉

5 일반동사의 의문문

- 현재시제 → Q: 〈⑤ ________ 나 ________ + 주어 + 동사원형 ~?〉
  A: 〈Yes, 주어 + do[does].〉 / 〈No, 주어 + don't[doesn't].〉
- 과거시제 → Q: 〈⑥ ________ + 주어 + 동사원형 ~?〉
  A: 〈Yes, 주어 + did.〉 / 〈No, 주어 + didn't.〉

일반동사의 부정문 & 의문문은 'do/does/did'와 동사원형을 함께 쓴다는 것 기억하기!

문제로 개념 다지기

다음 ( ) 안에서 알맞은 말을 고르시오.

1 Julie and Brian (do not / not do) like soda.
2 He (enjoys / enjoies) extreme sports.
3 I (go / went) to a concert last week.
4 (Does / Did) he buy a new T-shirt yesterday?
5 My brother (play / plays) the guitar as a hobby.
6 She was thirsty. She (drank / drinked) some water.
7 The bus (don't / doesn't) stop at Seoul Tower.
8 Does she (have / has) two cats and a dog?

개념 쏙쏙

I have ***an*** **umbrella**.	나는 한 개의 우산을 갖고 있다.
I have two **umbrellas**.	나는 두 개의 우산들을 갖고 있다.
The **umbrella** is blue.	그 우산은 파란색이다.

명사란?

사람, 사물, 장소 등을 나타내는 말로, 셀 수 있는 명사와 셀 수 없는 명사로 나뉩니다.

관사란?

명사 앞에 쓰여 명사의 의미나 성격에 대한 정보를 나타내는 말로, 부정관사 a/an과 정관사 the가 있습니다.

Point 01 셀 수 있는 명사 I – 규칙 변화 1

- 명사는 사람, 사물, 장소 등을 나타내는 말이다.
- 셀 수 있는 명사는 철자에 따라 복수형을 만드는 방법이 다르다.

대부분의 명사	명사+-s	cup → cup**s** book → book**s**	dog → dog**s** bottle → bottle**s**
〈-s, -sh, -ch, -x, -o〉로 끝나는 명사	명사+-es	bus → bus**es** church → church**es** potato → potato**es** 〈예외〉 piano → piano**s**	dish → dish**es** box → box**es** photo → photo**s**

A 다음 명사의 복수형을 쓰시오.

1 cat ________ 2 tomato ________
3 box ________ 4 flower ________
5 star ________ 6 present ________
7 friend ________ 8 watch ________
9 shirt ________ 10 plan ________
11 class ________ 12 idea ________
13 fox ________ 14 card ________
15 piano ________ 16 ship ________
17 address ________ 18 hero ________

B 다음 밑줄 친 부분을 어법에 맞게 고쳐 쓰시오.

1 An octopus has eight arm.
2 I have two map of Seoul.
3 I ate five chocolate cookie.
4 Nancy made four sandwich.
5 These two house look the same.
6 We need an eggs and two potato.
7 Albert always asks me many question.
8 There are many bananaes in the picnic basket.
9 Look at those beautiful boat over there.
10 The singer sang a lot of song at the jazz festival.
11 He put two shirt and three jacket in his bag.

Point 02 셀 수 있는 명사 II – 규칙 변화 2

〈자음+y〉로 끝나는 명사	y를 i로 바꾸고+-es	city → cit**ies** baby → bab**ies**	lady → lad**ies** cherry → cherr**ies**
〈모음+y〉로 끝나는 명사	명사+-s	boy → boy**s** day → day**s**	toy → toy**s** monkey → monkey**s**
〈-f, -fe〉로 끝나는 명사	f, fe를 v로 바꾸고+-es	leaf → lea**ves** wife → wi**ves** 〈예외〉 roof → roof**s**	thief → thie**ves** knife → kni**ves**

A 다음 명사의 복수형을 쓰시오.

1 country ________
2 comb ________
3 factory ________
4 shelf ________
5 mirror ________
6 body ________
7 picture ________
8 wallet ________
9 hobby ________
10 party ________
11 key ________
12 mouth ________
13 wolf ________
14 window ________
15 diary ________
16 family ________
17 puppy ________
18 brush ________

B 다음 밑줄 친 부분을 어법에 맞게 고쳐 쓰시오.

1 You made several mistake.
2 Lots of bus go to the stadium.
3 Please move these box for me.
4 The boy got a lot of toy for his birthday.
5 The birds are on the roofes of the houses.
6 My aunt has two baby. They are twins!
7 Be careful with those knifes and forks.
8 A lot of citys have many tall building.
9 My grandfather tells me many interesting story.
10 The leaf change color in the fall.
11 There are two big holiday in Korea — New Year's Day and Chuseok.

Point 03 셀 수 있는 명사 III – 불규칙 변화

■ 셀 수 있는 명사 중에 복수형이 불규칙하게 변화하는 것들이 있다.

man → m**en** woman → wom**en** child → child**ren** tooth → t**ee**th

foot → f**ee**t mouse → m**ice** goose → g**ee**se ox → ox**en**

■ 복수형이 불규칙하게 변화하는 명사 중에는 단수형과 복수형이 같은 것들도 있다.

sheep → **sheep** deer → **deer** fish → **fish**

A 다음 밑줄 친 부분을 어법에 맞게 고쳐 쓰시오.

1 She has white <u>tooth</u>.
2 My <u>foots</u> are very small.
3 This section is for <u>family</u>.
4 Those <u>cliff</u> look dangerous.
5 I joined three <u>club</u> last year.
6 The boy takes care of four <u>sheeps</u>.
7 Young <u>mans</u> wear masks.
8 There are a lot of <u>bug</u> in the old house.
9 Both of her <u>childs</u> are middle school students.
10 Seoul, Beijing, and Tokyo are big <u>city</u>.

B 다음 우리말과 같은 뜻이 되도록 ( ) 안의 말을 이용하여 문장을 완성하시오.

1 쥐들은 정말 치즈를 좋아하나요? (mouse)
Do __________ really love cheese?

2 사슴 두 마리가 갑자기 나타났다. (deer)
Two __________ suddenly appeared.

3 많은 큰 물고기들이 강에 산다. (fish)
Many large __________ live in the river.

4 그는 여자들에게 인기가 있다. (woman)
He is popular with __________.

5 그 농부는 많은 닭들과 거위들을 가지고 있다. (chicken, goose)
The farmer has many __________ and __________.

6 목장에 세 마리의 황소가 있다. (ox)
There are three __________ on the farm.

Point 04 셀 수 없는 명사

- 셀 수 없는 명사는 '하나, 둘, 셋, …' 등으로 셀 수 없는 명사를 뜻한다.
- 셀 수 없는 명사는 항상 단수형으로 쓰고, 앞에 부정관사 a/an을 쓰지 않는다.

추상명사	형체가 없는 추상적인 개념을 나타내는 명사 love, luck, beauty, truth, peace, hope, news 등
고유명사	사람의 이름, 지명, 월, 요일 등 고유한 것을 나타내는 명사 Alex, London, August, Friday 등
물질명사	재료, 음식, 입자 등 형태는 있지만 나누어 셀 수 없는 물질을 나타내는 명사 water, snow, rice, sand, bread, money, information 등

A 다음 밑줄 친 부분을 어법에 맞게 고쳐 쓰시오.

1 She came from a France.
2 A sugar tastes sweet.
3 They listened to the musics.
4 He wished me a luck on the test.
5 The printer is out of inks.
6 Cheese are my favorite food.
7 People need more informations.
8 Pancakes are great with honeys.
9 I have coffees and doughnuts every morning.
10 These are question about children's healthes.

B 다음 〈보기〉에서 알맞은 말을 골라 빈칸에 적절한 형태로 써넣으시오. (단, 한 번씩만 사용할 것)

〈보기〉 news America spoon water time money

1 The __________ gives us information.
2 Give me some __________. I'm thirsty.
3 There are two __________ on the table.
4 Tom is rich. He makes a lot of __________.
5 Do you have enough __________ for the meeting?
6 In __________, people eat turkey on Thanksgiving Day.

Point 05

명사 – 수량 표현 I

■ 셀 수 없는 명사의 수량은 그 명사를 측정하는 단위나 담는 용기 등을 나타내는 어구를 이용해서 표현한다. 복수형은 단위나 용기를 나타내는 명사에 -(e)s를 붙여서 나타낸다.

a piece of paper[cheese/bread/cake/pizza/advice/information/furniture]
a loaf of bread / **two slices of** bread[pizza/cheese]
a bowl of rice / **three bottles of** beer[wine]
a glass of water[juice/milk] / **two cups of** coffee[tea]
(glass는 차가운 음료에, cup은 따뜻한 음료에 주로 사용된다.)

★ PLUS TIP glasses(안경), scissors(가위), pants(바지), shoes(신발) 등은 항상 복수형으로 쓰며, pair를 이용해 수량을 나타낸다. (**a pair of** glasses, **two pairs of** pants)

A 다음 〈보기〉와 같이 주어진 말을 적절한 형태로 바꾸어 쓰시오.

〈보기〉 a glass of water → two glasses of water

1 a slice of pizza → six ______________
2 a loaf of bread → two ______________
3 a piece of cake → three ______________
4 a carton of milk → three ______________
5 a pair of scissors → two ______________

B 다음 밑줄 친 부분을 어법에 맞게 고쳐 쓰시오.

1 Tim bought a pair of pant and a shirt.
2 Mary brought three bottles of wines.
3 I was hungry, so I ate two bowl of rices.
4 Give me two glass of apple juices, please.
5 You had two piece of cheese and an orange.

C 다음 〈보기〉에서 알맞은 말을 골라 빈칸에 적절한 형태로 써넣으시오. (단, 한 번씩만 사용할 것)

〈보기〉 bottle cup pair piece slice

1 I gave him a __________ of advice.
2 They need two __________ of cheese.
3 David bought a new __________ of sunglasses.
4 My father drank two __________ of beer.
5 Chris drinks four __________ of tea a day.

Point 06 명사 – 수량 표현 II

■ 명사 앞에 쓰이는 표현 중에는 정해지지 않은 수량을 대략적으로 나타내는 것들이 있다.

많은	조금 있는, 약간의	거의 없는	
many	a few	few	+ 셀 수 있는 명사의 복수형
much	a little	little	+ 셀 수 없는 명사

Peter took **many pictures**. / I have **a few problems**.
Joan didn't do **much work**. / This soup needs **a little salt**.

★ 내신만점 *TIP* 셀 수 있는 명사나 셀 수 없는 명사와 함께 사용되는 수량 표현들을 확실히 구분하여 기억하자.

A 다음 밑줄 친 부분을 어법에 맞게 고쳐 쓰시오.

1 A water is important to life.
2 We have much things to do.
3 I can see smokes in the air.
4 I saw many child in the park.
5 Brian works six day a week.
6 There are butters on the table.
7 I had a few sandwich this morning.
8 We can help the children with a few money.
9 I poured a little milks into my brother's glass.
10 We don't have many time. Please hurry up.

B 다음 우리말과 같은 뜻이 되도록 ( ) 안의 말을 이용하여 문장을 완성하시오.

1 그 어려운 시험을 통과한 학생은 거의 없었다. (student)
_________ _________ passed the difficult test.

2 그 아이는 많은 용기가 필요하다. (courage)
The child needs _________ _________.

3 내 주머니 안에 열쇠 몇 개가 있다. (key)
There are _________ _________ _________ in my pocket.

4 그 두 개의 상자 안에 많은 장난감들이 있다. (toy, box)
There _________ _________ _________ in the two _________.

5 나는 우유 두 잔과 약간의 치즈를 먹었다. (milk, cheese)
I had two _________ of _________ and _________ _________ _________.

Point 07

관사 I – 부정관사 a/an

- 관사는 명사 앞에서 명사의 의미나 성격에 대한 정보를 나타내는 말로, 부정관사 a/an과 정관사 the가 있다.
- 부정관사 a나 an은 셀 수 있는 명사의 단수형 앞에 사용된다.
  - 막연한 하나를 나타낼 때: She is **a** doctor.
  - 하나(one)를 나타낼 때: I have **an** orange and two apples.
  - ~마다(= per): He plays basketball twice **a** week.

★ PLUS TIP
a+첫 발음이 자음인 명사: **a** house, **a** week, **a** student
an+첫 발음이 모음인 명사: **an** egg, **an** orange, **an** hour

A 다음 빈칸에 a와 an 중 알맞은 말을 쓰시오. (불필요하면 X 표시할 것)

1 He is ________ actor in this movie.
2 It is ________ nice suit.
3 She is full of ________ love.
4 Molly is ________ honest person.
5 They have ________ exam on Friday.
6 I stayed in Sokcho for ________ month.
7 Sue doesn't wear ________ uniform.
8 There is ________ old woman in the park.
9 Lilly sent me ________ invitation.
10 I had ________ cookie for dessert.

B 다음 우리말과 같은 뜻이 되도록 ( ) 안의 말을 이용하여 문장을 완성하시오.

1 그는 하루에 한 번 나에게 전화를 했다. (once, day)
He called me ________ ________ ________.

2 나는 재미있는 이야기를 읽었다. (interesting, story)
I read ________ ________ ________.

3 나는 어제 잡지 한 권을 샀다. (buy, magazine)
I ________ ________ ________ yesterday.

4 우리 언니는 대학생이다. (university student)
My sister ________ ________ ________ ________.

5 저에게 종이 한 장을 주세요. (piece, paper)
Please give me ________ ________ ________ ________.

Point 08

관사 II – 정관사 the

- 정관사 the는 특정한 것이나 명확한 것을 가리킬 때 쓴다.
  - 앞에 나온 명사를 가리킬 때: He sang a song. **The** song was great.
  - 서로 알고 있는 것을 가리킬 때: Close **the** window, please.
  - 수식어가 뒤에서 꾸며주고 있을 때: **The** book on the desk is yours.
  - 관용적으로 쓰이는 경우: **the** Internet, **the** sky, **the** sun, play **the** flute(악기명) 등

★ 내신만점 TIP 관사 a와 the를 사용하는 경우를 구분하자.

A 다음 ( ) 안에서 알맞은 말을 고르시오.

1 Mimi is (a / the) friendly pet.
2 (A / The) notebook on the desk is mine.
3 I was (a / an) hour late for the meeting.
4 Did you walk around under (a / the) sun yesterday?
5 Tim plays (a / the) guitar, and I play (a / the) piano.
6 Tony gave me (a / the) rose. (A / The) rose was white.
7 I got a box. There was a photo in (a / the) box.
8 (A / The) sky is cloudy. Take your umbrella with you.
9 This morning (a / the) girl said hello to me. But I didn't know (a / the) girl.
10 Mom bought me (a / the) new violin. Now I play (a / the) violin every day.

B 다음 우리말과 같은 뜻이 되도록 ( ) 안의 말을 이용하여 문장을 완성하시오.

1 너는 인터넷 없이 살 수 있니? (Internet)
Can you live without ________ ________?

2 아버지는 거실에 계신다. (living room)
My father is in ________ ________ ________.

3 Joe는 좋은 음악가이다. (good, musician)
Joe is ________ ________ ________.

4 의자 옆에 있는 가방은 내 것이다. (bag)
________ ________ next to the chair is mine.

5 달은 지구 주위를 돈다. (moon, earth)
________ ________ moves around ________ ________.

Point 09

관사의 생략 I

■ 식사나 운동경기 이름을 나타내는 명사 앞이나 〈by+교통/통신수단〉의 형태로 쓸 때는 관사를 쓰지 않는다.

I already had **lunch**.

We play **soccer** after school.

I came here by **bus**.

■ 건물이나 장소가 본래의 용도로 사용될 때도 관사를 쓰지 않는다.

I usually go to **school** at 8:30.

★ PLUS TIP 식사명 앞에 수식하는 말이 오면 관사를 쓰기도 한다.

I had **a** great breakfast.

A 다음 빈칸에 a와 an 중 알맞은 말을 쓰시오. (불필요하면 X 표시할 것)

1 Helen sat down on __________ bench.

2 He bought __________ used car.

3 Do you want to play __________ tennis?

4 We usually have __________ breakfast at six o'clock.

5 My grandparents went to Jeju Island by __________ plane.

6 What time do you go to __________ work?

7 Jennifer goes to Daejeon by __________ train.

8 I called you __________ hour ago.

9 My family has __________ special dinner once a month.

10 Students go to __________ school five days __________ week.

B 다음 우리말과 같은 뜻이 되도록 ( ) 안의 말을 배열하여 문장을 완성하시오.

1 나는 Jane과 함께 점심을 먹었다. (lunch, with, had, I, Jane)

____

2 당신은 여기에 택시를 타고 왔나요? (taxi, did, come, you, here, by)

____

3 Bill은 어젯밤에 10시에 잠자리에 들었다. (bed, at ten, Bill, went to, last night)

____

4 기독교인들은 일요일에 교회를 간다. (church, on Sunday, Christians, go to)

____

5 Paula는 수요일마다 배드민턴을 친다. (badminton, plays, every Wednesday, Paula)

____

Point 10 관사의 생략 II

■ 부정관사 a/an, 정관사 the를 쓰거나 생략하는 경우는 상황에 따라 달라지므로 의미에 유의해야 한다.
I want **a cello**. (막연한 첼로 하나를 의미하는 경우)
I play **the cello**. (악기를 연주한다는 의미인 경우)
Alison went to **bed** a minute ago. (잠을 자러 가는 경우)
Alison went to **the bed** to get her pillow. (가구인 '침대'로 가는 경우)

A 주어진 단어의 앞에 a, an, the를 쓰거나 관사를 생략하여 문장을 완성하시오.

1 (bus) She came home by __________.
I took __________ to the mall. The bus was full.

2 (car) Do you have __________?
He bought a new car. He washed __________ yesterday.

3 (salt) This soup needs __________.
Pass me __________, please.

4 (novel) This is her famous novel. A lot of people read __________.
Tim gave me __________. It was touching.

5 (restaurant) Sally was at __________ downtown.
He went to __________ again.

B 다음 빈칸에 a, an, the 중 알맞은 말을 쓰시오. (불필요하면 X 표시할 것)

1 Rome is __________ capital of Italy.
2 What time does __________ sun rise?
3 Our town is near __________ sea.
4 We had __________ wonderful dinner.
5 Please close __________ door.
6 Ken played __________ soccer after school.
7 There are millions of stars in __________ sky.
8 We can send you the file by __________ email.
9 I visit my grandparents four times __________ year.
10 I had __________ sandwich. __________ sandwich was good.
11 He plays __________ golf with Alexa on weekends.
12 __________ cat on the sofa is my pet.

[01-03] 다음 빈칸에 알맞은 말을 고르시오.

01

There is a ________.

① love ② luck
③ lions ④ water
⑤ coin

02

We saw a few ________.

① news ② child
③ snow ④ goose
⑤ wolves

03

He doesn't make much ________.

① idea ② money
③ friends ④ cookies
⑤ problem

04

다음 중 밑줄 친 복수형이 잘못된 것은?

① We caught three fish in the river.
② Their wives talked together.
③ There are two grand pianos in the shop.
④ Those childs had fun.
⑤ I want to visit many cities in England.

[05-07] 빈칸에 들어갈 말이 순서대로 알맞게 짝지어진 것을 고르시오.

05

• Dave bought a ________ of scissors.
• Please give me two ________ of juice.

① pair – loaves ② loaf – pairs
③ slice – cups ④ pair – glasses
⑤ piece – glasses

06

• Turn off ________ TV, please.
• I saw you on ________ TV yesterday.

① a – the ② the – 관사 없음
③ a – 관사 없음 ④ the – a
⑤ 관사 없음 – the

07

• There are ________ sheep.
• Did you play ________ tennis?

① much – the ② many – the
③ a little – the ④ little – 관사 없음
⑤ a few – 관사 없음

[08-09] 다음 빈칸에 a나 an이 들어갈 수 없는 문장을 고르시오.

08

① It was ________ mistake.
② People need ________ air.
③ Jamie is ________ English actor.
④ There is ________ bank near here.
⑤ I saw ________ accident this morning.

09

① I was ________ teacher.
② She is ________ fashion model.
③ My mother loves ________ coffee.
④ He had ________ apple in the morning.
⑤ My grandparents have two dogs and ________ cat.

10

다음 우리말을 영어로 바르게 옮긴 것은?

꽃병 안의 그 꽃은 약간의 물이 필요하다.

① A flower in the vase needs a few waters.
② A flower in the vase needs little water.
③ The flower in the vase needs few water.
④ The flower in the vase needs a little water.
⑤ The flower in the vase needs a little waters.

[11-13] 다음 빈칸에 공통으로 들어갈 말을 고르시오.

11

- ________ woman on your left is our new homeroom teacher.
- ________ sun rises in the east.

① A ② An
③ The ④ Few
⑤ Many

12

- Mrs. Robinson gave me a ________ of advice.
- Jessica had a ________ of cake for dessert.

① slice ② pair
③ piece ④ little
⑤ many

13

- We received ________ good information.
- There is ________ snow on the street.

① a ② an
③ a few ④ 관사 없음
⑤ many

기출응용

14

다음 우리말과 같은 뜻이 되도록 주어진 말을 배열할 때 네 번째에 올 단어는?

> 우리는 가구 두 점을 샀다.
> (bought, furniture, two, of, we, pieces)

① bought ② two ③ furniture
④ of ⑤ pieces

[15-17] 다음 중 어법상 틀린 것을 고르시오.

15

① She wears a uniform at work.
② Tim went to bed early.
③ Julie had a wonderful lunch.
④ I took a walk for an hour.
⑤ Dorothy wore a pairs of glasses.

16

① Maggie loves cookies.
② There is sand on the beach.
③ They work eight hour a day.
④ I brush my teeth after meals.
⑤ There are many benches in the park.

17

① She drank a cup of juice.
② My parents gave me a piece of advice.
③ My mother baked two loaves of bread.
④ Jack spent a few week in London.
⑤ My aunt put a little salt in the hot soup.

18

다음 〈보기〉의 밑줄 친 부분과 쓰임이 같은 것은?

> 〈보기〉 Let's take a taxi.

① I drink tea twice a day.
② She cried for an hour.
③ Chris is a singer.
④ This car goes 50 km an hour.
⑤ Ann has a son and two daughters.

19

다음 밑줄 친 부분의 쓰임이 잘못된 것은?

① Look at the sky. It's so blue.
② I saw a man. The man was a designer.
③ Those girls were talking in front of the church.
④ I found some information on the Internet.
⑤ Did you have the breakfast with your little brother?

고난도

20

다음 중 어법상 옳은 것끼리 짝지어진 것은?

> (a) Paris is a capital of France.
> (b) The children drink milk every day.
> (c) I'm waiting for three womans.
> (d) Kevin works at a small company.
> (e) I need a little sugar.

① (a), (b), (d) ② (a), (c), (d)
③ (b), (c), (e) ④ (b), (d), (e)
⑤ (c), (d), (e)

서술형 따라잡기

01
주어진 두 문장을 한 문장으로 바꾸어 쓸 때, 빈칸에 알맞은 말을 쓰시오.

I found a mouse in the kitchen.
I found three more in the bathroom.

→ I found four ________ in the house.

02
어법상 틀린 부분을 모두 찾아 바르게 고쳐 쓰시오.

(1) I can go see a movie today. I don't have many work to do. (1군데)

(2) There were a few monkey at the zoo. I took some photoes with them. (2군데)

03
다음 그림을 보고, 문장을 완성하시오.

There is a farm in my town. It has four ________ and two ________. There are also three ________. Yesterday, a ________ joined the other animals at the farm.

04
주어진 말을 알맞게 배열하여 대화를 완성하시오.

A: Did Gary eat rice?
B: Yes, he did. He ____________________.
(bowls, ate, of, rice, two)

05
다음 Paul과 Jane이 점심으로 먹은 것을 보고, 빈칸에 알맞은 말을 쓰시오.

Paul | Jane

(1) Paul had ________ ________ ________ ________ and ________ ________ ________ ________ for lunch.

(2) Jane had ________ ________ ________ ________ and ________ ________ ________ ________ for lunch.

고난도
06
다음 Willy의 일기를 읽고, 빈칸에 알맞은 관사를 쓰시오. (불필요하면 X 표시할 것)

Last night, my brother hid my smartphone. I looked for it for ________ hour and found it in the kitchen. So I went to ________ bed late. Today, I was very sleepy at ________ school.

SELF NOTE

핵심 포인트 정리하기

1 명사

- 의미: 사람, 사물, 장소 등을 나타내는 말
- 종류: 셀 수 있는 명사, 셀 수 없는 명사(추상명사, 고유명사, 물질명사)
- 셀 수 있는 명사의 복수형
  - 규칙 변화: 명사 + -(e)s

    book → ① ________ / potato → ② ________
  - 불규칙 변화

    deer → ③ ________ / mouse → ④ ________ / tooth → teeth / man → ⑤ ________
- 셀 수 없는 명사의 수량 표현
  - a ⑥ ________ of paper[cheese / bread / cake 등] / two slices of bread[pizza / cheese]
  - three bottles of beer[wine] / a glass of water[juice / milk]
  - two cups of coffee[tea]
- 정해지지 않은 수량에 대한 표현
  - many, a few, few + 셀 수 ⑦ ________ 명사의 복수형 / much, a little, little + 셀 수 ⑧ ________ 명사

이것만은 꼭! 셀 수 있는 명사나 셀 수 없는 명사와 함께 쓰이는 수량 표현 알아두기!

2 관사

- 의미: 명사의 의미나 성격에 대한 정보를 나타내는 말
- 부정관사와 정관사
  - 부정관사(a/an): 셀 수 있는 명사의 단수형 앞에 사용('막연한 하나', '하나', '~마다'의 의미)

    a doctor / ⑨ ________ orange / once a week
  - 정관사(the): 특정한 것이나 명확한 것을 가리킬 때 사용

    play the flute / ⑩ ________ book on the desk

관사의 사용 유무에 따라 달라지는 의미를 예문으로 익히기!

문제로 개념 다지기

밑줄 친 부분이 어법상 맞으면 O, 틀리면 X 표시하고 바르게 고치시오.

1 I ate three piece of cakes.
2 We saw many sheeps on the hill.
3 She plays the piano once a week.
4 There are a lot of clouds in the sky.
5 A sun heats the water in the lake.
6 It takes a hour to get there by car.

개념 쏙쏙

This is my notebook, and **that** is my pen.	[지시대명사]
They are expensive, but I really want **one**.	[부정대명사]
The cookies are homemade. I baked them **myself**.	[재귀대명사]

대명사란?

명사를 대신해서 쓰는 말로, 주로 명사의 반복을 피하기 위해 씁니다. 특정한 사람이나 사물을 가리키는 지시대명사, 불특정한 사람이나 사물을 가리키는 부정대명사, '~ 자신'이나 '직접'이라는 의미의 재귀대명사가 있다는 것을 알아 두세요!

지시대명사 – this / that

■ 지시대명사란 특정한 사람이나 사물을 가리키는 말로, 대상과의 거리 및 대상의 수에 따라 다르게 쓰인다.

	단수 / 복수	의미
가까이 있는 사람 · 사물	**this / these**	이것(들), 이 사람(들)
멀리 있는 사람 · 사물	**that / those**	저것(들), 저 사람(들)

This is Luna. / **These** are my friends.
Is **that** your car? / **Those** are oranges.

★ PLUS TIP this[these]와 that[those]은 명사를 앞에서 수식하는 지시형용사 역할을 하기도 하며, '이 ~', '저 ~'라는 의미로 쓰인다.
I like **this** picture. / **Those** T-shirts are on sale.

A 다음 ( ) 안에서 알맞은 말을 고르시오.

1 What's (this / that) right here?
2 Is (that / those) Steve's sister?
3 I got (this / these) flowers from Jim.
4 He made (that / those) wonderful shoes.
5 Do you know (that / those) children?

B 다음 우리말과 같은 뜻이 되도록 ( ) 안의 말을 배열하여 문장을 완성하시오.

1 이 배낭은 네 것이니? (backpack, yours, this, is)

____

2 저 아이들은 행복하다. (those, are, children, happy)

____

3 이것들은 여성들을 위한 재킷이다. (for, these, women, are, jackets)

____

4 저 사람은 Julie의 남자친구이다. (boyfriend, is, Julie's, that)

____

5 저 나무는 정말 크다. (tree, so, big, is, that)

____

6 너는 이 약속들을 지키니? (do, promises, keep, these, you)

____

7 우리 어머니가 저 머핀들을 만드셨다. (muffins, made, mother, those, my)

____

Point 02 부정대명사 I – one

- 부정대명사란 정해지지 않은 불특정한 사람이나 사물을 가리키는 말이다.
- 부정대명사 one은 앞에 나온 명사와 같은 종류의 불특정한 사물을 가리킬 때 사용된다. 복수명사를 받는 경우에는 ones를 쓴다.
  I need a blue pen. Can you lend **one** to me? (one = a blue pen)
  She has pretty earrings. I want the same **ones**. (ones = earrings)
- 부정대명사 one은 일반인을 가리킬 때도 사용된다.
  One should be honest. (one = a person)

★ PLUS TIP 앞에 나온 특정한 사물을 가리킬 때는 it을 사용한다.
This coat is too small. I can't wear **it**. (it = this coat)

A 다음 ( ) 안에서 알맞은 말을 고르시오.

1 Do you need a paper clip? I have (it / one).
2 Did you see my key? I lost (it / one).
3 My bag is old. I need a new (it / one).
4 This game is boring. Do you have a fun (it / one)?
5 A: Do you have a red pin? — B: No, but I have a few green (one / ones).

B 다음 빈칸에 one, ones, it, them 중 알맞은 말을 쓰시오.

1 I don't like cold drinks. I like hot __________.
2 My keyboard doesn't work. I want to buy a new __________.
3 Let's watch these romantic movies together. You'll love __________.
4 Let's have the seafood pizza at Mama's. I like __________ very much.

C 다음 우리말과 같은 뜻이 되도록 ( ) 안의 말을 배열하여 문장을 완성하시오.

1 사람은 신중하게 결정을 내려야 한다. (decisions, carefully, should make, one)
____

2 내가 알록달록한 컵케이크를 만들었다. 나는 분홍색 컵케이크가 마음에 든다.
(like, pink, the, I, ones)
I made colorful cupcakes. ______________________________

3 그녀는 예쁜 컵을 모은다. 그래서 나는 그녀를 위해 컵을 하나 샀다.
(one, I, her, for, bought)
She collects beautiful cups. So ______________________________.

Point 03

부정대명사 II – some/any

- some과 any는 '약간(의)', '얼마간(의)', '어떤'이라는 뜻으로 대명사나 형용사로 사용된다. some과 any가 형용사로 사용될 경우 셀 수 있는 명사와 셀 수 없는 명사 앞에 올 수 있다.
  - some: 긍정의 평서문과 긍정의 대답을 예상하는 의문문이나 권유문에서 사용된다.
    Are there pens? – Yes, there are **some**.
    There are **some** biscuits on the table. / Will you have **some** biscuits?
  - any: 주로 부정문, 의문문, 조건문에서 사용된다.
    Do you want **any** (of the books)?
    Do you have **any** questions? / I don't have **any** questions.

A 다음 빈칸에 some과 any 중 알맞은 말을 쓰시오.

1 Do you have __________ ideas?
2 Would you like __________ cake?
3 I want __________ water.
4 Give me __________ bread, please.
5 The doctor didn't have __________ time.
6 Are there __________ giraffes in this zoo?
7 Don't put __________ sugar in her coffee.
8 They got __________ sleep after working all day.
9 He didn't get __________ messages from his friends.
10 I don't have __________ toys, but my brother has __________.

B 다음 우리말과 같은 뜻이 되도록 ( ) 안의 말을 배열하여 문장을 완성하시오.

1 오늘 밤 무슨 계획 있니? (plans, you, have, tonight, do, any)
____

2 너 아이스크림 좀 먹을래? (ice cream, you, do, want, some)
____

3 Brian은 나를 위해 약간의 간식을 샀다. (me, bought, snacks, for, some)
Brian ____.

4 그 밴드는 좋은 노래가 하나도 없다. (have, any, doesn't, good songs)
The band __________________________________.

5 너 Sue와 무슨 문제가 있니? (you, any, problems, do, have)
____ with Sue?

Point 04 비인칭 주어 it

■ 비인칭 주어 it은 시간, 날씨, 계절, 거리, 명암 등을 나타낼 때 쓰인다. 이때, it을 '그것'이라고 해석하지 않는다.

What time is **it**? (시간)

It is very cold now. (날씨)

It's Monday today. (요일)

★ 내신만점 TIP 특정 대상을 가리키는 인칭대명사 it과는 분명한 쓰임의 차이가 있음을 기억하자.
This pen is very good. **It**'s for you. (인칭대명사 it) / **It** rained all day. (비인칭 주어 it)

A 다음 질문에 알맞은 대답을 〈보기〉에서 골라 쓰시오.

〈보기〉	It's Thursday.	It is about five kilometers.	It's 5:30.
	It is cloudy.	It takes half an hour.	It's May 8.

1 What time is it now? ______________

2 What day of the week is it? ______________

3 How is the weather today? ______________

4 What is today's date? ______________

5 How far is it from your house to school? ______________

6 How long does it take to get to the station? ______________

B 다음 우리말과 같은 뜻이 되도록 ( ) 안의 말을 이용하여 문장을 완성하시오.

1 밖이 어둡다. (dark, outside)

_______ _______ _______ _______.

2 오늘은 내 생일이다. (birthday)

_______ _______ _______ _______ today.

3 5시 10분 전이다. 나는 늦었다. (ten to five)

_______ _______ _______ _______ _______. I'm late.

4 기차로 한 시간 걸린다. (take, an hour)

_______ _______ _______ _______ by train.

5 여기서 시청까지는 10km이다. (kilometer)

_______ _______ _______ _______ from here to City Hall.

6 오늘 아침에는 비가 왔는데, 지금은 화창하다. (rainy, sunny)

_______ _______ _______ this morning, but _______ _______

_______ now.

Point 05 재귀대명사

- 재귀대명사란 '~ 자신'이라는 의미의 대명사로, 주어가 주어 자신에게 행위를 할 때 혹은 주어의 행위를 강조할 때 사용한다.
- 재귀대명사의 단수형은 인칭대명사의 소유격 또는 목적격에 -self를, 복수형은 -selves를 붙여서 만든다.

인칭	단수	복수
1인칭	myself	ourselves
2인칭	yourself	yourselves
3인칭	himself / herself / itself	themselves

A 다음 밑줄 친 부분을 알맞은 재귀대명사로 고쳐 쓰시오.

1 Rachel her made dinner.
2 My cat cleans it.
3 I don't think about me much.
4 We enjoyed us at the party.
5 Some people don't love them.
6 We made ourself look gentle.
7 The children dressed theirselves.

B 다음 우리말과 같은 뜻이 되도록 문장을 완성하시오.

1 나는 나 자신을 잘 표현한다.
I express __________ well.

2 당신 자신에 관한 에세이를 쓰세요.
Write an essay about __________.

3 Betty는 그녀 자신의 사진을 찍었다.
Betty took a picture of __________.

4 그들은 그들의 방을 직접 청소했다.
They cleaned their rooms __________.

5 우리는 우리 자신에 대해 배우려고 노력했다.
We tried to learn about __________.

6 Ben은 그 자신에 대해 이야기하는 것을 좋아하지 않는다.
Ben doesn't like to talk about __________.

7 우리는 그들에게 직접 편지를 썼다.
We wrote letters to them __________.

Point 06 재귀대명사의 용법 – 재귀 / 강조

- 재귀 용법은 주어와 목적어가 같을 때 동사나 전치사의 목적어로 쓰인다.
  Emily loves **herself**. (동사 love의 목적어)
  She felt proud of **herself**. (전치사 of의 목적어)
- 강조 용법은 주어나 목적어를 강조할 때 '직접', '스스로'라는 뜻으로 사용된다. (생략 가능)
  My dad **himself** made the spaghetti. (주어 강조)
  They enjoyed the music **itself**. (목적어 강조)

★ 내신만점 *TIP* 재귀 용법으로 쓰인 재귀대명사는 문장에서 반드시 필요한 요소로, 생략할 수 없다는 것을 잊지 말자.
You should trust **yourself**. (O) / You should trust. (X)

A 다음 우리말과 같은 뜻이 되도록 문장을 완성하고, 생략할 수 있는 부분을 찾아 ( ) 표시 하시오. (단, 없으면 X 표시할 것)

1 나는 실수로 나를 베었다.
I cut __________ by mistake.

2 우리가 직접 이 노래들을 만들었다.
We wrote these songs __________.

3 그들은 그들 자신을 영웅이라고 생각했다.
They thought of __________ as heroes.

4 음식 자체는 훌륭했다. 하지만 서비스가 형편없었다.
The food __________ was great. But the service was terrible.

B 다음 문장을 우리말로 해석하고, 재귀대명사가 어떤 용법으로 쓰였는지 〈 〉 안에 써넣으시오.

1 Susan washed the dishes herself.
__________________________________ 〈 〉

2 My brother talked to himself.
__________________________________ 〈 〉

3 Mom made this cake herself.
__________________________________ 〈 〉

4 The student introduced herself to the class.
__________________________________ 〈 〉

5 The artist himself explained the paintings.
__________________________________ 〈 〉

[01-03] 다음 빈칸에 알맞은 말을 고르시오.

01

Do you have a watch? I need _______.

① it ② them
③ one ④ ones
⑤ some

02

You have a lot of comic books! I want _______.

① it ② any
③ some ④ itself
⑤ themselves

03

Do you like the movie? I saw _______ several times.

① it ② them
③ one ④ ones
⑤ some

04

다음 밑줄 친 this의 쓰임이 나머지와 다른 것은?

① Will you buy this necklace?
② I didn't find the book in this library.
③ My son visited this toy store before.
④ Is this a present for your brother?
⑤ This room is my favorite place in my house.

[05-07] 빈칸에 들어갈 말이 순서대로 알맞게 짝지어진 것을 고르시오.

05

A: Do you have _______ good ideas for our team project?
B: Yes, I have _______.

① a – some ② any – it
③ some – it ④ any – some
⑤ some – any

06

A: My sister gave me this purse. She got a new _______.
B: _______ looks cool. I envy you.

① one – One ② one – Ones
③ one – It ④ it – One
⑤ one – They

07

A: There are _______ muffins on the table.
B: I baked them for you _______.

① a – me ② some – myself
③ any – myself ④ some – themselves
⑤ any – yourself

08
다음 대화 중 자연스럽지 <u>않은</u> 것은?

① A: What is Molly doing?
B: She is looking at herself in the mirror.
② A: Would you like some coffee?
B: Yes, please.
③ A: Do you have any pens?
B: Sorry, I don't have some.
④ A: When is your birthday?
B: It's August 9.
⑤ A: Do you like golf?
B: No, I don't like it.

[09-10] 다음 〈보기〉의 밑줄 친 부분과 쓰임이 <u>다른</u> 것을 고르시오.

09

〈보기〉 <u>It</u> is 10 a.m.

① <u>It</u> is a gift for you.
② <u>It</u> is spring now.
③ <u>It</u> is a lovely day.
④ <u>It</u> is September 14.
⑤ <u>It</u> is about 3 kilometers from here to the mall.

10

〈보기〉 Eric did all the work <u>himself</u>.

① Joe wrote the book <u>himself</u>.
② Holly calls <u>herself</u> a princess.
③ I <u>myself</u> made this website.
④ We grow the tomatoes <u>ourselves</u>.
⑤ They came up with the idea <u>themselves</u>.

기출응용

11
다음 밑줄 친 부분을 바르게 고친 것끼리 짝지어진 것은?

(a) Are <u>this</u> shoes his?
→ these
(b) There aren't <u>some</u> books on the desk.
→ any
(c) Your tie is very nice. I want the same <u>it</u>.
→ ones
(d) <u>That's</u> going to be dark soon.
→ It's
(e) They don't take care of <u>themself</u>.
→ itself

① (a), (b), (d) ② (a), (b), (e)
③ (b), (c), (d) ④ (b), (c), (e)
⑤ (c), (d), (e)

12
다음 우리말을 영어로 바르게 옮긴 것은?

우리는 우리 자신을 자랑스러워한다.

① We are proud of ourself.
② We are proud of ours.
③ We are proud of us.
④ We are proud of ourselves.
⑤ We are proud of ourselfs.

13
다음 밑줄 친 부분이 어법상 <u>틀린</u> 것은?

① I can't find <u>any</u> boxes here.
② Will you have <u>some</u> orange juice?
③ Did you use <u>any</u> of these coupons?
④ He read <u>some</u> of those books.
⑤ There aren't <u>some</u> people in the theater.

[14-16] 다음 빈칸에 공통으로 들어갈 말을 고르시오.

14

A: Wow! ________ is snowing.
B: Yes! ________ is a white Christmas!

① This ② That
③ There ④ It
⑤ One

15

• The children enjoyed ________ on the swings.
• Many people don't know ________ very well.

① itself ② myself
③ himself ④ yourselves
⑤ themselves

16

• I didn't read ________ novels.
• Are there ________ pigeons in the park?

① one ② some
③ any ④ ones
⑤ it

17

다음 밑줄 친 부분을 생략할 수 있는 것은?

① I blamed myself.
② We believe in ourselves.
③ He had lunch by himself.
④ She learned things about herself.
⑤ They did their homework themselves.

고난도

[18-19] 다음 중 어법상 틀린 것을 고르시오.

18

① The artist loves herself.
② It was very cold last winter.
③ There are any elephants here.
④ I paid for the ticket myself.
⑤ Would you like a sandwich? I bought one for you.

19

① She fixed the television myself.
② Look at that over there.
③ Help yourself to the apple pies.
④ He didn't get any gifts on his birthday.
⑤ I made a lot of bread. Please have some.

20

(A), (B), (C)의 괄호 안에서 알맞은 것끼리 바르게 짝지어진 것은?

(A) [One / It] is ten o' clock now.
(B) There were [some / any] cars on the street.
(C) [The child / The children] talks to herself.

	(A)		(B)		(C)
①	One	……	any	……	The children
②	It	……	any	……	The child
③	One	……	some	……	The child
④	It	……	some	……	The child
⑤	It	……	some	……	The children

서술형 따라잡기

01

다음 문장을 지시대로 바꾸어 쓰시오.

(1) Is that your pet? (pet을 pets로)

→ ________ ________ ________ ________?

(2) This is my new tablet PC. I sold the old one yesterday. (tablet PC를 tablet PCs로)

→ ________ ________ my new ________ ________. I sold ________ ________ ________ yesterday.

02

다음 〈보기〉에서 알맞은 말을 골라 빈칸을 완성하시오.

〈보기〉 it them one ones

(1) ________ should always keep promises.

(2) That is a nice bag. ________ is Tony's.

03

다음 그림을 보고, 빈칸에 적절한 대명사를 쓰시오.

(1) ________ was rainy. I was going to wear my black jacket, but I couldn't find (2) ________. So I wore my blue (3) ________ instead.

04

주어진 말을 알맞게 배열하여 우리말과 뜻이 같도록 문장을 완성하시오.

(1) 그는 자신에 대해서 신경 쓴다.
(himself, cares, he, about)

→ ________________

(2) 책상 위에 연필 몇 자루가 있었다.
(pencils, on, there, some, the desk, were)

→ ________________

05

다음 조건에 맞게 우리말을 영어로 옮겨 쓰시오.

〈조건〉 1. 재귀대명사를 이용할 것
2. 표현 move the box, look at, in the mirror를 이용할 것

(1) Mike가 그 상자를 직접 옮겼니?

→ ________________

(2) 그들은 거울 속의 자기 자신들을 봤다.

→ ________________

고난도

06

다음 대화의 밑줄 친 부분을 어법에 맞게 고쳐 쓰시오.

A: Do you have (1) <u>some</u> raincoats?
B: Yes, we have (2) <u>any</u>.
A: (3) <u>Those</u> pink one looks good.
B: We are out of pink ones in your size, but we do have the same design in a different color.

SELF NOTE

핵심 포인트 정리하기

1 지시대명사

- 의미: 특정한 사람이나 사물을 가리키는 말
- 형태

	단수	복수
대상이 가까울 때	①________	these
대상이 멀 때	that	②________

2 부정대명사

- 의미: 정해지지 않은 불특정한 사람이나 사물을 가리키는 말
- 형태

  - one (복수형: ③________)
  - ④________ (긍정의 평서문, 긍정의 대답을 예상하는 의문문이나 권유문에 사용)
  - ⑤________ (부정문, 의문문, 조건문에 사용)

부정대명사 one, some, any의 쓰임을 구분하기!

3 비인칭 주어 it

- 시간, 날씨, 계절, 거리, 명암 등을 나타낼 때 사용 ('그것'이라고 해석하지 않음)

인칭대명사 it과 비인칭 주어 it의 쓰임 바로 알기!

4 재귀대명사

- 주어와 목적어가 같을 때나 주어·목적어를 강조할 때 사용 ('~ 자신', '직접', '스스로'의 의미)

인칭	단수	복수
1인칭	myself	⑥________
2인칭	⑦________	yourselves
3인칭	himself / herself / itself	⑧________

대명사가 가리키는 대상을 파악할 때 앞에 나온 명사가 무엇인지 살펴보기!

문제로 개념 다지기

밑줄 친 부분이 어법상 맞으면 O, 틀리면 X 표시하고 바르게 고치시오.

1 How about going to <u>those</u> house on the hill?
2 Kelly doesn't have <u>any</u> plans this weekend.
3 She bought three skirts: a red one and two black <u>some</u>.
4 Mike <u>himself</u> made a plan for a field trip.
5 The children enjoyed <u>yourselves</u> at the show.
6 <u>It's</u> getting cold outside.

CHAPTER 05 시제

I	**go**	to school.	나는 학교에 간다.
I	**went**	to school.	나는 학교에 갔다.
I	**am going**	to school.	나는 학교에 가는 중이다.
I	**was going**	to school.	나는 학교에 가는 중이었다.

시제란?

'~한다', '~했다', '~하는 중이다', '~하는 중이었다' 등과 같이 동작이나 사건이 언제 일어나는지 보여주는 것으로, 동사의 형태를 변화시켜서 나타냅니다. 동사의 형태는 규칙적으로 변하기도 하지만, 불규칙적으로 변하기도 한답니다.

Point 01 현재시제

- 현재시제는 현재의 상태나 지속적인 성질, 일상적인 행동이나 습관, 과학적 사실이나 불변의 사실 등을 나타낼 때 사용된다.
  I **am** hungry now. (현재의 상태)
  My sister **walks** to school. (일상적인 습관)
  Water **freezes** at 0 ˚C. (과학적 사실)

A 다음 〈보기〉에서 알맞은 말을 골라 적절한 형태로 써넣으시오. (단, 한 번씩만 사용할 것)

〈보기〉 go open be take play be eat get have be

1 Whales __________ mammals.
2 Hanna __________ tennis.
3 My father __________ on TV now!
4 The shop __________ at 9 a.m. every day.
5 There __________ four seasons in Korea.
6 Jessica __________ two little sisters.
7 He __________ for a walk every day.
8 Joan __________ up early every morning.
9 It __________ 15 minutes to get to the fitness center.
10 I __________ breakfast at seven o'clock every morning.

B 다음 우리말과 같은 뜻이 되도록 ( ) 안의 말을 이용하여 문장을 완성하시오.

1 템스강은 런던에 있다. (be)
The Thames __________ in London.

2 Brian은 시험 전에 열심히 공부한다. (study, hard)
Brian __________ __________ before his exams.

3 우리 부모님은 저녁이면 피곤해 보이신다. (look, tired)
My parents __________ __________ in the evening.

4 마드리드는 스페인의 수도이다. (be, capital)
Madrid __________ __________ __________ of Spain.

5 물은 섭씨 100도에서 끓는다. (boil)
__________ __________ at 100 °C.

6 그 밴드의 멤버들은 키가 크고 잘생겼다. (be, tall, handsome)
The members of the band __________ __________ and __________.

Point 02

과거시제

■ 과거시제는 이미 끝난 과거의 동작이나 상태, 역사적 사실을 나타낼 때 사용된다. 주로 과거를 나타내는 시간의 부사(구)가 함께 쓰인다.

They **went** to the concert *yesterday*. (과거의 동작)
He **was** sick *last week*. (과거의 상태)
World War I **broke** out *in 1914*. (역사적 사실)

★ 내신만점 *TIP* 시제를 판단할 때는 현재시제 또는 과거시제와 함께 쓰이는 부사구가 있는지 확인하자.
She **looks** so tired **now**. / She **looked** so tired **last night**.

A 다음 ( ) 안의 동사를 알맞은 형태로 고쳐 쓰시오.

1 It __________ yesterday. (snow)
2 She __________ back to Korea last week. (come)
3 Anne Frank __________ her diary in the 1940s. (write)
4 Vincent van Gogh __________ sunflowers several times. (paint)
5 He __________ *The Little Prince* last month. (read)

B 다음 ( ) 안에서 알맞은 말을 고르시오.

1 I (am / was) slim now, but I (am / was) much heavier last year.
2 I was happy because Laura (sits / sat) next to me.
3 Paul (puts / put) his beach towel on the bench, but it disappeared.
4 It (is / was) Jane's birthday yesterday. We (give / gave) her a cute pencil case.
5 He usually (drives / drove) slowly, but he (drives / drove) fast yesterday.

C 다음 우리말과 같은 뜻이 되도록 ( ) 안의 말을 이용하여 문장을 완성하시오.

1 Donald는 어젯밤 악몽을 꿨다. (have)
Donald __________ a nightmare last night.

2 나는 지난 주말에 빵을 구웠다. (bake)
I __________ bread last weekend.

3 나는 그 배우에게 여러 통의 팬레터를 보냈다. (send)
I __________ several fan letters to the actor.

4 Sue는 오늘 아침에 어머니에게 거짓말을 했다. (lie)
Sue __________ to her mother this morning.

Point 03

진행형 만드는 법

- 진행형은 ⟨be동사+v-ing⟩의 형태로 특정 시점에 진행 중인 일을 나타낼 때 쓴다.
- ⟨v-ing⟩는 동사원형에 -ing를 붙여서 만든 형태이다.

대부분의 동사	동사원형+-ing	eat → eat**ing**
-e로 끝나는 동사	**e**를 빼고+-**ing**	come → com**ing**
-ie로 끝나는 동사	**ie**를 **y**로 고치고+-**ing**	lie → l**ying**
⟨단모음+단자음⟩으로 끝나고 그 모음에 강세가 오는 동사	자음을 한 번 더 쓰고+-**ing**	begin → begin**ning**
1음절 동사 중 ⟨단모음+단자음⟩으로 끝나는 동사		stop → stop**ping** get → get**ting**

A 다음 주어진 동사를 ⟨v-ing⟩의 형태로 바꾸어 쓰시오.

1 sleep __________ 2 say __________
3 make __________ 4 bring __________
5 have __________ 6 meet __________
7 buy __________ 8 take __________
9 win __________ 10 sit __________
11 drive __________ 12 stay __________
13 open __________ 14 die __________
15 run __________ 16 fly __________

B 다음 진행형 문장에서 ( ) 안의 동사를 알맞은 형태로 고쳐 쓰시오.

1 What are you __________ right now? (do)
2 Billy is __________ a glass of milk. (drink)
3 The food is __________ on the stove. (burn)
4 The train is __________ now. (arrive)
5 He is __________ a text message. (send)
6 They are __________ for the show. (wait)
7 I can't go now. I'm __________ lunch. (eat)
8 I'm __________ for my student ID. (look)
9 Vicky is __________ her hands. (wash)
10 The teacher is __________ the classroom. (enter)
11 My boyfriend is __________ in front of our school. (stand)

Point 04

현재진행형과 과거진행형

- 현재진행형은 〈be동사의 현재형+v-ing〉의 형태로, 현재 진행 중인 일을 나타낸다.
  Charlie **is sleeping** now.
- 과거진행형은 〈be동사의 과거형+v-ing〉의 형태로, 과거의 특정 시점에 진행 중이던 일을 나타낸다.
  I **was swimming** at that time.

★ PLUS TIP 소유나 상태를 나타내는 동사(have, know, want 등)는 진행형으로 쓰지 않는다. 단, have가 '먹다'의 뜻으로 쓰이면 진행형으로 쓸 수 있다.
I **want** a good grade on the exam. (O) / I'm wanting a good grade on the exam. (X)

A 다음 문장을 진행형으로 바꾸어 쓰시오.

1 I flew to Hawaii. → ____________________
2 She learns French. → ____________________
3 He held a big box. → ____________________
4 The monkey climbs the tree. → ____________________
5 You smiled at me. → ____________________
6 We make Christmas cards. → ____________________
7 They talk on the phone. → ____________________
8 Ted drove to the gas station. → ____________________
9 Susie and Dean had dinner. → ____________________
10 Gary sang a song for me. → ____________________

B 다음 우리말과 같은 뜻이 되도록 ( ) 안의 말을 이용하여 문장을 완성하시오.

1 Peter는 액세서리를 고르고 있었다. (choose)
Peter __________ __________ accessories.

2 그 아이들은 소파 위에서 뛰고 있었다. (jump)
The children __________ __________ on the sofa.

3 Cathy는 그때 울고 있었다. (cry)
Cathy __________ __________ at the time.

4 그들은 낮잠을 자는 중이다. (take a nap)
They __________ __________ __________ __________.

5 그녀는 인터넷을 사용하고 있다. (use the Internet)
She __________ __________ __________ __________.

6 그는 지금 수학 문제를 푸는 중이다. (solve math problems)
He __________ __________ __________ __________ right now.

Point 05 진행형의 부정문

- 진행형의 부정문은 〈be동사+not+v-ing〉의 형태이다.
  I'm not taking a bath. (현재진행형의 부정문)
  He **wasn't looking** at you. (과거진행형의 부정문)

A 다음 문장을 부정문으로 바꾸어 쓰시오.

1 I'm going shopping.
→ ______________________

2 She is packing her bag.
→ ______________________

3 Andrew was driving his car.
→ ______________________

4 They were wearing uniforms.
→ ______________________

B 다음 문장을 지시대로 바꾸어 쓰시오.

1 I'm waiting for her speech. (부정문)
→ ______________________

2 Kate and Alex weren't lying to each other. (긍정문)
→ ______________________

3 The dog wasn't playing with a ball. (현재진행형)
→ ______________________

4 You aren't wasting my time. (과거진행형)
→ ______________________

C 다음 우리말과 같은 뜻이 되도록 ( ) 안의 말을 이용하여 문장을 완성하시오.

1 David는 아무것도 숨기고 있지 않다. (hide)
David ________ ________ anything.

2 나는 너의 일기를 읽고 있지 않았다. (read)
I ________ ________ your diary.

3 그는 최선을 다하고 있지 않았다. (do)
He ________ ________ his best.

Point 06 진행형의 의문문

- 진행형의 의문문은 〈be동사+주어+v-ing ~?〉의 형태이다.

  A: **Are you making** pancakes? (현재진행형의 의문문)

  B: Yes, I am. / No, I'm not.

  A: **Were they dancing** to the music? (과거진행형의 의문문)

  B: Yes, they were. / No, they weren't.

A **다음 문장을 의문문으로 바꾸어 쓰시오.**

1 He is exercising. → ______________________

2 They were speaking Chinese. → ______________________

3 She is winking at you. → ______________________

4 Tony was fixing his computer. → ______________________

5 You were sleeping at the library. → ______________________

6 They are running on the playground. → ______________________

7 The boy was eating potato chips. → ______________________

B **다음 질문에 대한 알맞은 대답을 쓰시오.**

1 A: Are you writing a new novel?
B: No, ________ ________.

2 A: Pat, were you drinking a Coke?
B: ________, ________ ________. I was drinking grape juice.

3 A: Are Dan and Sarah dating?
B: ________, ________ ________. They like each other very much.

C **다음 우리말과 같은 뜻이 되도록 ( ) 안의 말을 이용하여 문장을 완성하시오.**

1 그는 땅 위에 누워 있었나요? (lie)
________ ________ ________ on the ground?

2 그들은 케이크를 자르고 있나요? (cut)
________ ________ ________ the cake?

3 너는 이 반지를 찾고 있었니? (look for)
________ ________ ________ ________ this ring?

[01-03] 다음 빈칸에 알맞은 말을 고르시오.

01

Steven ________ a blue shirt yesterday.

① wear ② wears
③ wore ④ wearing
⑤ is wearing

02

Your phone ________. Answer it, please.

① is ringing ② rang
③ ring ④ was ringing
⑤ are ringing

03

We ________ about ghosts last night.

① talk ② talks
③ are talking ④ were talking
⑤ was talking

04
다음 밑줄 친 동사의 형태가 잘못된 것은?

① I was tying my scarf.
② She is moveing to a new house.
③ He is drinking a cup of coffee.
④ Is your son holding a trophy in his hand?
⑤ We were making dinner for our family yesterday.

[05-06] 다음 빈칸에 들어갈 수 없는 말을 고르시오.

05

She was ________ Jerry.

① visiting ② knowing
③ helping ④ talking to
⑤ looking for

06

They ________ advice from him.

① want ② wanted
③ are wanting ④ don't want
⑤ didn't want

[07-08] 다음 질문에 대한 알맞은 대답을 고르시오.

07

A: Are you checking your email?
B: ________ I'm playing computer games.

① Yes, I am. ② Yes, I was.
③ No, I'm not. ④ No, I wasn't.
⑤ No, you weren't.

08

A: Was it raining at this time yesterday?
B: ________ It was raining very hard.

① Yes, it is. ② Yes, it was.
③ No, it isn't. ④ No, it wasn't.
⑤ No, it rained.

09

다음 빈칸에 공통으로 들어갈 말은?

- Where ________ you sitting in the theater this afternoon?
- They ________ sleeping at ten o'clock last night.

① was ② do
③ did ④ are
⑤ were

[10-11] 빈칸에 들어갈 말이 순서대로 알맞게 짝지어진 것을 고르시오.

10

A: What are you ________ right now?
B: I'm ________ a travel show.

① do – watch ② do – watching
③ doing – watches ④ did – watching
⑤ doing – watching

11

A: ________ they sending the text messages?
B: No, they aren't. They ________ them 10 minutes ago.

① Are – send ② Are – sends
③ Are – sent ④ Were – send
⑤ Were – sent

12

다음 우리말과 같은 뜻이 되도록 주어진 말을 배열할 때 네 번째에 올 단어는?

그 아이들은 우리에게 손을 흔들고 있지 않았다.
(us, at, were, waving, the children, not)

① at ② waving
③ us ④ were
⑤ not

13

다음 대화 중 자연스럽지 않은 것은?

① A: Did you study last night?
B: Yes, I did. I studied English.
② A: Was she absent from school?
B: Yes, she was. She was sick.
③ A: What do you do after school?
B: I take piano lessons every day.
④ A: What was one plus one?
B: One plus one was two.
⑤ A: What were you doing at that time?
B: I was having lunch.

고난도

14

다음 중 어법상 옳은 것을 모두 고르면? (2개)

① Was you reading a book at the library?
② The dance club meets at 3 p.m. on Mondays.
③ I buy a pair of shoes last month.
④ She not was using the laptop then.
⑤ We're looking for new members these days.

[15-17] 다음 중 어법상 틀린 것을 고르시오.

15

① I watch the news at 9 a.m.
② Japan has four seasons.
③ Daniel has a talent for music.
④ The earth moves around the sun.
⑤ The Korean War breaks out in 1950.

16

① Everybody was running.
② We were looking at you then.
③ Larry loves the *Friday Night Show*.
④ I'm having a lot of nicknames.
⑤ He read the magazine last night.

17

① I'm not listening to music.
② They went to the zoo yesterday.
③ The sun sets in the west.
④ Did they swimming at that time?
⑤ We were looking after the baby.

18

다음 우리말을 영어로 바르게 옮긴 것은?

Ian과 Sue는 전화로 수다를 떨고 있지 않았다.

① Ian and Sue don't chat on the phone.
② Ian and Sue aren't chatting on the phone.
③ Ian and Sue weren't chatting on the phone.
④ Ian and Sue not was chatting on the phone.
⑤ Ian and Sue were chatting not on the phone.

기출응용

19

다음 중 어법상 옳은 것끼리 짝지어진 것은?

(a) I met my old friend yesterday.
(b) Are you lying to me?
(c) She take a walk every morning.
(d) I was recording with guests now.

① (a), (b) ② (a), (d) ③ (b), (c)
④ (b), (d) ⑤ (c), (d)

고난도

20

(A), (B), (C)의 괄호 안에서 알맞은 것끼리 바르게 짝지어진 것은?

(A) Hangeul [is / was] the Korean alphabet.
(B) I [am finding / found] the keys this morning.
(C) They [had / were having] a nice house then.

	(A)		(B)		(C)
①	is	……	am finding	……	had
②	is	……	found	……	were having
③	is	……	found	……	had
④	was	……	found	……	had
⑤	was	……	am finding	……	were having

서술형 따라잡기

01
다음 〈보기〉에서 알맞은 말을 골라 적절한 형태로 써넣으시오.

〈보기〉 clean　be　bring

(1) It ________ very chilly tonight.

(2) Max ________ his friend to the party yesterday.

(3) Rose ________ her room every day these days.

02
주어진 말을 알맞게 배열하여 우리말과 뜻이 같도록 문장을 완성하시오.

내 친구들은 무대에서 춤을 추고 있지 않았다.
(not, on stage, were, dancing, friends, my)

→ ______________________________

03
다음 문장을 지시대로 바꾸어 쓰시오.

(1) He pays 400 dollars a month for this apartment.

→ ______________________________
(현재진행형 평서문)

→ ______________________________
(과거진행형 의문문)

(2) They ate strawberries for dessert.

→ ______________________________
(현재진행형 의문문)

→ ______________________________
(과거진행형 부정문)

04
다음 그림을 보고, 문장을 완성하시오.

(1) A woman ________ ________ on the bench.

(2) A man ________ ________ on the grass.

(3) The children ________ ________ along the river.

05
다음 표를 보고, 물음에 답하시오.

Name	An Hour Ago	Now
Amy	draw a picture	listen to music
Julie	exercise at the gym	make some food

(1) Q: Was Amy listening to music an hour ago?
A: ________, ________ ________. She ________ ________ ________ ________.

(2) Q: Is Julie exercising at the gym right now?
A: ________, ________ ________. She ________ ________ ________ ________.

06
다음 대화를 읽고, (　) 안의 동사를 적절한 형태로 써넣으시오.

A: Where ________ (be) you yesterday?
I ________ (call) you many times.
B: Sorry, I ________ ________ (go out) to go shopping in the afternoon.

S E L F N O T E

핵심 포인트 정리하기

1 현재시제는 이럴 때 사용한다!

- 현재의 상태나 지속적인 성질을 나타낼 때
- 일상적인 행동이나 습관을 나타낼 때
- 과학적 사실이나 불변의 사실을 나타낼 때

2 과거시제는 이럴 때 사용한다!

- 과거의 동작을 나타낼 때
- 과거의 상태를 나타낼 때
- 역사적 사실을 나타낼 때

3 진행형은 이렇게 사용한다!

- 특정 시점에 진행 중인 일을 나타낼 때
- 현재진행형: 〈be동사의 현재형 + ① ________〉
- 과거진행형: 〈② ____________ + v-ing〉
- 진행형의 부정문: ③ 〈________ + ________ + ________〉
- 진행형의 의문문: Q. ④ 〈________ + 주어 + ________ ~?〉

  A. 〈Yes, 주어 + be동사.〉 / 〈No, 주어 + be동사 + ⑤ ________.〉

현재[과거]시제와 함께 쓰이는 부사(구) 알아두기!
진행형의 형태 기억하기!

문제로 개념 다지기

다음 ( ) 안에서 알맞은 말을 고르시오.

1 Miri usually (goes / went) to bed at 10 p.m. these days.

2 Our team (lose / lost) the game last night.

3 King Sejong (invents / invented) Hangeul in 1443.

4 Henry (is / was) cooking in the kitchen right now.

5 My sister (wants / is wanting) a robot for her birthday.

6 We (not were / were not) walking through the museum.

7 (Did / Were) you watching TV this morning?

01 will
02 be going to
03 can
04 can과 be able to
05 may
06 must
07 have to
08 should

Sally		swims.	Sally는 수영을 한다.
Sally	**will**	swim.	Sally는 수영을 할 것이다.
Sally	**can**	swim.	Sally는 수영을 할 수 있다.
Sally	**must**	swim.	Sally는 수영을 해야 한다.

조동사란?

동사의 앞에 쓰여 동사에 미래, 가능, 추측, 허가, 의무 등의 의미를 더해주는 말이에요. 조동사는 주어의 인칭이나 수에 따라 변하지 않고 항상 같은 형태로 쓰며, 조동사 뒤에는 동사원형을 쓴다는 것을 기억해 두세요.

Point 01 will

- 조동사란 동사에 미래, 가능, 추측, 허가, 의무 등의 의미를 더해주는 말이다. 주어의 인칭이나 수에 관계없이 형태가 변하지 않으며, 조동사 뒤에는 항상 동사원형이 온다.
- will은 '~할 것이다', '~하겠다'라는 의미로 미래의 일이나 주어의 의지를 나타낸다.
  He **will** be fifteen next year. (미래)
  I **will** not do it again. (주어의 의지)
- will의 의문문은 〈Will+주어+동사원형 ~?〉이고, 부정형은 〈will+not+동사원형〉 혹은 〈won't+동사원형〉으로 쓴다.
  A: **Will** you **come** to the party?
  B: Yes, I **will**. / No, I **will not[won't]**.

★ PLUS TIP 〈주어+will〉은 주어'll로 줄여 쓰기도 한다. (I'll, You'll 등)

A 다음 밑줄 친 부분을 어법에 맞게 고쳐 쓰시오.

1 Linda will visits us soon.
2 Tony won't not give it to me.
3 I will am a high school student next year.
4 They will ask not me that question.

B 다음 문장을 지시대로 바꾸어 쓰시오.

1 I'll wear a raincoat. (부정문) → ______________________
2 They will join us. (의문문) → ______________________
3 He is in the kitchen. (미래시제) → ______________________
4 She invites a lot of people. (미래시제) → ______________________

C 다음 우리말과 같은 뜻이 되도록 ( ) 안의 말을 이용하여 문장을 완성하시오.

1 오늘 밤 Lucy는 노래를 부르지 않을 것이다. (sing)
Lucy __________ __________ a song tonight.

2 그 뮤지컬은 6시에 시작할 것이다. (begin)
The musical __________ __________ at six o'clock.

3 A: 내년 이맘때 당신은 여기에 있을 건가요? (be)
__________ you __________ here this time next year?
B: 아니요, 저는 아프리카에 있을 거예요.
No, __________ __________ in Africa.

Point 02

be going to

- be going to는 '~할 것이다', '~할 예정이다'라는 의미로 가까운 미래의 일이나 계획을 나타낸다.
  I'**m going to** clean my room.
- be going to의 의문문은 〈be동사+주어+going to+동사원형 ~?〉, 부정형은 〈be동사+not+going to+동사원형〉으로 쓴다.
  Are you **going to** call him?
  He'**s not going to** meet her.

A **다음 문장을 be going to를 이용하여 미래시제로 바꾸어 쓰시오.**

1 Dad makes lunch for us. → Dad ____________________ lunch for us.
2 Betty shows me her photos. → Betty ____________________ me her photos.
3 The train arrives in Osaka. → The train ____________________ in Osaka.
4 We visit our grandparents. → We ____________________ our grandparents.
5 He goes to the bookstore. → He ____________________ to the bookstore.

B **다음 우리말과 같은 뜻이 되도록 be going to와 ( ) 안의 말을 이용하여 문장을 완성하시오.**

1 나는 설거지를 할 것이다. (wash the dishes)
I ____________________________________.

2 너는 집에서 저녁 먹을 거니? (have dinner)
____________________________________ at home?

3 오늘 오후에는 날씨가 좋을 겁니다. (nice)
The weather ____________________________________ this afternoon.

4 Helen과 Dave는 그 영화를 보지 않을 것이다. (watch)
Helen and Dave ____________________________________ the movie.

C **다음 우리말과 같은 뜻이 되도록 ( ) 안의 말을 배열하여 문장을 완성하시오.**

1 너는 나를 도와줄 거니? (are, you, me, going, help, to)
____

2 그녀는 그녀의 헤어스타일을 바꾸지 않을 것이다.
(going, she, change, to, her hairstyle, isn't)
____

3 나는 일본에 있는 내 친구를 만날 것이다. (my friend, I'm, meet, going, in Japan, to)
____

Point 03 can

- can은 '~할 수 있다'라는 의미로, 주어의 능력이나 가능을 나타낸다.
  Jake **can** drive a car.
  A: **Can** you speak Spanish?
  B: Yes, I **can**. / No, I **can't**.
- can은 '~해도 좋다'라는 허가의 의미를 나타내기도 한다.
  Can I use your camera?
  You **can't** swim in this river.

★ PLUS TIP
- can의 의문문은 〈Can+주어+동사원형 ~?〉, 부정형은 cannot[can't]으로 나타낸다.
- can의 과거형은 could이고, 부정형은 could not[couldn't]이다.

A 다음 질문에 대한 알맞은 대답을 쓰시오.

1 A: Can you play the guitar?
B: Yes, __________ __________.

2 A: Can I use your cell phone?
B: __________, __________ __________. Go ahead.

3 A: Can I go to Andrew's?
B: __________, __________ __________. It's too late.

4 A: Can your brother cook Italian food?
B: __________, __________ __________. But he loves to eat it.

B 다음 우리말과 같은 뜻이 되도록 ( ) 안의 말을 이용하여 문장을 완성하시오.

1 당신은 이 병을 열 수 있나요? (open)
__________ __________ __________ this bottle?

2 Dorothy는 수화를 할 수 있다. (use)
Dorothy __________ __________ sign language.

3 Steve는 높은 산에 올라가지 못한다. (climb)
Steve __________ __________ high mountains.

4 너는 오후 8시 이후에 외출할 수 없다. (go outside)
You __________ __________ __________ after 8 p.m.

5 너는 한 손으로 문자메시지를 보낼 수 있니? (send a text message)
__________ __________ __________ __________ __________ __________ with one hand?

Point 04 can과 be able to

- be able to는 능력이나 가능을 나타내는 조동사 can과 같은 의미로 사용된다.
  Jake **is able to** drive a car. → Jake **can** drive a car.
- 능력이나 가능을 나타내는 조동사 can의 과거형 could는 was[were] able to로 바꾸어 쓸 수 있다.
  We **could** see the stars. → We **were able to** see the stars.

★ PLUS TIP 조동사 can은 미래형이 없으므로 will be able to로 미래의 의미를 나타낸다.

A 다음 〈보기〉와 같이 be able to를 이용한 문장으로 바꾸어 쓰시오.

〈보기〉 Stella can do magic. → Stella is able to do magic.

1 Can you do this job? → ______________ this job?
2 Peter can't play golf. → Peter ______________ golf.
3 I can make egg tarts. → I ______________ egg tarts.
4 They could hear my voice. → They ______________ my voice.
5 He couldn't use the machine. → He ______________ the machine.
6 We can deliver it for you. → We ______________ it for you.

B 다음 빈칸에 be able to를 적절한 형태로 바꾸어 쓰시오.

1 They ______________ pay for it. They are rich.
2 I need your help. ______________ read Chinese?
3 I ______________ drink my green tea. It was too hot.
4 Kate left her home early, so she ______________ catch the train.
5 Ted knows everything about computers. He ______________ fix yours tomorrow.

C 다음 우리말과 같은 뜻이 되도록 ( ) 안의 말을 이용하여 문장을 완성하시오.

1 나는 그 이야기를 영어로 말할 수 있다. (tell)
______ ______ ______ ______ the story in English.

2 Joe는 빨리 달릴 수 있나요? (run)
______ ______ ______ ______ ______ fast?

3 그들은 그 상자를 들어 올릴 수 없었다. (lift)
They ______ ______ ______ ______ the box.

Point 05

may

- may는 '~해도 좋다'라는 허가의 의미를 나타낸다.
  You **may** come to my office.
  May I see your passport?
- may는 '~일지도 모른다'라는 추측의 의미를 나타내기도 한다.
  He **may** fall in love with her.
  She **may not** be here in time.

★ PLUS TIP 허가의 의미인 can과 may에 대한 부정형 대답은 No, you can't[may not].과 같이 직설적인 표현 대신 I'm afraid[sorry] you can't[may not].라고 하는 것이 좋다.

A 다음 〈보기〉에서 알맞은 말을 골라 대화를 완성하시오.

〈보기〉 That may not be true. May I use your laptop?
She may be sick. May I have some ice cream?

1 A: ______________________
B: Sure. Vanilla or chocolate?

2 A: ______________________
B: I'm sorry, but I left it at home.

3 A: Brad is going to leave here soon.
B: ______________________ He likes this town.

4 A: I can't find Grace in the classroom.
B: She's absent today. ______________________

B 다음 우리말과 같은 뜻이 되도록 may와 ( ) 안의 말을 이용하여 문장을 완성하시오.

1 당신은 여기 앉으시면 안 됩니다. (sit)
You ________ ________ ________ here.

2 저 노인은 100세일지도 모른다. (be)
That old man ________ ________ 100 years old.

3 제가 이 모자를 써봐도 되나요? (try on)
________ ________ ________ ________ this hat?

4 그는 네 전화번호를 모르고 있을지도 모른다. (know)
He ________ ________ ________ your phone number.

5 제가 당신과 함께 사진을 찍어도 될까요? (take a picture)
________ ________ ________ ________ ________ with you?

Point 06 must

- must는 '~해야 한다'라는 의미로 의무를 나타낸다. 부정형 must not은 '~하면 안 된다'라는 금지를 나타낸다.
  You **must** wear a swimsuit here. (의무)
  You **must not** make any noise. (금지)
- must는 '~임이 틀림없다'라는 강한 추측을 나타내기도 한다.
  He **must** be hungry. (강한 추측)

★ PLUS TIP cannot[can't]는 '~일 리가 없다'라는 강한 부정적 추측을 나타낸다.
It **cannot[can't]** be true. (그것은 사실일 리가 없다.)

A 다음 <보기>에서 각 문장에 쓰인 must의 의미를 골라 그 기호를 쓰시오.

<보기> ⓐ 의무 ⓑ 금지 ⓒ 강한 추측

1 You must not write your answer with a pencil. ( )
2 We don't have much time. We must leave here now. ( )
3 That restaurant must be great. People love to eat there. ( )
4 We must not touch this machine. It is very dangerous. ( )
5 The alarm is ringing. It must be seven o'clock. ( )
6 All students must bring gym clothes tomorrow. ( )

B 다음 우리말과 같은 뜻이 되도록 ( ) 안의 말을 배열하여 문장을 완성하시오.

1 우리는 택시를 타야 한다. (a taxi, must, we, take)

____

2 너는 차를 운전하면 안 된다. (drive, you, a car, not, must)

____

3 나는 경주를 마쳐야 한다. (must, I, finish, the race)

____

4 너는 다시 지각하면 안 된다. (you, late, must, again, be, not)

____

5 저 영화는 틀림없이 재미있을 것이다. (interesting, be, that film, must)

____

6 그가 지금 병원에 있을 리가 없다. (now, cannot, at the hospital, be, he)

____

Point 07 have to

- have to는 '~해야 한다'라는 의무를 나타내는 조동사 must와 같은 의미로 사용된다.
  They **have to** wear uniforms. → They **must** wear uniforms.
- have to의 의문문은 〈Do[Does/Did]+주어+have to ~?〉로 쓴다.
  have to의 부정형인 don't[doesn't/didn't] have to는 '~할 필요가 없다'라는 의미로 금지를 나타내는 must not의 의미와 다름에 유의한다.
  You **don't have to** study tonight.

★ PLUS TIP 의무를 나타내는 조동사 must는 미래형과 과거형이 없으므로 각각 will have to와 had to를 사용해서 미래와 과거의 의미를 나타낸다.
You **will have to** do it again. (너는 그것을 다시 해야 할 것이다.)
Brian **had to** get up early. (Brian은 일찍 일어나야 했다.)

A 다음 〈보기〉와 같이 have to를 이용한 문장으로 바꾸어 쓰시오.

〈보기〉 Sue must meet her teacher. → Sue has to meet her teacher.

1 You must go to bed early. → You ____________ early.
2 They must stop smoking. → They ____________ smoking.
3 I must call my parents first. → I ____________ my parents first.
4 We must clean the classroom. → We ____________ the classroom.
5 He must go to the dentist. → He ____________ to the dentist.

B 다음 우리말과 같은 뜻이 되도록 ( ) 안의 말을 이용하여 문장을 완성하시오.

1 그는 9시부터 6시까지 일해야 한다. (work)
He ________ ________ ________ from 9 to 6.

2 Jane이 해외에 가야 하나요? (go)
________ Jane ________ ________ ________ abroad?

3 Tom은 Karen을 만나서 이야기해야 한다. (meet)
Tom ________ ________ ________ Karen and talk to her.

4 Jacob은 안경을 쓸 필요가 없었다. (wear)
Jacob ________ ________ ________ ________ glasses.

5 저희가 이것을 오늘 끝내야 하나요? (finish)
________ we ________ ________ ________ this today?

6 나는 지갑을 잃어버려서 어제 집에 걸어와야 했다. (walk)
I lost my wallet, so I ________ ________ ________ home yesterday.

Point 08 should

- should는 '~해야 한다'라는 의미로 의무나 충고, 제안 등을 나타낸다. 단, should는 must보다 의무의 정도가 약하다.
  You **should** wash your hands.
- should의 의문문은 〈Should+주어+동사원형 ~?〉이고, 부정형은 〈should not[shouldn't]〉이다.
  Should I **pay** you now?
  You **shouldn't** run in this building.

★ 내신만점 *TIP* must not과 don't have to의 의미를 구분하자.

A 다음 〈보기〉에서 알맞은 말을 골라 should나 shouldn't를 이용하여 문장을 완성하시오.

〈보기〉 apologize take wear believe

1 A: Oh, it's snowing a lot.
B: ________ I ________ the subway today?

2 A: I lied to my girlfriend. She is angry with me.
B: You ________ ________ to her.

3 A: I'm going to ride a motorcycle.
B: Okay, but you ________ ________ a helmet.

4 A: I heard some bad news about a singer.
B: You ________ ________ rumors.

B 다음 우리말과 같은 뜻이 되도록 〈보기〉와 ( ) 안의 말을 이용하여 문장을 완성하시오. (단, 한 번씩만 사용할 것)

〈보기〉 should don't have to must not cannot

1 그는 어제 일찍 잠자리에 들었다. 그는 피곤할 리가 없다. (tired)
He went to bed early yesterday. ________ ________ ________ ________.

2 우리는 사실대로 말할 필요가 없다. (tell, the truth)
________ ________ ________ ________ ________ ________ ________.

3 너는 박물관 안으로 음식을 가져와서는 안 된다. (bring, food)
________ ________ ________ ________ ________ into the museum.

4 너는 이 노래를 들어봐야 해. (listen to, this song)
You ________ ________ ________ ________ ________.

[01-03] 다음 빈칸에 알맞은 말을 고르시오.

01

The light is red! You ________ cross the street.

① will　② can
③ must　④ must not
⑤ cannot be

02

It ________ rain this afternoon. Bring an umbrella with you.

① don't have to　② have to
③ will　④ may not
⑤ must not

03

Eric ________ be tired. He played sports all day yesterday.

① must not　② must
③ may not　④ cannot
⑤ doesn't have to

[04-05] 다음 밑줄 친 부분과 바꾸어 쓸 수 있는 말을 고르시오.

04

<u>Can</u> I have a cookie?

① Should　② Must　③ May
④ Will　⑤ Do

05

John <u>is going to</u> enter college.

① will　② must　③ can
④ may　⑤ should

[06-07] 다음 우리말을 영어로 바르게 옮긴 것을 고르시오.

06

당신은 대전에서 기차를 갈아다야 해요.

① You can change trains in Daejeon.
② You may change trains in Daejeon.
③ You will change trains in Daejeon.
④ You should change trains in Daejeon.
⑤ You're going to change trains in Daejeon.

07

그는 게으른 학생이 틀림없다.

① He can be a lazy student.
② He must be a lazy student.
③ He will be a lazy student.
④ He may be a lazy student.
⑤ He doesn't have to be a lazy student.

[08-09] 다음 질문에 대한 알맞은 대답을 고르시오.

08

A: Will you tell me the secret?
B: No, ________________.

① I will　② I won't
③ I don't　④ you will
⑤ you'll not

09

A: Can I see you tomorrow?
B: ______________ How about next Saturday?

① Sure.
② No, you will not.
③ Why not?
④ Yes, you can.
⑤ I'm afraid not.

10

다음 대화 중 자연스럽지 않은 것은?

① A: Will you go to the party?
B: No, I won't.
② A: Can I use your phone?
B: Yes, you can.
③ A: May I go out now?
B: I'm afraid you may not.
④ A: Must I read this book now?
B: No, you don't have to.
⑤ A: Should we go and see him?
B: Yes, we had to.

기출응용

11

다음 밑줄 친 must의 의미가 나머지와 다른 것은?

① Kids like this song. It must be funny.
② You must take the school bus.
③ You must put your trash in the trash can.
④ The pot is very hot. We must be careful.
⑤ They must do their homework themselves.

12

다음 우리말을 영어로 옮긴 것 중 잘못된 것은?

① 제가 놀이공원에 가도 되나요?
Can I go to the amusement park?
② 그 둘은 자매일 리가 없다.
Those two can't be sisters.
③ 나는 커피 한 잔을 마셔야 했다.
I had to drink a cup of coffee.
④ 그녀는 그를 초대하지 않을지도 모른다.
She may not invite him.
⑤ 그는 한국에서 유명한 피아니스트임이 틀림없다.
He can be a famous pianist in Korea.

[13-14] 빈칸에 들어갈 말이 순서대로 알맞게 짝지어진 것을 고르시오.

13

A: Does your mother ________ to wake you up every morning?
B: No, she ________. I have an alarm clock.

① has – doesn't
② has – must not
③ have – doesn't
④ have – can't
⑤ have – not

14

Chris got up late, so he ________ able to be there on time. He ________ apologize to everyone.

① was – could
② is – should
③ wasn't – had to
④ could – couldn't
⑤ couldn't – has to

15

다음 빈칸에 공통으로 들어갈 말은?

- You ________ talk loudly in the library.
- I'm afraid you ________ borrow this book.
- You are 14 years old, so you ________ drive a car.

① can't ② may
③ must ④ can
⑤ don't have to

기출응용

16

다음 짝지어진 두 문장의 의미가 같지 않은 것은?

① She can ride a horse.
→ She is able to ride a horse.
② We will have a piece of cake.
→ We are going to have a piece of cake.
③ May I borrow your pencil?
→ Can I borrow your pencil?
④ You must not waste your money.
→ You don't have to waste your money.
⑤ All parents should take care of their children.
→ All parents have to take care of their children.

[17-18] 다음 중 어법상 틀린 것을 고르시오.

17

① Tim must be busy now.
② Can you speak English?
③ Do we have to wait for him?
④ Jane mays go to Scotland.
⑤ She should leave tomorrow.

18

① May I put on this T-shirt?
② We can able to make a website last year.
③ Sam has to meet her right now.
④ Students must follow the rules of the school.
⑤ Are you going to go to church this Sunday?

19

다음 대화의 순서로 알맞은 것은?

(a) You have to go to the service center.
(b) No, I am not able to.
(c) Can you fix this camera?
(d) Then what should I do?

① (a) – (c) – (b) – (d)
② (a) – (d) – (c) – (b)
③ (c) – (a) – (d) – (b)
④ (c) – (b) – (d) – (a)
⑤ (d) – (a) – (c) – (b)

고난도

20

다음 중 어법상 옳은 것끼리 짝지어진 것은?

(a) We can won the game.
(b) She won't change her mind.
(c) You must cleaned your room yesterday.
(d) They must stay inside today.
(e) He was able to download the music file yesterday.

① (a), (b), (c) ② (a), (d), (e)
③ (b), (c), (d) ④ (b), (d), (e)
⑤ (c), (d), (e)

내신대비 TEST

서술형 따라잡기

01

주어진 말을 이용하여 대화를 완성하시오.

(1) A: I wasn't able to have anything for lunch.
B: Oh, you ________ ________ ________.
(hungry) I'll prepare some food now.

(2) A: Look at that boy. Isn't that Luke?
B: That ________ ________ Luke. (be)
He is in China right now.

02

다음 문장을 지시대로 바꾸어 쓰시오.

(1) He is going to say hello to her.
→ ________________________________ (부정문)
→ ________________________________ (의문문)

(2) She had to come back home by ten.
→ ________________________________ (부정문)
→ ________________________________ (의문문)

03

주어진 말을 알맞게 배열하여 우리말과 뜻이 같도록 문장을 완성하시오.

너는 좋은 자리를 잡을 수 있었니?
(able, a good seat, were, get, to, you)

→ ________________________________

04

다음 표를 보고, 공연장에서 지켜야 할 규칙을 〈보기〉와 같이 완성하시오.

Do	Don't
Turn off your cell phone	Eat any food
(1) Stay silent during the show	(2) Take pictures during the show

〈보기〉 You must turn off your cell phone.

(1) You ________________________________.

(2) You ________________________________.

05

다음 그림을 보고, Yuna가 할 수 있는 일과 할 수 없는 일을 적어보시오.

O

X

(1) Yuna ________ ________ a car.

(2) Yuna ________ ________ ________ ________ ________ the guitar.

06

주어진 말과, 상자 안에 제시된 표현을 한 번씩 사용하여 〈보기〉와 같이 문장을 완성하시오. (단, 필요하면 부정형으로 쓸 것)

~~go out and play~~ / go to school / be kind

〈보기〉 He already finished his homework.
So he can go out and play. (can)

(1) She always helps her classmates.
She ________________________. (must)

(2) It's Sunday. He ________________________.
(have to)

S E L F N O T E

핵심 포인트 정리하기

1 조동사

- 의미: 동사에 미래, 가능, 허가, 추측, 의무 등의 의미를 더해주는 말
- 형태: 조동사 + ① ____________

  *인칭이나 수에 따라 변하지 않음 (be going to, be able to, have to 제외)

2 조동사의 종류

will	- 미래의 일: ② ____________ - 주어의 의지: ~하겠다
be going to	- 가까운 미래의 일이나 계획: ~할 것이다, ~할 예정이다
can	- 주어의 능력이나 가능: ~할 수 있다 (= ③ ____________) - 허가: ~해도 좋다
④ ________	- 허가: ~해도 좋다 - 추측: ~일지도 모른다
must	- 의무: ~해야 한다 / 금지 ⑤ ____________: ~하면 안 된다 - 강한 추측: ~임이 틀림없다 / 강한 부정적 추측 cannot[can't]: ~일 리가 없다
⑥ ________	- 의무: ~해야 한다 (=must) - don't have to: ~할 필요가 없다
should	- 의무, 충고, 제안: ~해야 한다

같은 의미로 바꿔 쓸 수 있는 조동사 기억하기!
must not과 don't have to의 의미 구분하기!

문제로 개념 다지기

1 다음 우리말과 같은 뜻이 되도록 ( ) 안에서 알맞은 말을 고르시오.

(1) 너의 남동생은 그녀를 좋아하는 게 틀림없다.
Your brother (can / must) like her.

(2) 너는 아직 떠날 필요가 없다.
You (must not / don't have to) leave yet.

(3) 그녀는 어제 파티에 올 수가 없었다.
She (was not able to / was not going to) come to the party yesterday.

2 밑줄 친 부분이 어법상 맞으면 O, 틀리면 X 표시하고 바르게 고치시오.

(1) May I introduces you to Ms. Gwen?
(2) Can I use the fax machine?
(3) James should is nicer to his mother.
(4) Have I to wear sunglasses?
(5) I'm getting better. So I not will go to see a doctor.

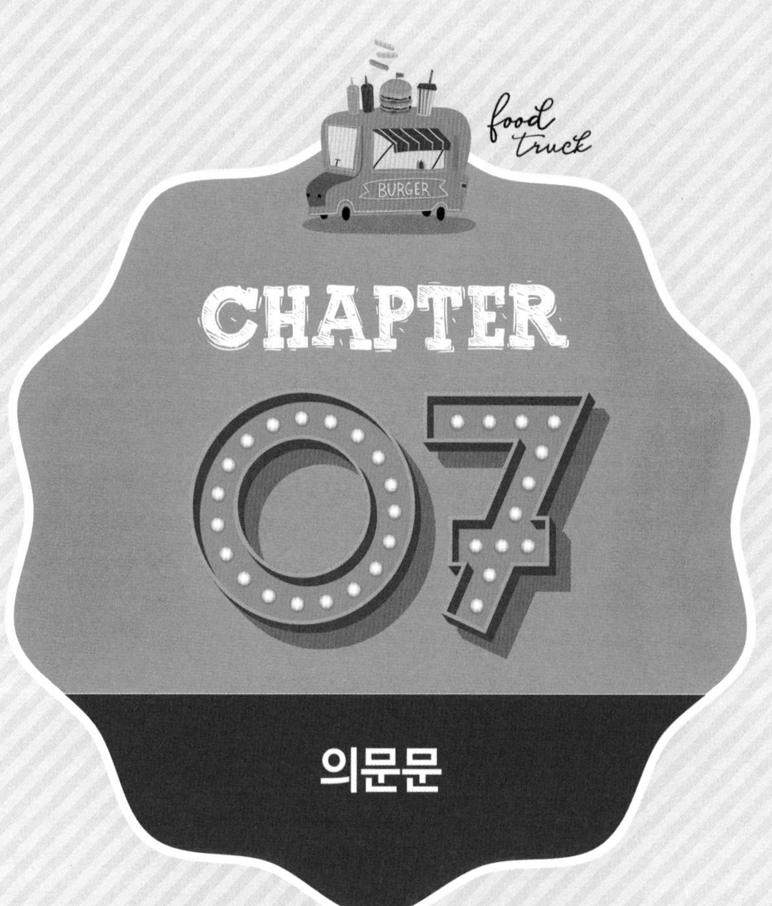

Who is the pretty girl? – She is ***my sister***.
누구

What did you have for lunch? – I had ***pasta*** for lunch.
무엇

How does he get to school? – He gets to school ***by bus***.
어떻게

의문사란?

who(누구), what(무엇), which(어느 것), when(언제), where(어디서, 어디에), why(왜), how(어떻게, 어떤)와 같이 특정 정보에 대해서 물어볼 때 쓰는 말이에요. 의문사가 있는 의문문은 <의문사+동사+주어 ~?>의 형태이고, 이에 대한 대답은 Yes나 No로 하지 않는답니다.

Point 01 who/what으로 시작하는 의문문

- 의문사란 who, what, which, when, where, why, how와 같은 말로, 의문사가 있는 의문문에는 Yes나 No로 대답하지 않는다.
- 의문사가 있는 의문문은 〈의문사+동사[be동사/do동사/조동사]+주어 ~?〉의 형태로 의문사가 맨 앞에 온다.
- who는 '누구'라는 뜻이다.
  Who is that handsome boy? / **Who** gave you the money? (의문사가 주어 역할을 하는 경우)
  (Who: 주어, gave: 동사)
- what은 '무엇'이라는 뜻이나, 명사 앞에 쓰일 때는 '무슨', '어떤'이라는 뜻을 나타낸다.
  What is your favorite color? / **What** color do you like most?

★ PLUS TIP 의문사가 주어 역할을 하는 경우에는 3인칭 단수로 취급한다.
Who ***lives*** here? / **What** ***is*** in your pocket?

A 다음 〈보기〉와 같이 밑줄 친 부분을 묻는 의문문을 쓰시오.

〈보기〉 I met Laura yesterday. → Who did you meet yesterday?

1 He is my boyfriend. → ____________________
2 My brother drew this. → ____________________
3 I bought a new shirt. → ____________________
4 They ate some bananas. → ____________________
5 The author is James Joyce. → ____________________
6 She can write songs. → ____________________

B 다음 우리말과 같은 뜻이 되도록 ( ) 안의 말을 이용하여 문장을 완성하시오.

1 너는 종이로 무엇을 만들었니? (make)
_______ _______ you _______ with paper?

2 너희 수학 선생님은 누구시니? (be)
_______ _______ your math teacher?

3 누가 이곳으로 오고 있나요? (come)
_______ _______ _______ here?

4 무슨 과목이 네가 가장 좋아하는 과목이니? (subject)
_______ _______ _______ your favorite?

5 누가 여우주연상을 탔어요? (win)
_______ _______ the Best Actress award?

6 너는 내일 무엇을 할 거니? (do)
_______ _______ you _______ tomorrow?

which로 시작하는 의문문

- which는 '어느 것'이라는 뜻으로, 정해진 범위 안에서 선택을 묻는 경우에 사용된다.
  Which do you like better, comedies or dramas?
- which가 명사 앞에 쓰일 때는 '어느'라는 뜻을 나타낸다.
  Which brand do you prefer?

★ PLUS TIP what은 정해지지 않은 대상, which는 정해진 대상 중에서 선택을 묻는 경우에 쓴다.

A **다음 ( ) 안의 말을 배열하여 의문문을 완성하시오.**

1 ______________________________, chicken or beef?
(you, better, which, like, do)

2 ______________________________, a window seat or an aisle seat?
(seat, you, do, want, which)

3 ______________________________, Google or Naver?
(you, which, use, do, search engine)

B **다음 ( ) 안에서 알맞은 말을 고르시오.**

1 A: (What / Who) did you eat for lunch?
B: I ate a tuna sandwich.

2 A: (What / Which) do you want, coffee or soda?
B: Coffee, please.

3 A: (Who / What) played the guitar at the concert?
B: Julian did.

4 A: (Which / What) do you like better, cats or dogs?
B: I like cats better.

C **다음 우리말과 같은 뜻이 되도록 ( ) 안의 말을 이용하여 문장을 완성하시오.**

1 누가 너에게 그 초콜릿을 줬니? (give)
__________ __________ __________ that chocolate?

2 너는 여름과 겨울 중에 어느 것을 더 좋아하니? (like)
__________ __________ __________ __________ better, summer or winter?

3 너는 야구와 농구 중 어느 스포츠를 더 자주 관람하니? (watch)
__________ __________ __________ __________ __________ more often, baseball or basketball?

Point 03 when / where로 시작하는 의문문

- when은 '언제'라는 뜻으로 시간이나 날짜 등을 묻는 의문사이다.
  When is your birthday?
  When does the café open? (시각을 묻는 when은 what time으로 바꿔 쓸 수 있다.)
  (→ **What time** does the café open?)
- where는 '어디서', '어디에'라는 뜻으로 장소를 묻는 의문사이다.
  Where is the subway station?

A 다음 〈보기〉와 같이 밑줄 친 부분을 묻는 의문문을 완성하시오.

〈보기〉 I went to Myeongdong. → Where did you go?

1 His birthday is July 9. → ______________ his birthday?
2 They're going to the bookstore. → ______________ going?
3 I bought the cake yesterday. → ______________ the cake?
4 I saw Lisa at the bus stop. → ______________ Lisa?
5 The movie starts at 5:30. → ______________ the movie start?

B 다음 밑줄 친 부분을 알맞은 의문사로 바꾸어 쓰시오.

1 A: Who are you from? — B: I'm from Australia.
2 A: What is City Hall? — B: It's around the corner.
3 A: Why is the Summer Festival? — B: It's this weekend.
4 A: Where are you going to see Diana again? — B: Next Sunday.
5 A: Which did you go with Steve? — B: We went to Green Park.

C 다음 우리말과 같은 뜻이 되도록 (   ) 안의 말을 이용하여 문장을 완성하시오.

1 그녀는 어디에 사니? (live)
_______ _______ _______ _______?

2 너는 점심시간에 어디에 있었니? (be)
_______ _______ _______ at lunch time?

3 Mark가 제게 언제 전화했나요? (call)
_______ _______ _______ _______ me?

4 너는 어제 몇 시에 Julia를 만났니? (meet)
_______ _______ _______ _______ _______ Julia yesterday?

Point 04

why로 시작하는 의문문

- why는 '왜'라는 뜻으로 이유를 묻는 의문사이다. 대답은 주로 '왜냐하면'이라는 뜻의 because로 시작한다.
  A: **Why** are you smiling?
  B: **Because** I got a present from Brian.

★ PLUS TIP 〈Why don't you ~?〉는 '너는 ~하는 것이 어때?'라는 뜻으로 상대방에게 권유할 때 쓰는 표현이고, 〈Why don't we ~?〉는 '우리 ~하지 않을래?'라는 뜻으로 〈Let's ~.〉나 〈How[What] about v-ing ~?〉와 같은 의미의 표현이다.

A 다음 ( ) 안의 말을 배열하여 의문문을 완성하시오.

1 ______________________ his mind? (he, did, change, why)
2 ______________________ of us? (this, took, who, picture)
3 ______________________ those earrings? (you, where, did, get)
4 ______________________ a new smartphone? (you, need, why, do)
5 ______________________ with Jeremy? (you, were, why, angry)

B 다음 대화의 빈칸에 알맞은 말을 쓰시오.

1 A: ________ ________ we take a break? B: That sounds great.

2 A: ________ didn't you come to the party?
B: ________ I was too busy.

3 A: ________ did he stay home yesterday?
B: ________ he was sick.

4 A: ________ did you last call your grandmother?
B: About two weeks ago.

C 다음 우리말과 같은 뜻이 되도록 ( ) 안의 말을 이용하여 문장을 완성하시오.

1 왜 기차가 멈췄나요? (stop)
________ did the train ________?

2 제가 왜 이것을 해야 하나요? (do)
________ do I ________ ________ ________ this?

3 너는 돈을 좀 모으는 게 어때? (save)
________ ________ you ________ some money?

4 너는 왜 그 가수를 좋아하니? (like)
________ ________ ________ ________ the singer?

5 우리 스키 타러 가지 않을래? (go)
________ ________ ________ ________ skiing?

Point 05 how로 시작하는 의문문

- how는 '어떻게', '어떤'이라는 뜻으로 수단이나 방법, 상태 등을 묻는 의문사이다.

A: **How** did you come here? (수단 · 방법)
B: By bus.

A: **How** are you? (상태)
B: I'm good.

A 다음 ( ) 안의 말을 배열하여 의문문을 완성하시오.

1 ______________________? (your, was, how, date)
2 ______________________ this salad? (she, how, make, did)
3 ______________________ to Europe? (how, your, was, trip)
4 ______________________ a model? (you, how, become, did)
5 ______________________ the alphabet? (people, did, how, invent)

B 다음 대화의 빈칸에 알맞은 의문사를 쓰시오.

1 A: __________ do you get to school? — B: By subway.
2 A: __________ made these lovely songs? — B: My sister did.
3 A: __________ is your mother? — B: She's great. Thanks.
4 A: __________ did you come home so early? — B: Because I'm tired.
5 A: __________ was your first day at school? — B: Not bad.
6 A: __________ did you buy those shoes? — B: At a department store.

C 다음 우리말과 같은 뜻이 되도록 ( ) 안의 말을 이용하여 문장을 완성하시오.

1 당신은 어떻게 그녀를 만났어요? (meet)
__________ __________ __________ __________ her?

2 서울의 날씨는 어때요? (the weather)
__________ __________ __________ __________ in Seoul?

3 그가 어떻게 제 이름을 알았나요? (know)
__________ __________ __________ __________ my name?

4 너는 수학을 어떻게 공부하니? (study)
__________ __________ __________ __________ math?

Point 06

〈how + 형용사 / 부사〉로 시작하는 의문문

■ how는 형용사나 부사와 함께 쓰여 '얼마나 ~한/하게'라는 뜻으로 다양한 의문문을 만든다.

How old are you? (나이를 물을 때)
How long is the program? (길이나 기간을 물을 때)
How often do you go to the movies? (빈도를 물을 때)
How many people were there at the party? (수를 물을 때)
How much money do you have now? (양이나 정도를 물을 때)

★ 내신만점 *TIP* How many 뒤에는 셀 수 있는 명사의 복수형, How much 뒤에는 셀 수 없는 명사가 온다는 것을 알아두자.

A 다음 대화의 빈칸에 알맞은 말을 쓰시오.

1 A: ________ ________ is your sister?
B: She is twenty years old.

2 A: ________ ________ is your holiday?
B: Ten days.

3 A: ________ ________ is the black jacket?
B: Oh, it's 25,000 won.

4 A: ________ ________ websites do you regularly visit?
B: About five or six.

5 A: ________ ________ do you go to the library?
B: Once a week.

B 다음 우리말과 같은 뜻이 되도록 문장을 완성하시오.

1 해변으로 가는 데 얼마나 걸리나요?
________ ________ does it take to get to the beach?

2 저 농구 선수는 키가 얼마나 크니?
________ ________ ________ that basketball player?

3 당신은 일본에 몇 년 동안 살았나요?
________ ________ ________ did you live in Japan?

4 우리는 매일 얼마나 많은 물을 마셔야 하나요?
________ ________ ________ should we drink every day?

5 너는 하루에 몇 번이나 휴대전화를 확인하니?
________ ________ ________ a day do you check your cell phone?

[01-03] 다음 빈칸에 알맞은 말을 고르시오.

01

A: ________ is my smartphone?
B: It's on the desk.

① Why ② What ③ Who
④ Where ⑤ When

02

A: ________ is in your right hand?
B: Nothing.

① Who ② What ③ How
④ Why ⑤ Where

03

A: ________ was the picnic yesterday?
B: It was great.

① What ② Why ③ How
④ Where ⑤ Who

04

다음 밑줄 친 부분의 쓰임이 나머지와 다른 것은?

① What did Sarah do last night?
② What food can you cook?
③ What languages can you speak?
④ What day is it today?
⑤ What movie is your favorite?

[05-06] 다음 대화의 빈칸에 알맞은 말을 고르시오.

05

A: Where did you travel?
B: ____________________

① Every year.
② I went to Canada.
③ About ten days.
④ I traveled by plane.
⑤ Because my boyfriend did it.

06

A: ____________________
B: We climbed Dobongsan.

① Who are you?
② What did you do?
③ Why did you do that?
④ Where are you going?
⑤ When did you climb a mountain?

07

다음 우리말을 영어로 바르게 옮긴 것은?

박물관까지 가는 데 얼마나 걸리나요?

① Where is the museum?
② How far is the museum?
③ How often do you go to the museum?
④ How long does it take to get to the museum?
⑤ How much does it cost to enter the museum?

[08-09] 다음 빈칸에 공통으로 들어갈 말을 고르시오.

08

- ________ is your favorite song?
- ________ time does the class start?

① What ② How ③ When
④ Which ⑤ Who

09

- ________ was your weekend?
- ________ tall is your boyfriend?

① What ② How ③ Which
④ Where ⑤ Why

[10-11] 빈칸에 들어갈 말이 순서대로 알맞게 짝지어진 것을 고르시오.

10

- ________ is going to the bakery?
- ________ don't we hold a party for Mom?

① Who – What ② Who – Why
③ Where – How ④ Where – Why
⑤ What – How

11

- How ________ people are there in your family?
- ________ do you like better, jazz or rock?

① long – What ② many – Why
③ much – What ④ many – Which
⑤ much – Which

12

다음 질문에 대한 대답으로 알맞은 것은?

Why don't we have a cup of coffee?

① Great. I'd love to.
② Three times a day.
③ I bought it for you.
④ I like coffee better.
⑤ Because we like coffee.

13

다음 대화의 빈칸에 들어갈 말이 순서대로 알맞게 짝지어진 것은?

A: ________ does he play soccer?
B: Once a month.
A: ________ do you like her?
B: Because she is kind and cute.

① When – Why ② When – Who
③ How often – Who ④ How often – Why
⑤ What – Why

기출응용

14

다음 중 어느 빈칸에도 들어갈 수 없는 것은?

(a) How ________ do you go shopping?
(b) How ________ milk do you drink?
(c) How ________ copies do you need?
(d) How ________ is your summer vacation?
(e) How ________ books did you read this month?

① long ② much ③ tall
④ often ⑤ many

[15-16] 다음 대화 중 자연스럽지 <u>않은</u> 것을 고르시오.

15

① A: What does he do?
B: He is a pilot.

② A: How do you get to work?
B: I like it.

③ A: How much time do you need?
B: Twenty minutes will be enough.

④ A: What time do you usually get up?
B: I usually get up at seven.

⑤ A: Which shirt do you like, the red one or the green one?
B: I like the red one.

16

① A: When did you visit London?
B: I went there last month.

② A: Why is she so happy?
B: Because she passed the exam.

③ A: Where is my cheesecake?
B: I put it in the refrigerator.

④ A: Which backpack did you buy?
B: I bought the one with frogs on it.

⑤ A: Why don't we go swimming?
B: Because you're not busy.

17

다음 우리말을 영어로 옮긴 것 중 <u>잘못된</u> 것은?

① 너는 무슨 야채를 가장 좋아하니?
What vegetable do you like the most?

② 너는 설탕이 얼마나 필요하니?
How many sugar do you need?

③ 저 책들을 읽는 게 어때?
Why don't you read those books?

④ 그는 교실에 무엇을 가져왔니?
What did he bring to the classroom?

⑤ 너는 왜 그에게 크리스마스 카드를 보냈니?
Why did you send him a Christmas card?

18

빈칸에 들어갈 말이 나머지와 <u>다른</u> 것은?

① ________ are you angry at me?
② ________ did she leave so early?
③ ________ don't you dance with him?
④ ________ was she late for the party?
⑤ ________ can I do for you?

기출응용

19

다음 중 어법상 <u>틀린</u> 문장의 개수는?

(a) Where does your cousin live?
(b) Why don't you join us?
(c) What time did you arrive here?
(d) Who want some cookies now?
(e) When did the accident happened?

① 0개 ② 1개 ③ 2개 ④ 3개 ⑤ 4개

고난도

20

다음 대화의 순서로 알맞은 것은?

(a) I prefer ice cream.
(b) I asked for the chocolate ice cream.
(c) What did you order for dessert?
(d) Why didn't you order the cherry pie?

① (a) – (c) – (d) – (b)
② (c) – (a) – (d) – (b)
③ (c) – (b) – (d) – (a)
④ (d) – (a) – (b) – (c)
⑤ (d) – (c) – (b) – (a)

내신대비 TEST

서술형 따라잡기

01

주어진 말을 이용하여 우리말과 뜻이 같도록 문장을 완성하시오.

(1) 누가 너에게 이 인형을 사줬니? (buy)

→ ________ ________ this doll for you?

(2) 너는 언제 치과에 갔니? (go)

→ ________ ________ ________ ________ to the dentist?

02

다음 대화를 읽고, 빈칸에 알맞은 의문사를 쓰시오.

A: ________ did you go to the concert hall?
B: I went there yesterday.
A: ________ had a concert?
B: My favorite band, Wanna Be, had a concert.
A: ________ was it?
B: It was really great.

03

주어진 말을 알맞게 배열하여 우리말과 뜻이 같도록 문장을 완성하시오.

(1) 너는 왜 모임에 늦었니? (were, why, late, you)

→ ________________ for the meeting?

(2) 네 수업에는 얼마나 많은 사람들이 있니? (are, how, there, people, many)

→ ________________ in your class?

기출응용

04

다음 그림을 보고, 대화를 완성하시오.

이름: David
나이: 30세
국적: 영국

(1) Q. ________ ________ his name?

A. His name is ________.

(2) Q. ________ ________ is he?

A. He is 30 years old.

(3) Q. ________ ________ he from?

A. ________ ________ from England.

05

다음 대화에서 어법상 <u>틀린</u> 부분을 모두 찾아 바르게 고쳐 쓰시오. (2군데)

A: What far is it to the airport? And how you got there?
B: It's 30 km from here. I went there by car.

06

주어진 말을 이용하여 각 질문을 완성하시오.

(1) go to yoga class
(2) see a doctor

(1) A: ________ ________ ________ ________ ________ ________ ________ ________?

B: I go there twice a week.

(2) A: ________ ________ ________ ________ ________ ________?

B: Because I had a headache.

SELF NOTE

핵심 포인트 정리하기

1 의문사

- 의미: 사람[사물], 때, 장소, 이유, 방법 등을 물을 때 쓰는 말
- 의문사가 있는 의문문 형태: 〈① __________ + 동사[be동사/do동사/조동사] + 주어 ~?〉

  * Yes나 No가 아닌 구체적인 정보로 대답

의문사가 있는 의문문의 어순(의문사 + 동사 + 주어) 기억하기!

2 의문사의 종류

② __________	'누구'	③ __________	'무엇', '무슨'
④ __________	'어느 것', '어느'	⑤ __________	'언제'(시간이나 날짜 등)
⑥ __________	'어디서', '어디에'(장소)		
why	• '왜'(이유) • 대답: 〈⑦ __________ +주어+동사〉		
how	• '어떻게', '어떤'(수단, 방법, 상태) • 〈how+형용사 / 부사〉: '얼마나 ~한/하게' - how old(나이) - how long(길이나 기간) - ⑧ __________(빈도) - how many(수) - ⑨ __________(양이나 정도)		

how many 뒤에 셀 수 있는 명사, how much 뒤에는 셀 수 없는 명사가 오는지 확인하기!

문제로 개념 다지기

밑줄 친 부분이 어법상 맞으면 O, 틀리면 X 표시하고 바르게 고치시오.

1 A: When were you laughing in the classroom?
  B: Because Harry told me a funny story.

2 A: Where is she doing?
  B: She's watering the plants.

3 A: How often do you watch TV at home?
  B: I watch TV three times a week.

4 A: Who are going to work with me?
  B: I'm not sure. Why don't you ask Jimmy?

5 A: How many money do you need?
  B: I need just one dollar.

CHAPTER 08 문장의 종류

You will see a doctor, **won't you**?	[부가 의문문]
Didn't you hear the news?	[부정 의문문]
Are you drinking lemon tea **or** orange tea?	[선택 의문문]
What wonderful weather this is!	[감탄문]
Wear your coat, **or** you'll catch a cold.	[명령문]

다양한 문장의 종류란?

상대방으로부터 확인이나 동의를 구하기 위해 평서문 뒤에 붙이는 부가 의문문, 동사의 부정형으로 시작하는 부정 의문문, 선택을 요구하는 선택 의문문, 놀람이나 기쁨 등의 감정을 나타내는 감탄문, 그리고 상대방에게 지시나 명령, 권유를 할 때 쓰는 명령문 등이 있습니다.

부가 의문문의 형태

- 부가 의문문은 평서문 뒤에 덧붙이는 「~, 동사+주어?」 형태의 의문문으로 상대방의 동의를 구하거나 확인을 하기 위해 사용한다. 앞 문장이 긍정문일 때는 뒤에 부정문을, 앞 문장이 부정문일 때는 뒤에 긍정문을 쓴다. 이때 부가 의문문은 '그렇지?', '그렇지 않니?' 등으로 해석한다.
  He *is* a lucky person, **isn't he**?
  He *didn't* wash his face, **did he**?
- 부가 의문문 만드는 방법

문장의 주어 → 대명사	*Jennifer* likes milk tea, doesn't **she**?
be동사 → be동사 / 조동사 → 조동사 일반동사 → do동사	She *is* cool, **isn't** she? / You *won't* come back, **will** you? This steak *smells* fantastic, **doesn't** it?

*시제는 앞 문장과 일치시키고, 부정의 부가 의문문은 축약형으로 쓴다.

A 다음 밑줄 친 부분을 어법에 맞게 고쳐 쓰시오.

1 He talks a lot, don't he?
2 They can drive, do they?
3 She didn't pass the test, does she?
4 You don't eat meat, don't you?
5 You were very tired, didn't you?

B 다음 빈칸에 알맞은 부가 의문문을 쓰시오.

1 He doesn't know you, __________ __________?
2 Mike can teach drawing, __________ __________?
3 You won first prize, __________ __________?
4 She finished her work yesterday, __________ __________?
5 Susan and Steve will join our club, __________ __________?

C 다음 우리말과 같은 뜻이 되도록 문장을 완성하시오.

1 커피가 아주 뜨겁지는 않아, 그렇지?
The coffee isn't very hot, __________ __________?

2 당신이 피자를 주문하셨죠, 그렇지 않나요?
You ordered a pizza, __________ __________?

3 그녀는 Tim과 데이트를 하지 않을 거야, 그렇지?
She's not going out with Tim, __________ __________?

4 내 여동생은 높이 뛸 수 있어, 그렇지 않니?
My sister can jump high, __________ __________?

Point 02 부가 의문문의 응답

- 부가 의문문에 대한 응답은 부가의문문이 긍정문인지 부정문인지에 상관없이 대답하는 내용이 긍정이면 Yes, 부정이면 No로 답한다.

  A: Nicholas is a genius, **isn't he**?

  B: **Yes, he is.** (천재임)

  No, he isn't. (천재가 아님)

★ PLUS TIP 명령문의 부가 의문문은 긍정·부정에 상관없이 보통 〈~, will you?〉를 쓴다. Don't be late, **will you**?
〈Let's ~.〉 형태인 권유의 명령문은 부가 의문문으로 〈~, shall we?〉를 쓴다. Let's take a taxi, **shall we**?

A 다음 우리말과 같은 뜻이 되도록 문장을 완성하시오.

1 A: 그 영화는 정말 놀라웠어, 그렇지 않니?
The movie was amazing, __________ __________?
B: 아니, 놀랍지 않았어.
__________, __________ __________.

2 A: George가 그 시험에서 높은 점수를 받았지, 그렇지 않니?
George got a high score on the test, __________ __________?
B: 응, 높은 점수를 받았어.
__________, __________ __________.

3 A: 그 박물관은 월요일마다 문을 닫아요, 그렇지 않나요?
The museum is closed on Mondays, __________ __________?
B: 네, 월요일마다 닫아요. 우리 화요일에 가요.
__________, __________ __________. Let's go on Tuesday.

B 다음 빈칸에 알맞은 말을 넣어 대화를 완성하시오.

1 A: You didn't buy doughnuts for me, did you?
B: __________, __________ __________. I forgot.

2 A: Let's take a break, __________ __________?
B: Sure, let's do that.

3 A: Wash your hands before dinner, __________ __________?
B: Oh, okay.

4 A: She saw her favorite TV star on the street, __________ __________?
B: __________, __________ __________. She said he was really handsome.

5 A: You can't play hockey, __________ __________?
B: __________, __________ __________. But I can ice-skate.

Point 03 부정 의문문의 형태

■ 부정 의문문은 동사의 부정형으로 시작하는 의문문으로 '~이지 않니?'라는 뜻이다. 이때 동사의 부정형은 모두 축약형으로 쓴다.

Aren't you angry? (be동사)
Can't she try again? (조동사)
Didn't he catch the train? (일반동사)

A **다음 문장을 〈보기〉와 같이 부정 의문문으로 바꾸어 쓰시오.**

〈보기〉 It is cold. → Isn't it cold?

1 This is yours. → ______
2 It was expensive. → ______
3 He is a designer. → ______
4 You feel thirsty. → ______
5 They can deliver it. → ______
6 He took notes. → ______
7 She plays tennis well. → ______
8 She will move to New York. → ______
9 You were interested in animals. → ______

B **다음 우리말과 같은 뜻이 되도록 ( ) 안의 말을 배열하여 부정 의문문 형태의 문장을 완성하시오.**

1 생선을 좀 먹어보지 않겠니? (eat, you, some fish, won't)
______

2 너는 그와 함께 있지 않았니? (him, weren't, with, you)
______

3 그는 한국에 올 수 없니? (he, Korea, come, can't, to)
______

4 너는 나를 신뢰하지 않니? (trust, you, don't, me)
______

5 그녀가 창문을 닫지 않았나요? (the window, didn't, close, she)
______

6 그는 어제 학교에 가지 않았나요? (he, yesterday, go, didn't, school, to)
______

Point 04

부정 의문문의 응답

- 부정 의문문에 대한 응답은 질문에 대해 대답하는 내용이 긍정이면 Yes, 부정이면 No로 답한다.

  A: **Don't** you like pasta?

  B: **Yes, I do.** (파스타를 좋아함)

  No, I don't. (파스타를 좋아하지 않음)

A 다음 우리말과 같은 뜻이 되도록 문장을 완성하시오.

1 A: 그분이 너의 과학 선생님 아니시니?

_________ he your science teacher?

B: 네, 그분은 아니에요.

_________, _________ _________.

2 A: 그는 돌아오지 않았나요?

_________ he come back?

B: 네, 오지 않았어요.

_________, _________ _________.

3 A: 그녀가 다시는 나를 보지 않을까요?

_________ she see me again?

B: 아니에요, 볼 거예요.

_________, _________ _________.

4 A: 그는 음악을 좋아하지 않나요?

_________ he like music?

B: 네, 좋아하지 않아요.

_________, _________ _________.

B 다음 빈칸에 알맞은 말을 넣어 대화를 완성하시오.

1 A: Isn't it too crowded here?

B: _________, _________ _________. There are so many people here.

2 A: I bought this watch. Isn't it nice?

B: _________, _________ _________. It looks cool.

3 A: Didn't he invite you to the party?

B: _________, _________ _________. But he said he was sorry.

4 A: Can't she come to my house today?

B: _________, _________ _________. She has a lot of work.

what으로 시작하는 감탄문

- 감탄문은 '참 ~하구나!'라는 뜻으로 기쁨, 슬픔, 놀라움 등의 감정을 표현하는 문장이다.
- what으로 시작하는 감탄문은 〈What+a/an+형용사+명사(+주어+동사)!〉의 어순이다. 명사가 복수형이거나 셀 수 없는 명사인 경우 a나 an을 쓰지 않는다.

  What a tasty doughnut (this is)!
  What cute puppies (they are)!

A **다음 문장을 〈보기〉와 같이 감탄문으로 바꾸어 쓰시오.**

〈보기〉 They are very lovely flowers. → What lovely flowers they are!

1 This is very hot soup. → ______________________
2 He has very big hands. → ______________________
3 It is a very beautiful day. → ______________________
4 They are very nice people. → ______________________
5 Jack is a very witty man. → ______________________
6 It is a very pretty T-shirt. → ______________________
7 She sent a very long message. → ______________________

B **다음 우리말과 같은 뜻이 되도록 ( ) 안의 말을 배열하여 문장을 완성하시오.**

1 그건 참 영리한 개구나! (it, is, a, what, dog, clever)

____

2 너는 참 좋은 친구구나! (you, a, what, are, friend, good)

____

3 이건 정말 더러운 방이구나! (this, a, room, is, what, dirty)

____

4 너는 참 수줍음이 많은 소년이구나! (what, boy, are, you, a, shy)

____

5 너는 정말 매운 음식을 요리했구나! (you, spicy, cooked, what, food)

____

6 Jude는 정말 매력적인 목소리를 가지고 있구나! (a, what, voice, Jude, charming, has)

____

7 그는 정말 위대한 사람이구나! (he, man, is, great, what, a)

____

Point 08

how로 시작하는 감탄문

- how로 시작하는 감탄문은 〈How+형용사/부사(+주어+동사)!〉의 어순이다.
  How tall (the model is)!
  How high (he jumps)!

★ 내신만점 TIP what으로 시작하는 감탄문과 how로 시작하는 감탄문의 어순을 구분하자.

A 다음 밑줄 친 부분을 어법에 맞게 고쳐 쓰시오.

1 How a huge airplane it is!
2 How interesting is the story!
3 What peaceful this village is!
4 How these shoes small are!
5 What cute dress she is wearing!

B 다음 문장을 〈보기〉와 같이 감탄문으로 바꾸어 쓰시오.

〈보기〉 I was very foolish. → How foolish I was!

1 It is very cheap. → ______
2 You are very friendly. → ______
3 This lake is very deep. → ______
4 Her hair is very short. → ______
5 This problem was very difficult. → ______
6 The game was very exciting. → ______
7 The sofa is very comfortable. → ______

C 다음 우리말과 같은 뜻이 되도록 ( ) 안의 말을 이용하여 문장을 완성하시오.

1 이 만화는 정말 재미있구나! (funny)
______ ______ this cartoon is!

2 네 배낭은 정말 무겁구나! (heavy)
______ ______ your backpack is!

3 그건 정말 유용한 정보구나! (useful)
______ ______ information it is!

4 우리는 정말 멋진 시간을 보냈구나! (wonderful)
______ ______ ______ time we had!

명령문 I

- 명령문은 상대방에게 지시나 명령, 권유 등을 하는 문장으로, 주어(you)를 생략하고 동사원형으로 시작한다.
- 긍정 명령문은 '~해라'라는 의미이다. 부탁이나 요청을 공손하게 나타내는 경우에는 문장의 앞이나 뒤에 please를 쓴다.
  Go to bed early. / **Call** me back later, **please**.
- 부정 명령문은 '~하지 마라'라는 의미로, 동사원형으로 시작하는 명령문 앞에 Don't를 붙인 형태이다.
  Don't wear my clothes. / **Don't be** late for the concert.

★ PLUS TIP 명령문에 대한 긍정의 대답은 OK. / Sure. / No problem. / All right. 등으로 한다.

A 다음 문장을 지시대로 바꾸어 쓰시오.

1 You are nice to people. (긍정 명령문) → ______________________
2 You wear a seat belt. (긍정 명령문) → ______________________
3 Be in a hurry. (부정 명령문) → ______________________
4 Tell him the truth. (부정 명령문) → ______________________

B 다음 <보기>에서 알맞은 말을 골라 명령문 형태의 문장을 완성하시오.

<보기> get up turn on listen to go out

1 It's getting dark. Please ________ ________ the light.
2 ________ ________ ________ alone late at night.
3 ________ ________ ________ loud music. It's not good for your ears.
4 ________ ________ early tomorrow. You have a class in the morning.

C 다음 우리말과 같은 뜻이 되도록 ( ) 안의 말을 배열하여 문장을 완성하시오.

1 문을 열어주세요. (the, please, door, open)
____

2 저에 대해 걱정하지 마세요. (worry, me, don't, about)
____

3 같은 실수를 다시는 하지 마세요. (the same, again, mistake, make, don't)
____

4 여기에 당신의 차를 주차하지 마세요. (car, park, don't, here, your)
____

Point 10

명령문 II

- 〈명령문+and ~〉는 '…해라, 그러면 ~할 것이다'라는 뜻이다.
  Do it now, and you will finish by six. (→ If you do it now, you will finish by six.)
- 〈명령문+or ~〉는 '…해라, 그러지 않으면 ~할 것이다'라는 뜻이다.
  Do it now, or you won't finish by six. (→ If you don't do it now, you won't finish by six.)
- 권유의 긍정 명령문은 '~하자'라는 뜻으로 〈Let's+동사원형〉으로 나타내고, 부정 명령문은 '~하지 말자'라는 뜻으로 〈Let's not+동사원형〉으로 나타낸다.
  A: **Let's go** to the concert. B: Sounds great. (긍정의 답변) / I'm sorry, but I can't. (부정의 답변)
  Let's not go outside.

A 다음 ( ) 안에서 알맞은 말을 고르시오.

1 (Let's not / Not let's) swim in the lake.
2 Let's (had / have) lunch together.
3 Eat something, (and / or) you will be hungry later.
4 Ask Sally, (and / or) she'll lend you her notebook.
5 We are late! (Let / Let's) take a taxi.

B 다음 문장을 〈명령문+and/or ~〉로 바꾸어 쓰시오.

1 If you read this book, you'll learn many things.
→ ______________________________

2 If you don't study hard, you won't pass the exam.
→ ______________________________

3 If you visit the website, you will get a coupon.
→ ______________________________

C 다음 우리말과 같은 뜻이 되도록 ( ) 안의 말을 이용하여 문장을 완성하시오.

1 지하철역을 함께 찾아보자. (find)
_________ _________ the subway station together.

2 그것을 써 놓으세요, 그러지 않으면 당신은 그것을 잊어버릴 거예요. (forget)
Write it down, _________ _________ _________ it.

3 저 식당에 가지 말자. (go)
_________ _________ _________ to that restaurant.

4 일찍 오세요, 그러면 당신은 좋은 자리를 잡게 될 거예요. (get)
Come early, _________ _________ _________ a good seat.

[01-03] 다음 빈칸에 알맞은 말을 고르시오.

01

You got my email, _______?

① do you ② don't you
③ didn't you ④ aren't you
⑤ weren't you

02

_______ delicious this sandwich is!

① Does ② What
③ What a ④ How
⑤ How a

03

Is this baby a girl _______ a boy?

① or ② and ③ but
④ so ⑤ to

04

빈칸에 들어갈 말이 나머지와 다른 것은?

① _______ cold it is!
② _______ smart you are!
③ _______ deep the sea is!
④ _______ small your hat is!
⑤ _______ long fingers you have!

[05-06] 다음 두 문장이 같은 뜻이 되도록 빈칸에 알맞은 말을 고르시오.

05

The vegetables are very fresh.
→ _______ the vegetables are!

① How fresh ② How a fresh
③ What fresh ④ What a fresh
⑤ There are fresh

06

Why don't we go to the movies?
→ _______ go to the movies.

① Do ② Let ③ Let's
④ Don't ⑤ Let's not

[07-08] 다음 질문에 대한 알맞은 대답을 고르시오.

07

A: You can speak Chinese, can't you?
B: _______________ Do you need my help?

① Yes, I do. ② No, I don't.
③ Yes, I can. ④ No, I can't.
⑤ No, I won't.

08

A: Isn't she a great actress?
B: _______________ I love her movies.

① Yes, she is. ② Yes, she isn't.
③ No, she is. ④ No, she isn't.
⑤ Yes, she does.

[09-10] 빈칸에 들어갈 말이 순서대로 알맞게 짝지어진 것을 고르시오.

09

A: Frank will stay here, ________ he?
B: Yes, he ________.

① does – will ② will – won't
③ won't – won't ④ won't – will
⑤ doesn't – does

10

________ noisy you are! ________ quiet, please.

① How – Be ② What – Do
③ How a – Be ④ What a – Be
⑤ How – Do

[11-12] 다음 빈칸에 공통으로 들어갈 말을 고르시오.

11

• ________ a great song it is!
• ________ is the title of the book?

① What ② How ③ Which
④ Let's ⑤ Why

12

• Make a reservation, ________ you won't get a seat.
• Which do you want to read, a book ________ a magazine?

① and ② or ③ but
④ if ⑤ so

[13-14] 다음 우리말을 영어로 바르게 옮긴 것을 고르시오.

13

그들의 사랑 이야기는 정말 흥미롭구나!

① How interesting their love story!
② How interesting their love story is!
③ How is interesting their love story!
④ What an interesting is their love story!
⑤ What an interesting their love story is!

14

James는 운전 면허증이 없어, 그렇지?

① James has a driver's license, does he?
② James has a driver's license, doesn't he?
③ James doesn't have a driver's license, does he?
④ James doesn't have a driver's license, didn't he?
⑤ James doesn't have a driver's license, doesn't he?

15

다음 대화 중 자연스럽지 않은 것은?

① A: Which do you want, pork or beef?
B: I want beef.
② A: Won't she go to the beach?
B: Yes, she will.
③ A: He made a mistake, didn't he?
B: No, he didn't.
④ A: I'm worried about the exam.
B: Study hard, or you'll pass.
⑤ A: Let's go bungee jumping.
B: No, let's not. It looks dangerous.

기출응용

16

다음 밑줄 친 부분을 바르게 고치지 않은 것은?

① You were absent yesterday, did you?
→ weren't you

② Turn on the heater, do you?
→ don't you

③ Let's order chicken sandwiches, are we?
→ shall we

④ Your brother is wearing glasses, doesn't he?
→ isn't he

⑤ Kate works for a car company, does she?
→ doesn't she

17

(A), (B), (C)의 괄호 안에서 알맞은 것끼리 바르게 짝지어진 것은?

(A) [What / How] well they dance!
(B) Don't eat at night, [and / or] you will gain weight.
(C) Which do you want, hamburgers [and / or] pizza?

	(A)		(B)		(C)
①	What	······	and	······	or
②	What	······	or	······	and
③	How	······	or	······	and
④	How	······	or	······	or
⑤	How	······	and	······	or

[18-19] 다음 중 어법상 틀린 것을 고르시오.

18

① It is scary, isn't it?
② Don't run in the hall.
③ Let's not plays a computer game.
④ Is this cell phone yours or Maria's?
⑤ Take a taxi, or you'll be late for work.

19

① Let's go to the library.
② What lovely shoes they are!
③ Take a seat, will you?
④ You will come back, aren't you?
⑤ Walk fast, and you'll get there on time.

고난도

20

다음 중 어법상 옳은 것끼리 짝지어진 것은?

(a) What fast the train is!
(b) Let's be careful of the dogs.
(c) How lucky those people are!
(d) Let's don't buy the ring for Jenny.
(e) Take this medicine, and you will get well.

① (a), (b), (c)
② (a), (c), (e)
③ (b), (c), (d)
④ (b), (c), (e)
⑤ (c), (d), (e)

내신대비 TEST

서술형 따라잡기

01
다음 문장을 지시대로 바꾸어 쓰시오.

(1) They are very cute girls.

→ ______________________

(what으로 시작하는 감탄문)

(2) Go to the shopping center today.

→ ______________________

(권유의 명령문)

02
다음 두 문장이 같은 뜻이 되도록 빈칸에 알맞은 말을 쓰시오.

(1) If you exercise every day, you will be healthy.

→ ________ ________ ________, ________ you will be healthy.

(2) If you lie to your friends, you will lose them.

→ ________ ________ to your friends, ________ you will lose them.

03
주어진 말을 알맞게 배열하여 우리말과 뜻이 같도록 문장을 완성하시오.

(1) Bob은 빨리 달리지 않아, 그렇지?
(he, does, run, Bob, fast, doesn't)

→ ______________________

(2) 그 돌고래는 정말 영리하구나!
(clever, dolphin, how, is, the)

→ ______________________

04
다음 그림을 보고, 주어진 말을 이용하여 명령하는 문장을 완성하시오.

________ ________ ________ on the street. (throw trash)

05
다음 표를 보고, 빈칸에 알맞은 말을 쓰시오.

	사용 가능 언어	좋아하는 과목 / 싫어하는 과목
Mike	Korean, English	Music / Science

(1) Q: Can't Mike speak English?
A: ________, ________ ________.

(2) Q: Mike likes science, doesn't he?
A: ________, ________ ________.

기출응용

06
다음을 보고, 〈보기〉와 같이 문장을 완성하시오.

Dr. Joe's Advice:
- Write in your diary every day.
  → You can be a good writer.

(1) Don't go to bed late.
→ You can get up early.

(2) Turn your music off.
→ You can focus on your work.

〈보기〉 Write in your diary every day, and you can be a good writer.

(1) Don't go to bed late, or
______________________.

(2) Turn your music off, and
______________________.

SELF NOTE

핵심 포인트 정리하기

1 여러 가지 의문문

	부가 의문문	부정 의문문	선택 의문문
형태	〈긍정문+① ＿＿＿＿＿〉 〈부정문+② ＿＿＿＿＿〉	〈be동사/조동사/do동사+ ⑤ ＿＿＿＿의 축약형+주어 ~?〉	〈의문문+A ⑥ ＿＿＿＿ B?〉
의미	'그렇지 않니?'/'그렇지?'	'~이지 않니?'	'A니 B니?'
응답	대답하는 내용이 긍정이면 ③ ＿＿＿＿, 부정이면 ④ ＿＿＿＿		원하는 선택 사항으로 대답

부가 의문문의 형태와 응답 알아두기!

2 감탄문

- 형태: 〈What + ⑦ ＿＿＿＿ + 형용사 + 명사(+주어+동사)!〉
  〈⑧ ＿＿＿＿ + 형용사/부사(+주어+동사)!〉
- 의미: '참 ~하구나!'

what으로 시작하는 감탄문과 how로 시작하는 감탄문의 어순 구분하기!

3 명령문

- 종류

긍정 명령문	⑨ ＿＿＿＿으로 시작	'~해라'
부정 명령문	⑩ ＿＿＿＿ +동사원형	'~하지 마라'
권유의 긍정 명령문	⑪ ＿＿＿＿ +동사원형	'~하자'
권유의 부정 명령문	⑫ ＿＿＿＿ +동사원형	'~하지 말자'

- 〈명령문 + ⑬ ＿＿＿＿ ~〉: '…해라, 그러면 ~할 것이다'
- 〈명령문 + or ~〉: '…해라, 그러지 않으면 ~할 것이다'

문제로 개념 다지기

밑줄 친 부분이 어법상 맞으면 O, 틀리면 X 표시하고 바르게 고치시오.

1 What a nice bag!
2 Are kind to your neighbors.
3 Let's saw a movie together.
4 A: Didn't Kevin join the music club? — B: Yes, he did.
5 Wake Peter up now, and he will be late for school.
6 Let's don't go for a walk today. It's going to be rainy.
7 A: This food is delicious, isn't it? — B: No, it is. It's very tasty.

개념 쏙쏙

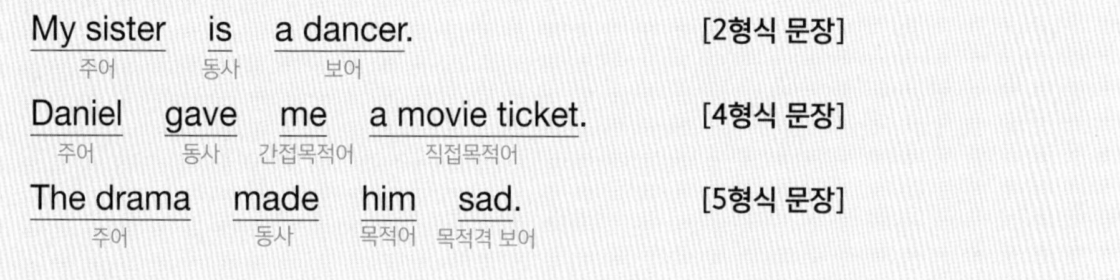
My sister (주어) is (동사) a dancer. (보어) [2형식 문장]

Daniel (주어) gave (동사) me (간접목적어) a movie ticket. (직접목적어) [4형식 문장]

The drama (주어) made (동사) him (목적어) sad. (목적격 보어) [5형식 문장]

문장이란?

각각의 단어가 일정한 순서로 모여 의미를 나타내는 것으로, 문장을 이루는 가장 기본적인 요소는 주어와 동사입니다. 그런데 때때로 주어와 동사 외에 '누구를[무엇을]'에 해당하는 목적어나, 주어 또는 목적어를 보충 설명해주는 보어가 필요하기도 합니다. 따라서 문장의 형태는 어떤 요소들이 포함되어 있는지에 따라 달라집니다.

Point 01 1형식 / 2형식 문장

- 문장은 일반적으로 문장 성분(주어 / 동사 / 보어 / 목적어)에 따라 5가지 형식으로 나눌 수 있다.
- 1형식 문장은 〈주어+동사〉로 이루어진 문장이다. 1형식 문장은 부사(구) 등과 함께 쓰이는 경우가 많다.
  The sun rises.
  The baby cried in the room.
- 2형식 문장은 〈주어+동사+보어〉로 이루어진 문장이다. 보어는 명사(구)나 형용사(구)로, 주어를 보충 설명해 주는 역할을 한다.
  Cristiano Ronaldo is **a soccer player**.
  He is **polite**.

A 다음 문장을 우리말로 해석하고, 몇 형식 문장인지 쓰시오.

1 Alex sings well.
______________________ 〈 〉 형식

2 Marie became a scientist.
______________________ 〈 〉 형식

3 Boseong is famous for green tea.
______________________ 〈 〉 형식

4 The dress in the shop is pretty.
______________________ 〈 〉 형식

5 The phone on the table rang.
______________________ 〈 〉 형식

B 다음 우리말과 같은 뜻이 되도록 ( ) 안의 말을 배열하여 문장을 완성하시오.

1 태양은 서쪽에서 진다. (the west, in, the sun, sets)
____

2 그들은 바닷가를 따라 거닐었다. (along, they, the beach, walked)
____

3 Chris는 고등학생이다. (a, student, Chris, high school, is)
____

4 그의 농담은 아주 재미있다. (very, are, jokes, his, funny)
____

5 나의 부모님은 보스턴에 살고 계신다. (live, my, Boston, parents, in)
____

Point 02 감각동사 + 형용사

■ 〈주어+동사+보어〉로 이루어진 2형식 문장에는 감각동사가 자주 사용된다.

■ 감각동사란 feel, look, smell, sound, taste 등과 같이 감각을 표현하는 동사로, 뒤에 보어로 형용사가 온다.

You **look tired**.

The herb tea **smells nice**.

• 감각동사 뒤에는 부사가 아닌 형용사가 온다는 것을 잊지 말자.

That **sounds *great***. (O)　That **sounds *greatly***. (X)

• 감각동사 뒤에 명사가 올 때는 '~처럼'의 뜻을 나타내는 전치사 like가 함께 쓰인다는 것을 알아두자.

The house **looks like** *a toy*. (그 집은 장난감처럼 보인다.)

A 다음 밑줄 친 부분을 어법에 맞게 고쳐 쓰시오.

1 I felt happily.

2 He looks like sick.

3 Her accent sounds strangely.

4 The curry smells deliciously.

5 These orange cookies taste awfully.

B 다음 〈보기〉에서 알맞은 말을 골라 문장을 완성하시오. (단, 한 번씩만 사용할 것)

〈보기〉 great　terrible　tastes　felt　sounded

1 After they swam, they __________ hungry.

2 He failed the test. His voice __________ sad.

3 That fruit smells __________, but it is very tasty.

4 The spaghetti __________ wonderful. You should try some.

5 You look __________ in your new suit. Where did you buy it?

C 다음 우리말과 같은 뜻이 되도록 (　) 안의 말을 이용하여 문장을 완성하시오.

1 레몬은 신맛이 난다. (sour)

Lemons __________ __________.

2 그 경찰은 친절해 보인다. (kind)

The police officer __________ __________.

3 그 옷감은 부드럽게 느껴진다. (soft)

The cloth __________ __________.

4 이 초콜릿 케이크는 달콤한 냄새가 난다. (sweet)

This chocolate cake __________ __________.

Point 03 3형식 / 4형식 문장

- 3형식 문장은 〈주어+동사+목적어〉로 이루어진 문장이다. 목적어는 주어가 하는 동작의 대상이 되는 말이다.
  He bought **a sandwich and some milk**. / She entered **the classroom**.
- 4형식 문장은 〈주어+수여동사+간접목적어+직접목적어〉로 이루어진 문장이다.
- 수여동사는 4형식 문장에 사용되는 동사로, '~에게(간접목적어)'와 '~을(직접목적어)'의 의미를 지니는 두 개의 목적어를 취한다. 대표적인 동사로는 give, buy, send, show, lend, bring, make, teach 등이 있다.
  Tony **gave me a watch**. / Alice **bought her son a toy**.

A 다음 ( ) 안의 말을 배열하여 대화를 완성하시오.

1 A: Is she a writer?
B: Yes, she is. ______________________ (she, novels, writes, for teenagers)

2 A: What do you do?
B: ______________________ (math, I, children, teach)

3 A: Are you ready to order?
B: Yes. ______________________, please. (a cheeseburger, want, I)

4 A: ______________________ (Kevin, a few days, saw, I, ago)
B: Oh, really? How was he?

5 A: How was your interview?
B: Not bad. ______________________ (a lot of, me, they, questions, asked)

B 다음 우리말과 같은 뜻이 되도록 ( ) 안의 말을 이용하여 문장을 완성하시오.

1 그녀는 새 가방을 하나 샀다. (buy, a new bag)
_______ _______ _______ _______ _______.

2 Rachel은 우리에게 파이를 만들어주었다. (make, a pie)
_______ _______ _______ _______ _______.

3 저에게 역으로 가는 길을 말씀해 주시겠어요? (tell, the way)
Can you _______ _______ _______ _______ to the station?

4 그는 유명한 사람들을 많이 알고 있다. (know, famous)
_______ _______ a lot of _______ _______.

5 부모님은 나에게 크리스마스 선물로 곰 인형을 주셨다. (give, a teddy bear)
My parents _______ _______ _______ _______ _______ as a Christmas gift.

Point 04 4형식 문장 → 3형식 문장으로의 전환 I

- 4형식 문장은 두 목적어의 순서를 바꾸어 3형식 문장으로 만들 수 있다. 간접목적어와 직접목적어의 순서를 바꾸고 간접목적어 앞에 전치사(to, for, of)를 쓰면 된다.
- 전치사 to를 사용하는 동사에는 give, send, pass, show, teach, tell, lend, write, bring 등이 있다.

Richard **gave** me a ring. (4형식: 동사+간접목적어+직접목적어)

Richard **gave** a ring **to** me. (3형식: 동사+직접목적어+전치사+간접목적어)

A 다음 두 문장이 같은 뜻이 되도록 문장을 완성하시오.

1 Bring us two glasses of water.
→ Bring ____________________.

2 I lent David an umbrella.
→ I lent ____________________.

3 Who told you the story?
→ Who told ____________________?

4 She showed them her room.
→ She showed ____________________.

5 My brother gave me his bicycle.
→ My brother gave ____________________.

6 Send me a text message about our field trip.
→ Send ____________________ about our field trip.

B 다음 우리말과 같은 뜻이 되도록 ( ) 안의 말을 이용하여 문장을 완성하시오.

1 나는 Ruth에게 내 사진을 보여주었다. (show, picture)
I ________ ________ ________ ________ Ruth.

2 Jake는 Linda에게 장미꽃 한 다발을 줬다. (give)
Jake ________ a bunch of roses ________ ________.

3 그는 고등학생들에게 역사를 가르친다. (teach, history)
He ________ ________ ________ high school students.

4 나에게 그 만화책을 건네줘. (the comic book)
Pass ________ ________ ________ ________ ________.

5 그에게 네 운동화를 빌려줘. (running shoes)
Lend ________ ________ ________ ________ ________.

Point 05

4형식 문장 → 3형식 문장으로의 전환 II

- 4형식 문장을 3형식 문장으로 바꿀 때 전치사 to 외에 for나 of를 사용하는 동사들이 있다.
- 전치사 for를 사용하는 동사에는 make, buy, get, cook 등이 있다.

  Ben **made** me hot chocolate. (4형식: 동사+간접목적어+직접목적어)

  Ben **made** hot chocolate **for** me. (3형식: 동사+직접목적어+전치사+간접목적어)
- 전치사 of를 사용하는 동사에는 ask가 있다. 단, ask의 직접목적어가 favor, question인 경우에만 전치사 of를 쓴다.

★ 내신만점 *TIP* 4형식 문장을 3형식 문장으로 바꿀 때 간접목적어 앞에 전치사 to, for, of를 사용하는 동사를 알아두자.

A **다음 빈칸에 알맞은 말을 넣어 대화를 완성하시오.**

1 A: Can I ask a favor __________ you?
B: Sure. What is it?

2 A: I made fresh salad __________ you.
B: Wow, it looks delicious.

3 A: Can you send me the file?
B: I already sent it __________ __________.

4 A: There are no eggs in the refrigerator.
B: Will you buy some eggs __________ me?

5 A: I didn't tell your secret __________ anybody.
B: Then how does Jack know?

6 A: What is she doing in China?
B: She is teaching Korean __________ Chinese students.

B **다음 두 문장이 같은 뜻이 되도록 문장을 완성하시오.**

1 Can I get you some orange juice?
→ Can I get ________________________________?

2 He bought us a box of doughnuts.
→ He bought ________________________________.

3 I made a doghouse for my dog.
→ I made ________________________________.

4 Dad cooked dinner for Mom.
→ Dad cooked ________________________________.

Point 06

5형식 문장의 목적격 보어 I

- 5형식 문장은 〈주어+동사+목적어+목적격 보어〉로 이루어진 문장이다.
- 목적격 보어는 목적어의 성질이나 상태를 보충 설명해 주는 말이다. 목적격 보어로는 명사(구)나 형용사(구)가 올 수 있다.

  People **call** her "**Pop Princess**." (목적격 보어: 명사구)

  We should **keep** it **safe**. (목적격 보어: 형용사)

A 다음 〈보기〉에서 알맞은 말을 골라 문장을 완성하시오. (단, 한 번씩만 사용할 것)

〈보기〉 clean   happy   an angel   interesting   a great tennis player

1 He found the book ____________________.
2 Lots of practice made her ____________________.
3 You have to keep your uniform ____________________.
4 Dan always helps people. His friends call him ____________________.
5 Ben and Diane love each other. That makes me ____________________.

B 다음 우리말과 같은 뜻이 되도록 (   ) 안의 말을 배열하여 문장을 완성하시오.

1 나는 창문을 열어두었다. (the window, I, kept, open)

____

2 그 소식은 그녀를 화나게 만들었다. (her, the news, angry, made)

____

3 그는 그의 딸을 'sweetie'라고 부른다. (calls, he, "sweetie", daughter, his)

____

C 다음 우리말과 같은 뜻이 되도록 (   ) 안의 말을 이용하여 문장을 완성하시오.

1 그의 눈물은 나를 슬프게 만들었다. (make)
His tears __________ __________ __________.

2 나는 그 문제가 쉽다는 것을 알게 되었다. (find)
I __________ the problem __________.

3 채소는 너를 건강하게 유지시켜 준다. (keep)
Vegetables __________ __________ __________.

5형식 문장의 목적격 보어 II

■ 목적어를 보충 설명해 주는 목적격 보어로 to부정사가 사용되기도 한다. to부정사를 목적격 보어로 취하는 동사에는 want, ask, tell, expect, order, allow 등이 있다.

I **want** you **to come** with me.

He **expected** me **to be** there.

★ PLUS TIP 목적어와 목적격 보어는 주어와 서술어의 관계이다.
I want **you** to **be my girlfriend**. (나는 네가 내 여자친구가 되었으면 좋겠어.)

A 다음 〈보기〉에서 알맞은 말을 골라 빈칸에 적절한 형태로 써넣으시오. (단, 한 번씩만 사용할 것)

〈보기〉 stop　come　be　take care of　call

1 She asked me ____________ her cat for two days.

2 Mr. Johnson told you ____________ to his office.

3 The police ordered me ____________ my car.

4 Do you want me ____________ him now?

5 They expected Betty ____________ late.

B 다음 우리말과 같은 뜻이 되도록 ( ) 안의 말을 배열하여 문장을 완성하시오.

1 나는 그에게 떠나라고 말하지 않았다. (tell, to, I, him, leave, didn't)

____

2 나는 네가 이 책을 읽었으면 해. (you, I, read, want, this, to, book)

____

3 그는 내가 자신감을 갖기를 원한다. (confident, wants, he, to, me, be)

____

4 나는 네가 토요일에 돌아올 거라고 예상했다.
(you, I, to, on Saturday, come back, expected)

____

5 그는 Helen에게 돈을 좀 빌려달라고 부탁했다.
(Helen, he, him, to, asked, lend, some money)

____

6 선생님은 내가 교실에 머무는 것을 허락하셨다.
(me, in the classroom, allowed, stay, the teacher, to)

____

Point 08 5형식 문장의 목적격 보어 III

- 목적어를 보충 설명해 주는 목적격 보어로 원형부정사(동사원형)가 사용되기도 한다. 원형부정사를 목적격 보어로 취하는 동사에는 have, make, let과 같은 사역동사와 see, watch, hear, feel 등과 같은 지각동사가 있다.
  Sad movies **make** me **cry**.
  I **saw** him **draw** a picture.
- help는 to부정사와 원형부정사를 모두 목적격 보어로 취할 수 있다.
  He **helped** me **(to) move** the chairs.

★ *PLUS TIP* 지각동사의 목적격 보어로 현재분사가 쓰이면 진행의 의미가 강조된다.
I **saw** him **delivering** a pizza. (나는 그가 피자를 배달하고 있는 것을 보았다.)

★ 내신만점 *TIP* 5형식 문장의 목적격 보어로 to부정사와 원형부정사를 쓰는 동사를 구분하여 알아두자.

A 다음 밑줄 친 부분을 어법에 맞게 고쳐 쓰시오.

1 My parents don't let me to eat too much.
2 I asked them be quiet in the theater.
3 I saw his hands to shake.
4 The doctor had her to stay in the hospital.
5 She heard someone to knock on the door.

B 다음 우리말과 같은 뜻이 되도록 ( ) 안의 말을 이용하여 문장을 완성하시오.

1 그의 농담은 사람들을 웃게 만든다. (make, laugh)
His jokes ________ ________ ________.

2 언니는 내가 그녀의 옷을 입지 못하게 한다. (let, wear)
My sister doesn't ________ ________ ________ her clothes.

3 나는 배들이 물 위에 떠 있는 것을 지켜보았다. (watch, float)
I ________ the boats ________ on the water.

4 그들은 그가 축제에서 노래 부르는 것을 허락했다. (allow, sing)
They ________ ________ ________ ________ at the festival.

5 나는 바람이 내 얼굴을 어루만지는 것을 느꼈다. (feel, touch)
I ________ the wind ________ my face.

6 David는 Maggie가 마술사가 되는 것을 도와주었다. (help, become)
David ________ Maggie ________ ________ a magician.

7 그녀의 친구들은 그녀가 외국에서 공부할 것이라고 예상하지 못했다. (expect, study)
Her friends didn't ________ ________ ________ ________ abroad.

[01-03] 다음 빈칸에 알맞은 말을 고르시오.

01

George bought a robot ________ his son.

① to ② of ③ for
④ on ⑤ in

02

We watched him ________.

① sleep ② slept ③ sleepy
④ to sleep ⑤ to be sleeping

03

I expected them ________ my house.

① visit ② to visit ③ visiting
④ be visiting ⑤ to be visit

04

빈칸에 들어갈 말이 나머지와 <u>다른</u> 것은?

① Pass the chili sauce _______ me.
② He gave his sunglasses _______ her.
③ She showed her accessories _______ us.
④ She told her daily plan _______ me.
⑤ I made tomato pasta _______ my sister.

[05-07] 다음 빈칸에 들어갈 수 <u>없는</u> 말을 고르시오.

05

His new hairstyle looks ________.

① good ② nicely ③ bad
④ terrible ⑤ strange

06

It ________ wonderful.

① feels ② looks ③ sounds
④ tastes ⑤ shows

07

The movie made Kate ________.

① happy ② bored ③ laugh
④ to cry ⑤ a star

08

다음 우리말을 영어로 바르게 옮긴 것은?

그들은 그가 뉴욕으로 여행하는 것을 허락했다.

① They let him travel to New York.
② They let him to travel to New York.
③ They had him travels to New York.
④ They had him to travel to New York.
⑤ They allowed him travel to New York.

[09-10] 빈칸에 들어갈 말이 순서대로 알맞게 짝지어진 것을 고르시오.

09

A: You should keep your kids ________.
B: Yes, I don't want them ________ hurt.

① safe – get ② safe – to get
③ safe – getting ④ safely – get
⑤ safely – to get

10

A: I'm ________.
B: I'm sorry, but they don't let us ________ the heater in this room.

① cold – use ② cold – to use
③ cold – using ④ coldly – use
⑤ coldly – to use

11

A: I saw Mike ________ with Emma yesterday.
B: I know. He already sent a message about that ________ me.

① dance – for ② to dance – of
③ to dance – to ④ dancing – to
⑤ dancing – for

[12-13] 다음 빈칸에 공통으로 들어갈 말을 고르시오.

12

• I lent my laptop ________ Chris.
• Linda asked him ________ turn off the TV.

① to ② of ③ for
④ on ⑤ with

13

• The song ________ the singer famous.
• He ________ every student wear a school uniform.

① kept ② found ③ made
④ wanted ⑤ taught

기출응용

14

다음 중 문장의 전환이 바르지 않은 것은?

① I'll bring you the thick coat.
→ I'll bring the thick coat to you.
② I showed them my old pictures.
→ I showed my old pictures to them.
③ They bought me a pair of skates.
→ They bought a pair of skates to me.
④ Dad made me blueberry pancakes.
→ Dad made blueberry pancakes for me.
⑤ They wrote their guests some letters.
→ They wrote some letters to their guests.

15
문장의 형식이 나머지와 다른 것은?

① I made the taxi driver angry.
② He asked me to wait outside.
③ People called him "Mr. President."
④ My boyfriend sent me that candy.
⑤ We let our children play on the sand.

[16-17] 다음 중 어법상 틀린 것을 고르시오.

16
① I found science difficult.
② You look wonderful today.
③ He wanted me to rest.
④ She got me some dessert.
⑤ I can teach you to Spanish.

17
① They saw me run away.
② He told me to walk fast.
③ Pass the paper to me, please.
④ Mike helped me carry the boxes.
⑤ I heard James to play the guitar.

기출응용
18
다음 중 어법상 틀린 것을 모두 고르면? (2개)

① The perfume smells terrible.
② Mr. Kang teaches us Chinese.
③ He lent a purple umbrella to me.
④ Emily had me to make dinner.
⑤ I thought the travel map usefully.

19
(A), (B), (C)의 괄호 안에서 알맞은 것끼리 바르게 짝지어진 것은?

(A) This bread tastes [great / greatly].
(B) He asked a small favor [for / of] me.
(C) I saw someone [to come / coming] towards me.

	(A)		(B)		(C)
①	great	……	of	……	coming
②	great	……	for	……	to come
③	greatly	……	for	……	coming
④	great	……	of	……	to come
⑤	greatly	……	of	……	coming

고난도
20
다음 중 어법상 옳은 것끼리 바르게 짝지어진 것은?

(a) Those dolls look lions.
(b) My parents don't let me go out at night.
(c) I made a cookie my brothers.
(d) Could you give the English menu for me?
(e) She asked me to join the surfing club.

① (a), (d)
② (b), (e)
③ (a), (b), (c)
④ (b), (c), (d)
⑤ (c), (d), (e)

서술형 따라잡기

01
다음 두 문장이 같은 뜻이 되도록 문장을 완성하시오.

(1) Peter passed the ball to Sam.
→ Peter passed ________ ________ ________.

(2) Did you get them some bread?
→ Did you get ________ ________ ________ ________?

02
다음 〈보기〉와 같이 두 문장을 한 문장으로 쓰시오.

〈보기〉 Tony was swimming.
Kim watched him.
→ Kim watched Tony swimming.

(1) Martin was following me.
I saw him.
→ I ______________________________.

(2) I washed the dishes.
Joan helped me.
→ Joan ______________________________.

03
주어진 말을 이용하여 우리말과 뜻이 같도록 문장을 완성하시오.

(1) 그는 Ned에게 조용히 있으라고 명령했다. (order, stay silent)
→ He ______________________________.

(2) 우리는 그녀가 사람들에게 소리치고 있는 것을 들었다. (hear, shout at people)
→ We ______________________________.

04
각 상자에서 알맞은 말을 골라 문장을 완성하시오. (단, 한 번씩만 사용할 것)

The soup	told	her happy
She	made	delicious
We	smells	us the big news

(1) The soup ______________________________.

(2) She ______________________________.

(3) We ______________________________.

05
다음을 보고, 〈보기〉와 같이 문장을 완성하시오.

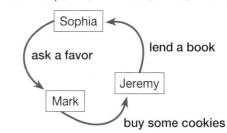

Sophia
ask a favor
Mark
buy some cookies
Jeremy
lend a book

〈보기〉 Sophia asked a favor of Mark.

(1) Mark bought ________ ________ ________ ________.

(2) Jeremy lent ________ ________ ________ ________.

06
다음 메모를 보고, Julie의 엄마가 Julie에게 시킨 일에 대한 문장을 완성하시오.

(1) read an English book
(2) clean the bathroom
(3) take care of her sister

(1) Julie's mom wanted her ______________________________.

(2) Julie's mom had her ______________________________.

(3) Julie's mom made her ______________________________.

S E L F N O T E

핵심 포인트 정리하기

1 문장의 5형식

1형식	주어+동사	Thomas smiled.
2형식	주어+동사+보어 (주어+감각동사+① ____________)	Michelle was a nurse. (The girls look happy.)
3형식	주어+동사+② ____________	They love Jennifer.
4형식	주어+수여동사+간접목적어+직접목적어	She gave him a blanket.
5형식	주어+동사+목적어+③ ____________	My grandmother called me "darling."

2 4형식 문장 → 3형식 문장으로의 전환

■ 형태: 주어 + 동사 + 간접목적어 + 직접목적어

주어 + 동사 + 직접목적어 + ④ ____________ + 간접목적어

■ 문장 전환 시 필요한 전치사

• 전치사 ⑤ __________ 를 쓰는 동사: give, send, pass, show, teach 등

• 전치사 ⑥ __________ 를 쓰는 동사: make, buy, get, cook 등

• 전치사 ⑦ __________ 를 쓰는 동사: ask

4형식 문장이 3형식 문장으로 바뀔 때 전치사 to / for / of를 쓰는 동사 구분하기!

3 목적격 보어가 될 수 있는 말

명사(구), 형용사(구), to부정사, 원형부정사(동사원형) 등이 목적격 보어가 될 수 있음

• 목적격 보어로 ⑧ ____________ 를 취하는 동사: want, ask, tell, expect, order, allow 등

• 목적격 보어로 ⑨ ____________ 를 취하는 동사: 사역동사(have, make, let), 지각동사(see, watch, hear, feel)

보어 자리에는 부사가 올 수 없다는 것 기억하기!
5형식 문장에서 목적격 보어로 to부정사 / 원형부정사를 취하는 동사 알아두기!

문제로 개념 다지기

밑줄 친 부분이 어법상 맞으면 O, 틀리면 X 표시하고 바르게 고치시오.

1 His voice sounded strangely.

2 I didn't expect you to come to the party.

3 They gave the present for Fred.

4 I kept the soup warmly for him.

5 We bought Nicole a lovely skirt.

6 I saw them making a sandcastle.

7 Let me to carry it for you.

to부정사와 동명사

To learn yoga is not easy. [to부정사]
Learning yoga is not easy. [동명사]

to부정사란?

〈to + 동사원형〉의 형태로, 동사의 의미와 성질을 가지면서 문장 안에서 명사, 형용사, 부사의 역할을 하는 것을 말합니다.

동명사란?

〈동사원형 + -ing〉의 형태로, 동사의 의미와 성질을 가지면서 문장 안에서 명사 역할을 하는 것을 말합니다.

Point 01 to부정사의 명사적 용법 I – 주어 역할

- to부정사란 ⟨to+동사원형⟩의 형태로 쓰여 문장에서 명사, 형용사, 부사의 역할을 하는 것이다.
- to부정사는 '~하는 것'이라는 의미로 명사처럼 주어, 목적어, 보어 역할을 할 수 있다.
- to부정사가 '~하는 것은'의 의미로 문장에서 주어 역할을 하는 경우에는 보통 주어 자리에 가주어 It을 쓰고 to부정사(구)는 뒤로 보낸다.

To watch fireworks is amazing.
→ **It** is amazing **to watch** fireworks.
가주어 / 진주어

★ PLUS TIP 주어로 쓰인 to부정사(구)는 3인칭 단수 취급한다.
To play online games *is* fun.

A 다음 문장을 가주어 It을 이용한 문장으로 고쳐 쓰시오.

1 To travel alone is dangerous.
→ ______________________________

2 To go on a picnic is exciting.
→ ______________________________

3 To ride the subway is easy.
→ ______________________________

4 To jog along the river is relaxing.
→ ______________________________

B 다음 우리말과 같은 뜻이 되도록 ( ) 안의 말을 이용하여 문장을 완성하시오.

1 약속을 지키는 것은 중요하다. (important, keep)
_____ _____ _____ _____ _____ promises.

2 간호사가 되는 것은 그녀의 꿈이다. (become, nurse)
_____ _____ _____ _____ _____ her dream.

3 나만의 옷 가게를 여는 것이 내 목표이다. (open)
_____ _____ my goal _____ _____ my own clothing store.

4 TV를 매일 보는 것은 불필요하다. (watch, unnecessary)
_____ _____ TV every day _____ _____.

5 그 상황을 이해하는 것은 어려웠다. (difficult, understand)
_____ _____ _____ _____ _____ the situation.

6 피라미드를 실제로 보는 것은 놀랍다. (amazing, see)
_____ _____ _____ _____ _____ the Pyramids in real life.

Point 02 to부정사의 명사적 용법 II – 보어 / 목적어 역할

- to부정사는 '~하는 것(이다)'라는 의미로 주어의 성질, 상태 등을 나타내는 보어 역할을 하기도 한다. 이때 주어와 보어는 동격 관계이다.
  My plan is **to lose** seven kilograms. (My plan = to lose seven kilograms)
- to부정사는 '~하는 것을'이라는 의미로 문장에서 목적어 역할을 하기도 한다. to부정사를 목적어로 취하는 동사에는 want, decide, plan, hope, refuse, expect 등이 있다.
  I want **to go** to the concert.
  We decided **to help** them.

★ PLUS TIP
to부정사의 부정형은 to부정사 앞에 not이나 never를 붙여 만든다.
She decided **not to meet** him. (그녀는 그를 만나지 않기로 결심했다.)

A 다음 문장을 to부정사의 사용에 유의하여 우리말로 해석하시오.

1 He needed to buy a new bicycle.
____

2 My plan is to read an English novel this month.
____

3 Ann refused to say anything.
____

4 His goal is to become a photographer.
____

B 다음 우리말과 같은 뜻이 되도록 ( ) 안의 말을 배열하여 문장을 완성하시오.

1 그의 일은 자동차를 수리하는 것이다. (to, repair, is, cars)
His job ______________________________.

2 나는 회사에 지각하고 싶지 않다. (be late, to, want, don't)
I ______________________________ for work.

3 우리는 조만간 이곳에 다시 올 수 있기를 바란다. (hope, here, again, come, to)
We ______________________________ soon.

4 그녀의 희망은 오케스트라에서 첼로를 연주하는 것이다. (is, the cello, play, to)
Her hope ______________________________ in an orchestra.

5 Martin은 베이글을 커피와 함께 먹지 않기로 결심했다. (not, have, to, a bagel, decided)
Martin ______________________________ with his coffee.

6 Jack은 고추장 없이 비빔밥을 먹고 싶어했다. (bibimbap, wanted, eat, to)
Jack ______________________________ without red pepper sauce.

Point 03 to부정사의 명사적 용법 Ⅲ – 의문사+to부정사

■ 〈의문사+to부정사〉는 what, when, where, how, who(m) 등의 의문사 뒤에 to부정사를 쓴 것이다. 문장 안에서 명사처럼 쓰이며, 주로 목적어 역할을 한다.

- 〈what+to부정사〉 '무엇을 ~할지'
- 〈when+to부정사〉 '언제 ~할지'
- 〈where+to부정사〉 '어디서 ~할지'
- 〈how+to부정사〉 '어떻게 ~할지'
- 〈who(m)+to부정사〉 '누구를 ~할지'

What to choose is an important question. (주어 역할)
The problem is **where to go** this weekend. (보어 역할)
Can you show me **how to make** waffles? (목적어 역할)

A 다음 밑줄 친 부분을 어법에 맞게 고쳐 쓰시오.

1 Dan understood to do what.
2 Can you tell me when go to the show?
3 I want to learn what to drive a car.

B 다음 우리말과 같은 뜻이 되도록 〈보기〉에서 알맞은 말을 골라 빈칸에 적절한 형태로 써넣으시오.

〈보기〉 buy   come   go   invite   use

1 저에게 언제 다시 올지 말씀해주세요.
Please tell me ______________ again.

2 그녀는 나에게 누구를 파티에 초대할지 물었다.
She asked me ______________ to the party.

3 Sally는 휴가로 어디를 갈지 결정했다.
Sally decided ______________ for her vacation.

4 나는 생일 선물로 그녀에게 무엇을 사줄지 모르겠다.
I don't know ______________ her for her birthday.

5 그는 나에게 그 세탁기를 어떻게 사용하는지 보여주었다.
He showed me ______________ the washing machine.

C 다음 문장을 to부정사의 사용에 유의하여 우리말로 해석하시오.

1 Ted told me where to stay in London.

____

2 Do you know how to play the guitar?

____

Point 04

to부정사의 형용사적 용법 – 명사 / 대명사 수식

- to부정사의 형용사적 용법은 to부정사가 형용사처럼 명사를 수식해서 '~하는', '~할'이라는 의미를 나타내는 것을 말한다. 이때 to부정사는 명사를 뒤에서 수식한다.

  There are many books **to read**.

- -thing, -one, -body로 끝나는 대명사의 경우 형용사가 대명사를 뒤에서 수식하며, 형용사와 to부정사가 함께 수식하는 경우에는 〈-thing[-one/-body]+형용사+to부정사〉의 순서로 쓴다.

  I want **something cold**. I want **something cold to drink**.

★ 내신만점 TIP -thing, -one, -body로 끝나는 대명사를 형용사와 to부정사가 함께 수식하는 경우 어순에 주의하자.

A 다음 밑줄 친 부분을 어법에 맞게 고쳐 쓰시오.

1 There is some fruit eat.
2 I have something show you.
3 I need someone love.
4 They have nothing to say important.
5 Do you have anyone talk to?
6 He's not going to come. He has a lot of things doing.

B 다음 우리말과 같은 뜻이 되도록 ( ) 안의 말을 배열하여 문장을 완성하시오.

1 그는 입을 정장이 없다. (doesn't, a suit, have, wear, to)
He ______________________________.

2 할 만한 재미있는 일이 있나요? (to, interesting, do, anything)
Is there ______________________________?

3 이제 작별 인사를 할 때이다. (goodbye, to, time, say)
It's ______________________________.

4 나는 사야 할 몇 가지 것들이 있다. (have, buy, things, to, several)
I ______________________________.

5 그녀는 마쳐야 할 숙제가 좀 있다. (homework, to, has, finish, some)
She ______________________________.

6 한국에는 방문할 곳이 많다. (places, visit, to, many)
There are ______________________________ in Korea.

7 냉장고에 먹을 것이 아무것도 없다. (to, nothing, is, eat, there)
______________________________ in the refrigerator.

Point 05 to부정사의 부사적 용법 I – 목적

- to부정사의 부사적 용법은 to부정사가 부사처럼 동사, 형용사, 부사를 수식하는 역할을 하는 것이다.
- 목적을 나타내는 to부정사의 부사적 용법은 '~하기 위해', '~하려'라는 뜻이다.

I went to Peru **to see** Machu Picchu.
They came to Korea **to teach** English.

★ PLUS TIP 목적을 나타내는 to부정사의 부사적 용법은 〈in order to-v〉를 써서 그 의미를 확실히 할 수 있다.
He studied hard **in order to get** a perfect score. (그는 만점을 받기 위해 열심히 공부했다.)

A 다음 우리말과 같은 뜻이 되도록 ( ) 안의 말을 이용하여 문장을 완성하시오.

1 나는 그들과 수영을 하러 해변에 갔다. (swim)
I went to the beach ________ ________ ________ ________.

2 그는 이탈리아어를 배우려고 이탈리아에 갔다. (learn, Italian)
He went to Italy ________ ________ ________.

3 Alice는 자기 소지품을 싸려고 상자 몇 개를 가져왔다. (pack, her things)
Alice brought some boxes ________ ________ ________ ________.

4 그녀는 깨어있으려고 커피를 마셨다. (stay awake)
She drank coffee ________ ________ ________.

5 Peter는 그의 아이디어를 공유하기 위해 블로그를 만들었다. (share, ideas)
Peter made a blog ________ ________ ________ ________.

6 우리는 그 소식을 너에게 알려주기 위해 이메일을 보냈다. (tell)
We sent the email ________ ________ ________ the news.

B 다음 문장을 to부정사의 사용에 유의하여 우리말로 해석하시오.

1 He came early to help me.
____

2 I saved money to buy a new cell phone.
____

3 She went to the market in order to buy some fruit.
____

4 I had to use a dictionary to read the English book.
____

5 Please write down your name to join this club.
____

Point 06 to부정사의 부사적 용법 II – 감정의 원인/결과

- to부정사의 부사적 용법에는 '~해서', '~하니'라는 뜻으로 감정의 원인을 나타내는 용법과 '(…해서) ~하다'라는 뜻으로 결과를 나타내는 용법도 있다.
  I'm glad **to see** you again. (감정의 원인)
  He grew up **to be** a pilot. (결과)
- 〈형용사/부사+enough+to부정사〉는 '…할 만큼 충분히 ~하다'라는 뜻이고, 〈too+형용사/부사+to부정사〉는 '너무 ~하여 …할 수 없다'라는 뜻이다.
  The boy is **tall enough to reach** the top shelf.
  → The boy is **so tall that he can reach** the top shelf.
  They are **too young to get married**.
  → They are **so young that they can't get married**.

A 다음 두 문장과 의미가 같도록 빈칸에 알맞은 말을 쓰시오.

1 They read the bad news. So they were upset.
→ They were upset __________ __________ the bad news.

2 She got a letter from him. So she was pleased.
→ She was pleased __________ __________ a letter from him.

3 He is weak. He can't run for an hour.
→ He is __________ weak __________ __________ for an hour.

4 Linda is strong. She can lift her brother.
→ Linda is strong __________ __________ __________ her brother.

B 다음 우리말과 같은 뜻이 되도록 ( ) 안의 말을 이용하여 문장을 완성하시오.

1 우리는 그 이야기를 듣고 슬펐다. (hear)
We were __________ __________ __________ the story.

2 그는 너무 바빠서 점심을 먹지 못했다. (have)
He was __________ __________ __________ __________ lunch.

3 그녀는 자라서 작가가 되었다. (grow up)
She __________ __________ __________ __________ a writer.

4 그들은 그 영화를 볼 만큼 충분히 나이가 들었다. (watch)
They are __________ __________ __________ __________ the movie.

5 나는 그녀와 데이트를 해서 행복했다. (go on a date)
I was __________ __________ __________ __________ __________ __________
with her.

동명사의 역할 I – 주어 / 보어 역할

- 동명사는 〈동사원형+-ing〉의 형태로, 문장에서 명사처럼 주어, 목적어, 보어의 역할을 한다.

Solving this problem is impossible. (주어 역할: '~하는 것은')
→ It is impossible to solve this problem.
One of my hobbies is **making** cookies. (보어 역할: '~하는 것(이다)')
→ One of my hobbies is to make cookies.

★ PLUS TIP 주어로 쓰인 동명사(구)는 3인칭 단수 취급한다.
Studying math *is* not easy.

A 다음 〈보기〉에서 알맞은 말을 골라 빈칸에 적절한 동명사 형태로 써넣으시오.

〈보기〉 read meet take play swim live drive

1 ________ tennis with my cousin is fun.
2 His job is ________ care of children.
3 ________ science magazines is difficult.
4 My favorite activity is ________ in the pool.
5 ________ new people is interesting.
6 ________ without water is impossible.
7 ________ safely is important for everyone.

B 다음 우리말과 같은 뜻이 되도록 ( ) 안의 말을 배열하여 문장을 완성하시오.

1 내 취미는 사진을 찍는 것이다. (taking, is, pictures)
My hobby ________________.

2 깊은 강에서 수영을 하는 것은 위험하다. (a, swimming, is, deep, in, river)
________________ dangerous.

3 영어 에세이를 쓰는 것은 그에게 어렵다. (is, English essays, difficult, writing)
________________ for him.

4 탄산음료를 마시는 것은 건강에 좋지 않다. (is, soda, good, not, drinking)
________________ for your health.

5 롤러코스터를 타는 것은 나를 두렵게 한다. (scares, roller coasters, riding)
________________ me.

6 Brian의 나쁜 습관 중 하나는 아침에 늦게 일어나는 것이다.
(in the morning, getting up, is, late)
One of Brian's bad habits ________________.

Point 08 동명사의 역할 II – 목적어 역할

- 동명사가 동사의 목적어로 쓰이는 경우 '~하는 것을'로 해석한다.
- 동명사를 목적어로 취하는 동사에는 enjoy, avoid, consider, mind, finish, give up, keep, stop, quit 등이 있다.
  I enjoy **going** shopping every weekend.

★ PLUS TIP 동명사는 전치사의 목적어로 쓰이기도 한다.
The restaurant is famous *for* **serving** traditional Korean food.

A 다음 밑줄 친 부분을 어법에 맞게 고쳐 쓰시오.

1 Do you mind to help me carry this bag?
2 He was interested in drive a car.
3 Maria thinks about to go abroad someday.
4 My grandparents wanted makes a garden.

B 다음 〈보기〉와 같이 두 문장과 의미가 같도록 동명사를 이용하여 빈칸에 알맞은 말을 쓰시오.

〈보기〉 I baked a cake. I enjoyed it. → I enjoyed baking a cake.

1 I worked for a shoe company. I quit the job.
→ I quit ______________________.

2 James might miss the train. He is worried about it.
→ James is worried about ______________________.

C 다음 우리말과 같은 뜻이 되도록 ( ) 안의 말을 이용하여 문장을 완성하시오.

1 나는 무대 위에서 노래를 잘한다. (be good at, sing)
_______ _______ _______ _______ on stage.

2 너 자신에게 도전하는 것을 멈추지 마라. (stop, challenge)
_______ _______ _______ yourself.

3 우리는 비닐봉지를 사용하는 것을 피해야 한다. (should, avoid, use)
_______ _______ _______ _______ plastic bags.

4 Peter가 드디어 설거지를 끝냈다. (finish, wash the dishes)
Peter finally _______ _______ _______ _______.

5 그녀는 라디오를 끄는 것을 개의치 않았다. (mind, turn off)
_______ _______ _______ _______ _______ the radio.

[01–03] 다음 빈칸에 알맞은 말을 고르시오.

01

________ is easy to use chopsticks.

① All ② It ③ That
④ This ⑤ What

02

Nick avoided ________ too much at night.

① eat ② ate ③ to eat
④ eating ⑤ to eating

03

I don't have a cookbook. Can you show me ________ to make mushroom soup?

① how ② what ③ why
④ when ⑤ where

04

다음 〈보기〉의 밑줄 친 부분과 쓰임이 같은 것은?

〈보기〉 She kept talking with James.

① Learning new languages is fun.
② I just finished making the bed.
③ His problem is wasting too much money.
④ Ann's dream is writing a book someday.
⑤ We are thinking about going bowling tonight.

[05–07] 빈칸에 들어갈 말이 순서대로 알맞게 짝지어진 것을 고르시오.

05

I plan ________ Japanese. ________ will be exciting to read Japanese books.

① learn – It ② to learn – It
③ learning – It ④ to learn – That
⑤ learning – That

06

A: Why don't you wear these shoes?
B: They are ________ big ________.

① enough – to wear ② not – wearing
③ enough – wear ④ too – to wear
⑤ too – wearing

07

I want ________ healthy. So I gave up ________ junk food.

① be – eating ② being – eating
③ to be – eating ④ to be – to eat
⑤ to be – eat

[08-09] 다음 대화의 빈칸에 알맞은 말을 고르시오.

08

A: Can you tell me ________ to get to Namsan Park?
B: Sure. Walk down that street and go up the stairs on your left.

① when ② what ③ whom
④ where ⑤ how

09

A: Would you like ________________?
B: Yes, please. I'm so thirsty.

① cold something drinking
② cold something to drink
③ drinking cold something
④ something cold to drink
⑤ something to drink cold

10
다음 우리말을 영어로 바르게 옮긴 것은?

그녀는 나를 도와줄 만큼 충분히 친절했다.

① She was too kind to help me.
② She was kind enough help me.
③ She was enough kind to help me.
④ She was kind enough to help me.
⑤ She was so kind that helped me.

[11-12] 다음 빈칸에 들어갈 수 없는 말을 고르시오.

11

I ________ to play outside.

① expected ② enjoyed ③ decided
④ wanted ⑤ hoped

12

Jessica ________ writing her essay.

① refused ② kept ③ finished
④ considered ⑤ avoided

[13-14] 다음 밑줄 친 부분의 용법이 나머지와 다른 것을 고르시오.

13

① I need someone to talk to.
② She has a dress to wear tonight.
③ She grew up to be a film director.
④ There are many things to do now.
⑤ There's no one to tell me the truth.

14

① I decided to study abroad.
② He lived to be 80 years old.
③ I'm sorry to bother you.
④ She was happy to pass the test.
⑤ I went to China to see the Great Wall.

[15-16] 다음 밑줄 친 부분이 어법상 틀린 것을 고르시오.

15

① She wanted to join the tennis club.
② He was glad to meet his old friend.
③ The man quit to smoke a few years ago.
④ We went to Mt. Baekdu to see the lake.
⑤ My dream is to become a computer engineer.

16

① I have something to show you.
② Please tell me where to go.
③ He grew up be a doctor.
④ It is fun to draw people on the street.
⑤ Stella kept looking at him.

17

다음 빈칸에 to가 들어갈 수 없는 것은?

① He refused ________ make a speech.
② I saw them ________ play baseball.
③ She helped me ________ find the bank.
④ It is good for one's health ________ exercise.
⑤ My plan is ________ master English grammar.

기출응용

18

다음 우리말과 같은 뜻이 되도록 주어진 말을 배열할 때 네 번째에 올 단어는?

나는 저녁으로 무엇을 요리할지 결정할 수 없다.
(for, what, cook, decide, to, I, dinner, can't)

① decide ② can't ③ to
④ cook ⑤ what

19

(A), (B), (C)의 괄호 안에서 알맞은 것끼리 바르게 짝지어진 것은?

(A) I don't mind [to eat / eating] alone.
(B) [To walk / Walking] is good for the environment.
(C) It is important [to go / go] to the dentist regularly.

	(A)		(B)		(C)
①	to eat	……	Walking	……	to go
②	to eat	……	To walk	……	go
③	eating	……	Walking	……	go
④	eating	……	To walk	……	go
⑤	eating	……	Walking	……	to go

고난도

20

다음 중 어법상 옳은 것끼리 짝지어진 것은?

(a) He decided to leave early.
(b) This is difficult to lose weight.
(c) Going camping will be a lot of fun.
(d) I'm interested in to protect animals.
(e) I need someone to help me.

① (a), (c), (d) ② (a), (c), (e)
③ (b), (c), (d) ④ (b), (d), (e)
⑤ (c), (d), (e)

내신대비 TEST

서술형 따라잡기

01
다음 두 문장이 같은 의미가 되도록 빈칸에 알맞은 말을 쓰시오.

(1) The tablet PC was so expensive that I couldn't buy it.
→ The tablet PC was ________ ________ ________ ________.

(2) Climbing mountains is difficult.
→ ________ ________ difficult ________ ________ ________.

02
다음 그림을 보고, 문장을 완성하시오.

(1) He is good at ________ ________ ________.

(2) It is difficult ________ ________ ________ ________.

03
주어진 말을 이용하여 우리말과 뜻이 같도록 문장을 완성하시오.

A: 너는 먹을 것이 있니?
B: 아니, 없어. 간식을 좀 사러 가게에 가자.

A: Do you ________ ________ ________ ________? (anything, eat)
B: No, I don't. Let's go to the store ________ ________ ________ ________. (snacks)

04
주어진 말을 알맞게 배열하여 우리말과 뜻이 같도록 문장을 완성하시오.

(1) 그는 그 소리를 듣고 놀랐다.
(the noise, surprised, he, hear, to, was)
→ ________________________

(2) 창문을 열어 주시겠어요?
(mind, do, the window, you, opening)
→ ________________________

기출응용

05
다음 행사표를 보고, 주어진 말과 to부정사를 이용하여 문장을 완성하시오.

행사	준비물	참가 가능 연령
Go hiking	Sneakers	8세 이상
Take a diving class	Swimsuit	17세 이상

(1) Emma is nine years old. She is ________ ________ ________ ________ ________. (old)

(2) Andy is fourteen years old. He is ________ ________ ________ ________ ________ ________ ________. (young)

06
대화를 읽고, 다음 질문에 답하시오.

A: Did you decide (A) 무엇을 할지 in Seoul?
B: Yes. I want to visit some palaces. But I don't know how I can get to them.
A: Don't you speak Korean?
B: No, I don't. So I need (B) (helpful, me, to, someone, guide)

(1) (A)의 우리말을 영어로 쓰시오.

____

(2) (B)를 문맥에 맞게 배열하시오.

____

SELF NOTE

핵심 포인트 정리하기

1 to부정사

- 형태: 〈① ________ + ________〉
- 용법
  - 명사적 용법 – 주어, ② ________, 보어 역할: '~ 하는 것(이다)'
  - 형용사적 용법 – 명사를 뒤에서 수식: '~하는', '~할'
    - * 〈-thing[-one / -body] + ③ ________ + to부정사〉
  - 부사적 용법
    - 동사, 형용사, 부사를 수식
    - ④ ________: '~하기 위해' = 〈in order to-v〉
    - 감정의 원인: '~해서','~하니'
    - 결과: '(…해서) ~하다'
    - * 〈형용사/부사 + enough + to부정사〉: '…할 만큼 충분히 ~하다'
    - * 〈⑤ ________________〉: '너무 ~하여 …할 수 없다'

to부정사의 세 가지 용법 구분하기!
enough to-v와 too ~ to-v의 어순과 쓰임 익히기!

2 동명사

- 형태: 〈⑥ ________ + ________〉
- 역할: 주어, 보어, 목적어 – '~하는 것(이다),' '~하는 것을'

3 to부정사 vs. 동명사

- to부정사를 목적어로 취하는 동사: want, decide, plan, hope, refuse 등
- 동명사를 목적어로 취하는 동사: enjoy, avoid, mind, finish, give up, keep 등

to부정사와 동명사를 각각 목적어로 취하는 동사 알아두기!

문제로 개념 다지기

밑줄 친 부분이 어법상 맞으면 O, 틀리면 X 표시하고 바르게 고치시오.

1 I have someone <u>introducing</u> to you.
2 I was lucky <u>to meeting</u> you here.
3 They kept <u>ask</u> me about the book.
4 My mother is too sick <u>to eat</u> anything.
5 The pool is <u>enough deep to swim</u> in.
6 Luna is afraid of <u>to see</u> a doctor.
7 He wanted <u>dancing</u> with Amy.

He is *my brother* **and** *my best friend*. [등위 접속사]

When *he arrived at home*, he was very hungry. [종속 접속사]

접속사란?

단어와 단어, 구와 구, 절과 절을 연결해 주는 말로, 등위 접속사와 종속 접속사가 있습니다. 등위 접속사에는 and, but, or, so 등이 있으며, 문법적으로 대등한 단어, 구, 절을 연결해 주는 역할을 합니다. 종속 접속사에는 when, before, because, that 등이 있으며, 주가 되는 절(주절)과 그 내용을 보충하는 절(종속절)을 연결해 주는 역할을 합니다.

등위 접속사 and

- 등위 접속사란 문법적으로 대등한 역할을 하는 단어, 구, 절을 연결하는 말로 and, but, or, so 등이 이에 속한다.
- and는 서로 비슷한 내용을 연결하는 말로 '그리고', '~와'라는 뜻이다.
  Chris **and** Laura are my classmates.
  We went to the cinema **and** had dinner.
- 〈both A and B〉는 'A와 B 둘 다'라는 의미이다.
  I like **both** bread **and** rice.

★ 내신만점 TIP 등위 접속사로 연결되는 부분은 문법적으로 대등해야 한다는 점에 유의하자.
We have cats(명사) **and** dogs(명사). / He likes(동사) strawberries **but** doesn't like(동사) strawberry milk.

A 다음 두 문장을 한 문장으로 만들 때, 빈칸에 알맞은 말을 쓰시오.

1 The man is gentle. The man is smart, too.
→ The man is ______________________.

2 I met Frank in Madrid. I met Sarah in Madrid, too.
→ I met ______________________ in Madrid.

3 She has blue eyes. She has long, blond hair.
→ She has blue eyes ______________________.

B 다음 밑줄 친 부분을 어법에 맞게 고쳐 쓰시오.

1 She is tall and beauty.
2 We swam in the river and eat sandwiches.
3 I like to ride my bicycle and playing online games.
4 Daniel will play the piano and sang a song.

C 다음 우리말과 같은 뜻이 되도록 ( ) 안의 말을 배열하여 문장을 완성하시오.

1 우리는 책을 읽고 사진을 찍었다. (and, books, took, read, pictures, we)

____

2 그는 중국어와 일본어를 둘 다 말할 수 있다.
(can, Chinese, both, Japanese, he, speak, and)

____

3 그녀는 노트북을 사고 인도로 여행을 가기 위해서 돈을 모았다.
(to buy, money, to travel, and, she, to India, saved, a laptop)

____

Point 02

등위 접속사 but

- but은 서로 반대되거나 대조되는 내용을 연결하는 말로 '그러나', '그런데'라는 뜻이다.
  It wasn't snowing, **but** it was very cold.
  I grew up in a big city, **but** I don't like big cities.

A 다음 우리말과 같은 뜻이 되도록 문장을 완성하시오.

1 나는 점심을 먹지 않았지만, 배가 고프지 않다.
I didn't have lunch, __________ I'm not hungry.

2 그는 나에게 이메일을 보내고 전화를 걸었다.
He sent me an email __________ gave me a call.

3 비가 오는데, 나는 우산이 없다.
It is raining, __________ I don't have an umbrella.

B 다음 두 문장을 한 문장으로 만들 때, 빈칸에 알맞은 말을 쓰시오.

1 I came early. I didn't get a good seat.
→ I came early, ______________________________.

2 He is handsome. He is not popular.
→ He is handsome, ______________________________.

3 Jay loves hip-hop music. I don't like it.
→ Jay loves hip-hop music, ______________________________.

C 다음 우리말과 같은 뜻이 되도록 ( ) 안의 말을 배열하여 문장을 완성하시오.

1 그녀는 슬펐지만 울지 않았다. (sad, but, cry, she, didn't, was, she)

____

2 나는 시험에 떨어졌지만, 다시 시도할 것이다. (I, again, I'll, the test, but, try, failed)

____

3 Susan은 Mike에게 잘해주었지만 그를 좋아하지는 않았다.
(Susan, Mike, she, him, but, like, nice, was, to, didn't)

____

Point 03 등위 접속사 or

- or는 둘 중 하나를 선택하는 경우에 사용하는 등위 접속사로, '또는', '~(이)거나'라는 뜻이다.
  Are you coming to Korea in July **or** August?
  Which kind of food do you like better, Chinese **or** Italian?
- ⟨either A or B⟩는 'A이거나 B'라는 뜻이다.
  Either my brother **or** I should do the dishes.

A 다음 두 문장을 한 문장으로 만들 때, 빈칸에 알맞은 말을 쓰시오.

1 Do you want to come with William? Do you want to come with Jack?
→ Do you want to come with William ______________________________?

2 Ben went on a picnic. Natalie didn't go on a picnic.
→ Ben went on a picnic, ______________________________.

3 We can go to the museum. We can go to Namdaemun Market, too.
→ We can go to the museum ______________________________.

B 다음 우리말과 같은 뜻이 되도록 문장을 완성하시오.

1 나는 예술가나 교사가 되고 싶다.
I want to be an artist __________ a teacher.

2 그는 호주인이거나 영국인이다.
He is __________ Australian __________ British.

3 따뜻한 것과 차가운 것 중에 어떤 커피를 원하세요?
Which kind of coffee do you want, hot __________ iced?

C 다음 우리말과 같은 뜻이 되도록 ( ) 안의 말을 배열하여 문장을 완성하시오.

1 오늘이 25일인가요, 26일인가요? (the 25th, the 26th, today, is, or)

____

2 저 여자아이의 이름은 Justine이거나 Julia이다.
(either, name, Justine, Julia, that, or, girl's, is)

____

3 그는 돈을 벌거나 여행을 갈 것이다. (going, go on a trip, make money, he, to, or, is)

____

Point 04 등위 접속사 so

- so는 절과 절을 연결하는 등위 접속사로 앞 내용에 대한 결과를 나타내고자 하는 경우에 사용하며, '그래서'라는 뜻이다.
  There was a lot of traffic, **so** I was twenty minutes late for work.
  It rained all day long, **so** we couldn't go on a picnic.

A 다음 우리말과 같은 뜻이 되도록 ( ) 안의 말을 이용하여 문장을 완성하시오.

1 수프가 짜서 나는 물을 추가했다. (add, water)
The soup was salty, __________ __________ __________ __________ to it.

2 그 방에서 좋지 않은 냄새가 나서 그는 창문을 열었다. (open, the window)
The room smelled bad, __________ __________ __________ __________ __________.

3 나는 외국인 친구가 많아서 너에게 그들을 소개해 줄 수 있어. (introduce)
I have a lot of foreign friends, __________ __________ __________ __________ __________ to you.

B 다음 ( ) 안에서 알맞은 말을 고르시오.

1 Mr. Jang is a famous writer (and / but) professor.
2 I knocked on the door, (and / but) no one answered.
3 My final exams are over, (but / so) I can go out to play.
4 The sneakers are good-looking (and / but) uncomfortable.
5 We'll either go paragliding (and / or) go skydiving on the trip.

C 다음 〈보기〉에서 알맞은 접속사를 골라 두 문장을 한 문장으로 만드시오. (단, 한 번씩만 사용할 것)

〈보기〉 and but or so

1 I stayed up late last night. I feel tired now.
→ ______________________________

2 I called her name. She didn't look at me.
→ ______________________________

3 I ordered ice cream. I ordered cheesecake too.
→ ______________________________

4 You can make an exchange. You can get a refund.
→ ______________________________

종속 접속사 when / while

- 종속 접속사는 절과 절을 연결하는 말로, 종속 접속사가 이끄는 절(종속절)이 다른 절(주절)의 내용을 보충하는 역할을 한다.
- 때를 나타내는 종속 접속사 when은 '~할 때', while은 '~하는 동안(에)'라는 뜻이다.

You were with James **when** I saw you.
종속절: when+주어+동사

While I'm out, please take care of my children.

- 때의 접속사가 이끄는 절에서는 미래의 일도 현재시제로 나타낸다.

I'll reply **when** I *get* back to my office.

★ PLUS TIP
when이 의문사로 쓰이면 '언제'라는 의미이다.
When did you see me? (너는 나를 언제 봤니?)

A 다음 〈보기〉와 같이 접속사 when을 이용하여 두 문장을 한 문장으로 만드시오.

〈보기〉 I'm thirsty. I drink water. → When I'm thirsty, I drink water.

1 I will get there. I'll call you.
→ ______________________________

2 Alice heard a strange sound. She felt scared.
→ ______________________________

3 David crossed the street. He saw the accident.
→ ______________________________

B 다음 우리말과 같은 뜻이 되도록 ( ) 안의 말을 이용하여 문장을 완성하시오.

1 나는 프랑스에 있을 때 와인을 샀다. (be)
I bought wine ________ ________ ________ in France.

2 우리는 저녁을 먹고 있는 동안에 우리의 여행에 대해 이야기했다. (eat, dinner)
________ ________ ________ ________ ________, we talked about our trip.

3 나는 공항에 도착했을 때 들떴다. (arrive)
________ ________ ________ at the airport, I was excited.

4 그녀는 책을 읽을 때 안경을 쓴다. (wear, read)
She ________ glasses ________ ________ ________ a book.

5 그는 길을 걷는 동안 자주 노래를 부른다. (walk)
________ ________ ________ ________ on the street, he often sings.

Point 06 종속 접속사 before / after

- before는 '~하기 전에', after는 '~한 후에'라는 뜻이다.

  I usually ask the price **before** I buy something.

  You can't exchange these shoes **after** you wear them.

★ PLUS TIP before/after가 접속사로 쓰일 때는 뒤에 절이 오지만, 전치사로 쓰일 때는 뒤에 (동)명사(구)가 온다.
I do homework **after** dinner. (나는 저녁 식사 후에 숙제를 한다.)

A 다음 우리말과 같은 뜻이 되도록 빈칸에 before, after, when, while 중 알맞은 말을 쓰시오.

1 우리는 어두워지기 전에 집에 가야 한다.
We should go home ________ it gets dark.

2 이 차를 마시고 나면 당신은 기분이 좋을 거예요.
You'll feel good ________ you drink this tea.

3 내가 장을 보러 갈 때면 너무 많은 물건을 산다.
________ I go shopping, I buy too many things.

4 나는 Chris가 외국으로 가기 전에 그를 보고 싶다.
I want to see Chris ________ he goes abroad.

5 그녀는 잠을 자는 동안에 돼지꿈을 꿨다.
________ she was sleeping, she dreamed of a pig.

B 다음 우리말과 같은 뜻이 되도록 ( ) 안의 말을 배열하여 문장을 완성하시오.

1 우리는 해가 지기 전에 도착했다. (the sun, before, arrived, set)
We ____.

2 Tim은 저녁을 먹고 나서 잠들었다. (after, dinner, fell asleep, he, had)
Tim ____.

3 네가 읽고 난 후에 그 책을 빌릴 수 있을까?
(I, you, borrow, read, after, the book, it)
Can ____?

4 너는 너무 늦기 전에 치과에 가야 해.
(the dentist, is, it, should, before, to, too, go, late)
You ____.

5 내가 어제 그를 만났을 때 그는 나에게 그의 전화번호를 줬다.
(his number, gave, when, met, yesterday, him, me, I)
He ____.

종속 접속사 because / if

- because는 원인이나 이유를 나타내는 접속사로 '~ 때문에'라는 뜻이며, if는 조건을 나타내는 접속사로 '만약 ~하다면'이라는 뜻이다.
- 조건을 나타내는 접속사가 이끄는 절에서는 미래의 일도 현재시제로 나타낸다.

I didn't go out **because** it was raining. (원인 · 이유)
If it rains, I won't go out. (조건)
~~will rain~~

★ 내신만점 TIP 때나 조건을 나타내는 접속사가 이끄는 절에서는 미래를 나타내더라도 현재시제를 쓴다는 것을 기억하자.

A 다음 우리말과 같은 뜻이 되도록 빈칸에 because, if, before, after 중 알맞은 말을 쓰시오.

1 나는 잠자리에 들기 전에 자명종을 맞춘다.
I set the alarm ________ I go to bed.

2 그는 교통 체증이 심했기 때문에 지각했다.
________ the traffic was bad, he was late.

3 그녀는 양치질을 한 후에는 아무것도 먹지 않는다.
She doesn't eat anything ________ she brushes her teeth.

4 당신이 이 일자리를 받아들인다면, 내일 일을 시작하시게 될 겁니다.
________ you accept this job, you'll start work tomorrow.

B 다음 우리말과 같은 뜻이 되도록 ( ) 안의 말을 이용하여 문장을 완성하시오.

1 그녀는 영화가 재미없어서 집에 가고 싶었다. (interesting)
She wanted to go home ________ the film ________ ________.

2 네가 일찍 떠나면, 그들이 실망할 것이다. (leave)
They will be disappointed ________ ________ ________ early.

3 그는 몸이 좋지 않아서 결석했다. (feel)
He was absent ________ ________ ________ ________ well.

4 당신이 배가 고프다면, 뭘 좀 먹읍시다. (hungry)
________ ________ ________ ________, let's eat something.

5 내가 운전면허증을 딴다면 차를 살 것이다. (get)
________ ________ ________ a driver's license, I will buy a car.

6 나는 안경이 없어서 잘 보이지 않는다. (have)
I can't see well ________ ________ ________ ________ my glasses.

Point 08 종속 접속사 that

- that은 명사절을 이끄는 접속사로 '~인 것', '~라는 것'이라는 뜻이다. 명사절을 이끈다는 것은 문장에서 주어, 목적어, 보어 역할을 한다는 것을 의미한다.

  That we are friends is important. (주어 역할)

  I think **(that)** his English is quite good. (목적어 역할 / that 생략 가능)

  The issue is **that** there's not enough money. (보어 역할)

- that절이 문장에서 주어 역할을 하는 경우에는 보통 그 자리에 가주어 It을 쓰고 that절을 문장 뒤에 쓴다.

  That he is my uncle is true. (주어 역할)

  → **It** is true **that** he is my uncle.

  가주어 진주어

A 다음 문장을 가주어 It을 이용한 문장으로 바꾸어 쓰시오.

1 That you like Tony is surprising.

→ ______________________________

2 That he often loses things is a problem.

→ ______________________________

3 That I broke the window is a secret.

→ ______________________________

4 That she became a comedian is amazing.

→ ______________________________

5 That she never eats nuts is true.

→ ______________________________

B 다음 우리말과 같은 뜻이 되도록 ( ) 안의 말을 배열하여 문장을 완성하시오.

1 그들이 무언가를 훔쳤다는 것은 심각한 문제이다. (they, something, that, stole)

______________________________ is a serious problem.

2 그녀를 초대하지 않은 것은 나의 실수였다. (invite, didn't, that, I, her)

______________________________ was my mistake.

3 나는 그 노래가 좋다고 생각하지 않는다. (good, the song, is, that)

I don't think ______________________________.

4 문제는 내가 휴대전화를 가져오지 않은 것이다. (didn't, that, I, my cell phone, bring)

The problem is ______________________________.

5 당신은 그녀가 농구 선수라는 것을 알고 있었나요? (that, a basketball player, she, is)

Did you know ______________________________?

[01-03] 다음 빈칸에 알맞은 말을 고르시오.

01

I like bananas ________ melons. They are sweet.

① and ② but ③ or
④ that ⑤ so

02

________ you don't have an umbrella, you can borrow mine.

① That ② Before ③ After
④ But ⑤ If

03

I enjoyed the film, ________ I didn't like the main character.

① and ② but ③ or
④ because ⑤ so

04

다음 두 문장을 한 문장으로 쓸 때 빈칸에 알맞은 말은?

My parents and I set up the tent. Then we built a fire.
→ ________ my parents and I set up the tent, we built a fire.

① Before ② Because ③ If
④ After ⑤ While

05

다음 빈칸에 because[Because]가 들어갈 수 없는 것은?

① I ate sandwiches ________ I was hungry.
② I was listening to music ________ she called me.
③ ________ it snowed a lot, we couldn't leave.
④ Be careful with the bottles ________ they break easily.
⑤ ________ there was nothing to eat, we ordered a pizza.

[06-07] 다음 우리말을 영어로 바르게 옮긴 것을 고르시오.

06

일을 끝낸 후에 내가 너에게 전화할게.

① I'll call you that I finish my work.
② I'll call you after I'll finish my work.
③ I'll call you before I finish my work.
④ I'll call you after I finish my work.
⑤ I finish my work before I'll call you.

07

나는 서점이나 미술관에 갈 것이다.

① I will go to both bookstore and art museum.
② I will go to either a bookstore and an art museum.
③ I will go to either a bookstore or an art museum.
④ I will go to a bookstore after I go to an art museum.
⑤ I will not go to a bookstore but to an art museum.

[08-10] 빈칸에 들어갈 말이 순서대로 알맞게 짝지어진 것을 고르시오.

08

- ________ he was sick, he couldn't go on the field trip.
- ________ you are interested in art, let's take the drawing class.

① When – That ② After – That
③ Because – If ④ After – Before
⑤ Because – That

09

- I heard ________ you like rock music.
- Is today Thursday ________ Friday?

① when – but ② when – after
③ if – or ④ that – but
⑤ that – or

10

A: What did you do ________ you came back home?
B: I ate dinner ________ watched a DVD.

① when – that ② before – that
③ after – and ④ when – but
⑤ after – but

기출응용

11

빈칸에 들어갈 말이 나머지와 다른 것은?

① I thought ________ you were busy.
② It is not true ________ he failed the test.
③ It is my fault ________ you missed the train.
④ Brush your teeth ________ you eat those chocolates.
⑤ The problem is ________ he plays computer games too much.

12

다음 대화 중 자연스럽지 않은 것은?

① A: Which do you like better, milk or juice?
B: I prefer juice.
② A: Do you like to dance?
B: Yes, but I'm not good at it.
③ A: Why did you walk home?
B: I couldn't take the bus because I lost my wallet.
④ A: What will you do on Sunday?
B: I'll either meet Julie or stay home.
⑤ A: Are you going to invite both Jason and Ann?
B: Yes. I'll invite only Jason.

13

다음 밑줄 친 부분이 어법상 옳은 것은?

① I like both skating or skiing.
② She sang a song, but nobody listened.
③ I took a shower after I went to bed.
④ He can buy either the shirt and the hat.
⑤ I will buy the book and borrow it from the library.

[14-15] 다음 빈칸에 공통으로 들어갈 말을 고르시오.

14

- ________ I was in Japan, I ate the best sushi.
- ________ did you move to Florida?

① Before ② After ③ If
④ When ⑤ That

15

- It is important _______ you prepare for the class.
- I thought _______ this umbrella was yours.

① before ② after ③ if
④ when ⑤ that

[16-17] 다음 중 어법상 틀린 것을 고르시오.

16

① I know they will meet at the airport.
② He lost his cell phone while he was sleeping on the bus.
③ If it is not expensive, I'll get it.
④ I'll dance with either Brad and Andrew.
⑤ She didn't answer my calls because she was angry with me.

17

① Try on the shirt before you buy it.
② If the rumor is true, Brian will marry Helen.
③ She drinks hot milk when she wants to sleep well.
④ I don't like vegetables, but they are good for my health.
⑤ I went to a nice restaurant and having a great dinner.

18

(A), (B), (C)의 괄호 안에서 알맞은 것끼리 바르게 짝지어진 것은?

(A) It is true [before / that] he took a taxi.
(B) You should put on your coat [and / because] it is cold.
(C) Did you go to a park or [watch / watched] a movie?

	(A)		(B)		(C)
①	before	……	and	……	watched
②	before	……	because	……	watched
③	that	……	because	……	watch
④	that	……	because	……	watched
⑤	that	……	and	……	watch

기출응용

19

다음 중 어법상 틀린 문장의 개수는?

(a) That Jake is a great cook is surprising.
(b) I will be very sad if my puppy will die.
(c) Turn off the lights when you will go out.
(d) I didn't swim in the river if I was afraid of the deep water.

① 0개 ② 1개 ③ 2개 ④ 3개 ⑤ 4개

고난도

20

다음 중 밑줄 친 부분을 생략할 수 없는 것은?

① I knew that he was lying.
② Tina said that she wanted to be an editor.
③ We hope that you will get better soon.
④ It is strange that Mike is absent from school.
⑤ Did you know that she is our teacher's daughter?

내신대비 TEST

서술형 따라잡기

01
주어진 말과 접속사를 이용하여 우리말과 뜻이 같도록 문장을 완성하시오.

(1) 만약 아프면 이 약을 드세요. (feel sick)
→ Take this medicine ________ ________ ________ ________.

(2) 나는 우리 팀이 우승할 것이라고 믿는다. (win)
→ I believe ________ ________ ________ ________ ________.

02
주어진 말을 알맞게 배열하여 대화를 완성하시오.

(1) A: Why didn't you come yesterday?
B: I ____________________ I had a cold.
(because, in, stayed, bed)

(2) A: Do you want something to eat?
B: No, thanks. I ____________________.
(I, here, had, came, before, lunch)

03
각 상자에서 알맞은 말을 골라 문장을 완성하시오.

and but or	I'll buy some at the bakery I won the gold medal you didn't reply

(1) I sent a text message to you, ____________ ____________.

(2) I'll bake some cookies, ____________ ____________.

(3) I ran in the marathon, ____________ ____________.

04
다음 일과표를 보고, 알맞은 접속사를 넣어 문장을 완성하시오.

Time	Things to do
10:00-11:30 a.m.	Take a ballet lesson
2:00-3:00 p.m.	Walk my dog
3:00-6:00 p.m.	Practice violin on Mon. Read books on Tue. & Fri.
6:00-8:00 p.m.	Watch TV
8:00-9:00 p.m.	Write in my diary

(1) I take a ballet lesson ________ I walk my dog.

(2) I ________ practice violin ________ read books from three o'clock to six o'clock.

(3) I write in my diary ________ I watch TV.

05
다음 조건에 맞게 우리말을 영어로 옮겨 쓰시오.

〈조건〉 1. 적절한 접속사를 이용할 것
2. 어휘 late, angry, a book, a camera 를 이용할 것

(1) 그녀가 늦는다면, 나는 화가 날 것이다.
→ ____________________

(2) 그는 책과 카메라 둘 다를 가지고 있다.
→ ____________________

고난도

06
다음 대화를 읽고, 어법상 틀린 부분을 모두 찾아 바르게 고쳐 쓰시오. (2군데)

A: Did you rest at home?
B: No. I went jogging or had a snack at a café.
A: What are your plans for tonight?
B: If my dad will come home early, I will eat out with him.

핵심 포인트 정리하기

1 등위 접속사

■ 의미: 문법적으로 대등한 역할을 하는 단어, 구, 절을 연결하는 말

■ 종류
- and: '그리고', '~와' (서로 비슷한 내용 연결)
- ① ________: '그러나', '그런데' (서로 반대 혹은 대조되는 내용 연결)
- or: '또는', '~(이)거나' (둘 중 하나 선택)
- so: '그래서' (앞 내용에 대한 결과 표현)

〈② ________________〉: 'A와 B 둘 다'

〈③ ________________〉: 'A이거나 B'

등위 접속사로 연결되는 부분은 문법적으로 대등해야 한다는 것 기억하기!

2 종속 접속사

■ 의미: 주절과 종속절을 연결하는 말

■ 종류

④________	'~할 때'
while	'~하는 동안(에)'
before	'⑤________'
after	'~한 후에'
because	'~ 때문에'
⑥________	'만약 ~하다면'
that	'~인 것', '~라는 것' - 명사절을 이끄는 접속사(주어, 목적어, 보어 역할) - 주어 역할인 경우 보통 그 자리에 가주어 ⑦________을 쓰고 that절을 문장 뒤에 씀 - 목적어 역할인 경우 접속사 that 생략 가능

때나 조건을 나타내는 부사절에서는 미래의 일도 현재시제로 표현한다는 것 잊지 말기!
종속 접속사 that의 여러 가지 역할 구분하기!

문제로 개념 다지기

밑줄 친 부분이 어법상 맞으면 O, 틀리면 X 표시하고 바르게 고치시오.

1 He took a shower and <u>watching</u> TV last night.

2 You can have either French fries <u>and</u> onion rings.

3 Do you want to have a snack or <u>drinking</u> some coffee?

4 It is surprising <u>if</u> the main character dies in the movie.

5 It is impossible <u>that</u> he got home so early.

6 <u>When</u> I got on the bus, I met Tim.

7 If it <u>will snow</u>, we will cancel the trip.

She plants **red** *roses*. [형용사]

Summer *is coming* **fast**. [부사]

형용사란?

명사나 대명사를 수식하거나 설명하는 말로, 명사나 대명사의 상태나 성질을 나타냅니다.

부사란?

동사, 형용사, 다른 부사 혹은 문장 전체를 수식하는 말로, 수식하는 말의 의미를 더 구체적으로 설명합니다. 부사는 문장 전체를 수식하기도 한답니다.

Point 01 형용사의 역할

- 형용사는 명사나 대명사를 수식하거나 설명하는 역할을 한다.
- 형용사는 명사를 주로 앞에서 수식하지만, -thing, -body, -one으로 끝나는 대명사는 뒤에서 수식한다.

  He has a **new** smartphone. (앞에서 수식)

  I want something **cold** to drink. (뒤에서 수식)
- 형용사는 주격 보어나 목적격 보어로 쓰여 사람이나 사물의 상태 · 성질을 나타낸다.

  She is **kind** and **pretty**. (주격 보어)

  I found this book **difficult**. (목적격 보어)

A **다음 밑줄 친 부분을 어법에 맞게 고쳐 쓰시오.**

1 I found him nicely.

2 The soup smells deliciously.

3 He is good a baseball player.

4 Her dress is really beautifully.

5 Be carefully with those knives.

6 There was new nothing in this magazine.

7 I heard interesting something from Jennifer.

8 It is very danger to ride a motorcycle without a helmet.

B **다음 우리말과 같은 뜻이 되도록 ( ) 안의 말을 배열하여 문장을 완성하시오.**

1 나는 창문을 열린 채로 두었다. (left, I, open, the window)

____

2 그녀는 이 퍼즐이 쉽다는 것을 알았다. (this, easy, found, puzzle, she)

____

3 그의 실수는 나를 화나게 만들었다. (made, his, angry, mistake, me)

____

4 나는 중요한 사람이 되고 싶다. (someone, I, to, important, be, want)

____

5 당신은 저녁 식사에 필요한 모든 것을 샀나요?
(you, everything, for dinner, did, buy, necessary)

____

Point 02 부사의 역할 / 형태 I

- 부사는 동사, 형용사, 다른 부사 혹은 문장 전체를 수식하는 말이다.

Thomas appeared **suddenly**. (동사 수식)

Strangely, we met at the same place several times. (문장 전체 수식)

- 대부분의 부사는 형용사에 -ly를 붙여 만든다.

대부분의 형용사	형용사+**-ly**	real – real**ly** serious – serious**ly**
-y로 끝나는 형용사	**y**를 **i**로 바꾸고+**-ly**	happy – happ**ily** lucky – luck**ily**
-le로 끝나는 형용사	**e**를 빼고+**-y**	gentle – gent**ly** simple – simp**ly**

A 다음 형용사의 부사형을 쓰시오.

1 special ________　　2 sad ________
3 different ________　　4 kind ________
5 usual ________　　6 loud ________
7 nice ________　　8 necessary ________
9 quiet ________　　10 easy ________
11 wise ________　　12 careful ________
13 strong ________　　14 terrible ________
15 clear ________　　16 heavy ________
17 important ________　　18 angry ________

B 다음 ( ) 안에서 알맞은 말을 고르시오.

1 She is very (kind / kindly).
2 He spoke (strange / strangely).
3 Can you speak (slow / slowly)?
4 She opened the bottle (easy / easily).
5 The couple lived (happy / happily).
6 The man entered the room (quiet / quietly).
7 I have a (simple / simply) question.
8 Your boyfriend looks (great / greatly).
9 (Lucky / Luckily), I found a cheap apartment.
10 This program keeps your computer (safe / safely).

Point 03

부사의 형태 II

■ 형용사와 형태가 같은 부사들이 있으므로 주의해야 한다.

fast	형 빠른 / 부 빠르게	early	형 이른 / 부 일찍
hard	형 어려운, 딱딱한, 열심인 / 부 열심히	near	형 가까운 / 부 가까이
late	형 늦은 / 부 늦게	high	형 높은 / 부 높게

He is a **fast** runner. (형용사: 빠른) / He runs **fast**. (부사: 빠르게)
It is **hard** to get up early. (형용사: 어려운) / They work **hard**. (부사: 열심히)

★ PLUS TIP 〈부사+-ly〉가 다른 뜻을 가지는 부사로는 hardly(거의 ~않다), lately(최근에), highly(매우), nearly(거의) 등이 있다.

A 다음 우리말과 같은 뜻이 되도록 문장을 완성하시오.

1 그는 공을 공중으로 높이 쳤다.
He hit the ball __________ in the air.

2 나는 오늘 아침에 또 늦었다.
I was __________ again this morning.

3 그녀는 거의 잠이 들 뻔했다.
She __________ fell asleep.

4 나는 지난 주말에 잠을 거의 못 잤다.
I __________ slept last weekend.

5 그렇게 빨리 차를 몰지 마.
Don't drive so __________.

B 다음 문장을 밑줄 친 부분에 유의하여 우리말로 해석하시오.

1 The train arrived a little late.

____

2 If you finish early, you can go home.

____

3 There were some hard questions on the exam.

____

4 He was born in the early nineteenth century.

____

5 I worked really hard, and I became successful.

____

Point 04

빈도부사

■ 빈도부사란 어떤 일이 얼마나 자주 일어나는지를 나타내는 말이다. be동사나 조동사의 뒤, 일반동사의 앞에 쓴다.

never(결코 ~않다) 〈 seldom(거의 ~않는) 〈 sometimes(가끔) 〈 often(자주) 〈 usually(대개, 보통) 〈 always(항상)

0% ←——————————————→ 100% (빈도)

Sarah is **usually** very cheerful. (be동사 뒤)
I will **always** love you. (조동사 뒤)
Nick **never** tells a lie. (일반동사 앞)

★ 내신만점 TIP 빈도부사는 be동사나 조동사 뒤, 일반동사 앞에 온다는 것을 기억하자.

A 다음 ( ) 안의 빈도부사가 들어갈 알맞은 위치를 고르시오.

1 (always) I ① can ② help ③ you.
2 (usually) She ① wears ② a ③ skirt.
3 (never) I'll ① forget ② this moment ③.

B 다음 우리말과 같은 뜻이 되도록 빈칸에 알맞은 빈도부사를 쓰시오.

1 Paul은 항상 안경을 쓴다.
Paul __________ wears glasses.

2 그는 수업에 자주 늦는다.
He is __________ late for classes.

3 3월에는 가끔 눈이 온다.
It __________ snows in March.

4 그녀는 결코 직장을 그만두지 않을 것이다.
She will __________ quit her job.

5 나는 보통 방과 후에 수영을 하러 간다.
I __________ go swimming after school.

C 다음 우리말과 같은 뜻이 되도록 ( ) 안의 말을 배열하여 문장을 완성하시오.

1 그녀는 거의 버스를 타고 등교하지 않는다. (goes, school, seldom, to)
She ______________________________ by bus.

2 너는 길을 건널 때 항상 조심해야 한다. (should, be careful, always)
You ______________________________ when you cross the street.

3 Mike는 그의 여자친구에게 전화를 자주 한다. (his, calls, girlfriend, often)
Mike ______________________________.

원급 비교

- 원급 비교는 형용사나 부사의 원급을 이용해서 '~만큼 …한[하게]'라는 뜻을 나타내는 비교 표현이다.
  원급 비교는 〈as+형용사/부사의 원급+as〉의 형태로 쓴다.
  I am **as tall as** my brother.
  Ben runs **as fast as** Tim.
- 〈not+as[so]+형용사/부사의 원급+as〉는 '~만큼 …하지 않은[않게]'라는 뜻이다.
  She is **not as[so] cute as** you are.

A 다음 우리말과 같은 뜻이 되도록 〈보기〉에서 알맞은 말을 골라 빈칸에 적절한 형태로 써넣으시오.

〈보기〉 comfortable expensive hot interesting much light

1 이 소파는 내 것만큼 편안하다.
This sofa is ______________ mine.

2 내 코트는 깃털처럼 가볍다.
My coat is ______________ a feather.

3 그 시계는 보이는 것만큼 비싸지 않다.
The watch is ______________ it looks.

4 당신은 원하는 만큼 가질 수 있어요.
You can have ______________ you want.

5 이번 방송분은 지난번 것만큼 재미있다.
This episode is ______________ the last one.

6 이번 여름은 작년 여름만큼 덥지 않다.
This summer is ______________ last summer was.

B 다음 〈보기〉와 같이 'as ~ as'를 이용하여 두 문장을 한 문장으로 만드시오.

〈보기〉 I'm 17 years old. Paul is 17 years old, too.
→ I'm as old as Paul.

1 Elizabeth is 150 cm tall. Her sister is 150 cm tall, too.
→ Elizabeth is ______________ her sister.

2 Your book is 13 cm thick. Mine is 20 cm thick.
→ Your book is ______________ mine.

3 This picture frame is one meter wide. That picture frame is one meter wide, too.
→ This picture frame is ______________ that picture frame.

Point 06 비교급과 최상급 만드는 방법

■ 형용사나 부사의 비교급은 -(e)r 또는 more를 붙이고, 최상급은 -(e)st 또는 most를 붙여 만든다.

대부분의 단어	+-er / -est	fast – fast**er** – fast**est**
-e로 끝나는 단어	+-r / -st	large – large**r** – large**st**
〈단모음+단자음〉으로 끝나는 단어	자음을 한 번 더 쓰고 +-er / -est	hot – hot**ter** – hot**test** big – big**ger** – big**gest**
〈자음+-y〉로 끝나는 단어	y를 i로 바꾸고 +-er / -est	happy – happ**ier** – happ**iest** easy – eas**ier** – eas**iest**
-ful/-ous/-less/-ing/-ive 등으로 끝나는 단어 3음절 이상의 단어	단어의 앞에 more / most	beautiful – **more** beautiful – **most** beautiful

■ 비교급과 최상급이 불규칙하게 변화하는 단어들도 있다.

many / much – **more** – **most**
good / well – **better** – **best**
little – **less** – **least**
bad – **worse** – **worst**

A 다음 단어의 비교급과 최상급을 순서대로 쓰시오.

1 heavy ________ ________
2 important ________ ________
3 loud ________ ________
4 careful ________ ________
5 busy ________ ________
6 small ________ ________
7 bad ________ ________
8 pretty ________ ________
9 cute ________ ________
10 terrible ________ ________

B 다음 밑줄 친 부분을 어법에 맞게 고쳐 쓰시오.

1 I feel much gooder.
2 It was the hotest summer in 10 years.
3 I have much money than you.
4 This exam was easyer than the last one.
5 It is the expensivest necklace in the world.
6 Emily is the most fast student in the class.

비교급

- 비교급을 이용한 비교 표현은 〈비교급+than〉의 형태로 '~보다 더 …한[하게]'라는 뜻을 나타낸다.
  Your cell phone is **better than** mine.
  Comic books are **more interesting than** novels.
- much, even, still, a lot, far 등을 비교급 앞에 써서 '훨씬 더 …한[하게]'라는 뜻으로 비교급을 강조할 수 있다.
  The white shoes look **much nicer** than the brown ones.

A ( ) 안의 말을 이용하여 비교급 문장을 완성하시오.

1 You look ________________ before. (thin)
2 Your room is ________________ mine. (big)
3 The plane is ________________ the train. (fast)
4 Math is ________________ English. (difficult)
5 Her dress is ________________ my dress. (pretty)
6 Her boyfriend is ________________ her. (young)
7 Happiness is ________________ money. (important)
8 The horror movie was ________________ the action movie. (exciting)
9 My new backpack was ________________ my old one. (cheap)
10 A near neighbor is ________________ a distant cousin. (good)

B 다음 우리말과 같은 뜻이 되도록 ( ) 안의 말을 이용하여 문장을 완성하시오.

1 더 천천히 말씀해 주시겠어요? (slowly)
Could you speak ________ ________?

2 나는 평소보다 더 일찍 잠자리에 들었다. (early)
I went to bed ________ ________ usual.

3 나는 가지고 있는 것보다 더 많은 돈이 필요하다. (more, money)
I need ________ ________ ________ I have.

4 이 노트북은 다른 것보다 훨씬 더 무겁다. (much, heavy)
This laptop is ________ ________ ________ the other one.

5 그의 문제가 네 것보다 더 심각해 보인다. (serious)
His problem seems ________ ________ ________ yours.

6 저 기타는 이것보다 훨씬 더 비싸다. (a lot, expensive)
That guitar is ________ ________ ________ ________ ________ this one.

최상급

- 최상급을 이용한 비교 표현은 〈the+최상급〉의 형태로 '가장 ~한[하게]'이라는 뜻을 나타낸다. 최상급 뒤에는 보통 of(~ 중에서)나 in(~ 안에서)을 써서 비교의 범위를 한정하는 경우가 많다.
  Robin is **the tallest** boy in my class.
- 〈one of the+최상급+복수명사〉는 '가장 ~한 … 중의 하나'라는 뜻이다.
  She is **one of the most famous designers** in the world.

★ 내신만점 *TIP* 〈one of the+최상급〉 뒤에 단수가 아닌 복수명사가 오는지 반드시 확인하자.

A ( ) 안의 말을 이용하여 최상급 문장을 완성하시오.

1 This is ______________ room in our hotel. (good)
2 It was ______________ day of my life. (happy)
3 Today is ______________ day of the year. (hot)
4 What is ______________ river in Korea? (long)
5 That is ______________ chair in my house. (comfortable)
6 It is one of ______________ buildings in Asia. (tall)
7 Brenda is ______________ girl in her family. (young)
8 Mt. Everest is ______________ mountain in the world. (high)
9 What is ______________ animal in the world? (dangerous)

B 다음 우리말과 같은 뜻이 되도록 ( ) 안의 말을 이용하여 문장을 완성하시오.

1 그것은 내 인생 최악의 실수였다. (bad, mistake)
It was ______ ______ ______ of my life.

2 김치는 가장 유명한 한국 음식이다. (famous)
Kimchi is ______ ______ ______ Korean food.

3 그의 책은 모든 것들 중에서 가장 인상 깊었다. (impressive)
His book was ______ ______ ______ of all.

4 미국에서 가장 인기 있는 운동 경기는 무엇인가요? (popular)
What is ______ ______ ______ sport in America?

5 그녀는 세계에서 가장 부유한 사람들 중 한 명이다. (rich)
She is one of ______ ______ ______ in the world.

6 이것은 서울에서 가장 오래된 집들 중 하나이다. (old, house)
This is ______ ______ ______ ______ ______ in Seoul.

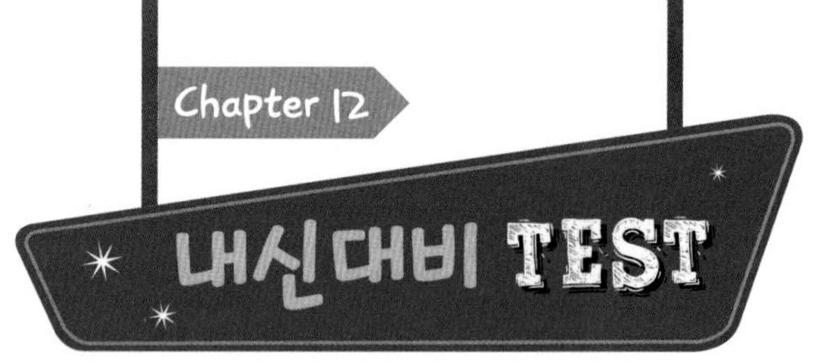

[01-03] 다음 빈칸에 알맞은 말을 고르시오.

01

She looked ________ yesterday.

① happily ② sadly ③ lovely
④ strangely ⑤ angrily

02

He is as ________ as David.

① brave ② braver ③ bravest
④ more brave ⑤ most brave

03

Today is ________ than yesterday.

① cold ② colder ③ coldest
④ more cold ⑤ coldly

기출응용

04

다음 짝지어진 두 단어의 관계가 나머지와 다른 것은?

① usual – usually
② loud – loudly
③ special – specially
④ friend – friendly
⑤ lucky – luckily

[05-07] 다음 빈칸에 들어갈 수 없는 말을 고르시오.

05

My jacket is ________ cheaper than his.

① much ② even ③ a lot
④ very ⑤ far

06

Mike is as ________ as his brother.

① tall ② fast ③ handsome
④ strong ⑤ worse

07

Helen is more ________ than Jennifer.

① patient ② wiser ③ famous
④ confident ⑤ intelligent

08

다음 중 원급–비교급–최상급이 잘못 연결된 것은?

① many – more – most
② ugly – uglyer – uglyest
③ true – truer – truest
④ light – lighter – lightest
⑤ useful – more useful – most useful

[09-10] 빈칸에 들어갈 말이 순서대로 알맞게 짝지어진 것을 고르시오.

09

• Russia is the ________ country in the world.
• The Amazon is ________ than the Nile.

① large – long ② larger – longer
③ larger – longest ④ largest – longest
⑤ largest – longer

10

• I'm cold. I need ________ to drink.
• They found the museum very ________.

① hot something – impressive
② hot something – impressively
③ something hot – impressive
④ something hot – impressively
⑤ hot thing – impressively

11

다음 대화의 빈칸에 공통으로 들어갈 말은?

A: Which do you like ________ for traveling, backpacks or suitcases?
B: I like backpacks ________.

① good ② better ③ best
④ much ⑤ well

12

다음 우리말을 영어로 바르게 옮긴 것은?

오늘은 내 인생에서 가장 기쁜 날들 중 하루이다.

① Today is the happiest day of my life.
② Today is the most happy day of my life.
③ Today is one of the happiest day of my life.
④ Today is one of the happier days of my life.
⑤ Today is one of the happiest days of my life.

13

빈칸에 들어갈 말이 나머지와 다른 것은?

① This is cheaper ________ that.
② I like rice better ________ bread.
③ Bob sleeps less ________ seven hours a day.
④ The robot is as small ________ a finger.
⑤ I think the book was more interesting ________ the movie.

14

다음 문장과 의미가 같은 것은?

I don't speak German as well as Joe.

① I speak German as well as Joe.
② I speak German better than Joe.
③ Joe speaks German better than me.
④ Joe speaks German worse than me.
⑤ Joe doesn't speak German as well as me.

[15-16] 다음 중 어법상 틀린 것을 고르시오.

15

① She is much busier than you.
② The news made my father happily.
③ Work hard and play hard.
④ They usually go shopping on Saturdays.
⑤ Sally comes to school much earlier than I do.

16

① Linda eats as less as I do.
② It is the oldest building in this city.
③ There is something sharp in the bag.
④ Speaking is a lot harder than listening.
⑤ Look at that bird. It is flying really high.

17

다음 우리말을 영어로 옮긴 것 중 잘못된 것은?

① 나는 방과 후에 자주 테니스를 친다.
I often play tennis after school.
② 그는 전보다 훨씬 더 크게 노래를 불렀다.
He sang a lot louder than before.
③ 나는 네 생각에 강하게 동의할 수 있다.
I can hardly agree with your idea.
④ 이 방이 이 건물에서 가장 어둡다.
This room is the darkest in this building.
⑤ 너는 정보를 더 쉽게 검색할 수 있다.
You can search for information more easily.

18

다음 밑줄 친 부분의 쓰임이 잘못된 것은?

① It won't take long.
② The cake smells wonderful.
③ Some people drive too fast.
④ I didn't know that it was so lately.
⑤ Everything is boring. There is nothing new!

기출응용

19

(A), (B), (C)의 괄호 안에서 알맞은 것끼리 바르게 짝지어진 것은?

(A) I found the food [horrible / horribly].
(B) She [near / nearly] fell down the stairs.
(C) Alex fixes things as [good / well] as Ian.

	(A)		(B)		(C)
①	horrible	……	nearly	……	good
②	horrible	……	near	……	well
③	horrible	……	nearly	……	well
④	horribly	……	near	……	well
⑤	horribly	……	nearly	……	good

고난도

20

다음 중 어법상 옳은 것끼리 짝지어진 것은?

(a) Listen carefully. It's important.
(b) It can sometimes happen.
(c) She is very cuter than Lynne.
(d) He finished the work late at night.
(e) The theater is so near as the post office.

① (a), (b), (d) ② (a), (c), (e)
③ (b), (c), (d) ④ (b), (c), (e)
⑤ (c), (d), (e)

서술형 따라잡기

01
다음 표를 보고, 문장을 완성하시오.

Jack	170 cm
Jenny	162 cm
Phillip	165 cm

(1) Jenny is ________ ________ Phillip.

(2) Jack is ________ ________ of the three students.

02
다음 Mark가 한가한 시간에 하는 일을 나타낸 그래프를 보고, 주어진 말을 이용하여 문장을 완성하시오.

(1) Mark ________ ________ ________ ________. (usually)

(2) Mark ________ ________ ________. (sometimes)

(3) Mark ________ ________ ________. (often)

03
다음 두 문장이 같은 뜻이 되도록 빈칸에 알맞은 말을 쓰시오.

(1) Seoul is not as big as New York.
→ New York is ________ ________ Seoul.

(2) Tony is more diligent than all the other boys in his class.
→ Tony is ________ ________ ________ boy in his class.

04
주어진 말을 알맞게 배열하여 우리말과 뜻이 같도록 문장을 완성하시오.

(1) 나는 절대 너를 잊지 않을 것이다.
(forget, never, you, will, I)
→ ________________________________

(2) 그녀는 우리 학교에서 가장 똑똑한 사람들 중 한 명이다. (is, of, one, people, smartest, the, she)
→ ________________________________ in my school.

05
다음 애견 콘테스트 심사표를 보고, 주어진 말을 이용하여 비교하는 문장을 완성하시오.

	Thomas	Max	Luis	Becky
Age	5	3	8	2
Weight	5.7 kg	4.1 kg	7.5 kg	3.0 kg
Speed	★★★	★★★	★	★★

(1) Luis is ________ ________ Becky. (old)

(2) Thomas is ________ ________ ________ Max. (fast)

(3) Becky is ________ ________ of the four dogs. (light)

고난도

06
주어진 말을 문맥에 맞게 알맞은 형태로 바꾸어 쓰시오.

I saw Matthew today. I could ________ (hard) believe my eyes. He looked much ________ (thin) than before. He told me about his terrible summer vacation. He said he was sick the whole time. It was one of ________ ________ (bad) vacations of his life.

SELF NOTE

핵심 포인트 정리하기

1 형용사

- 역할: 명사 · 대명사를 수식하거나 주격 보어 · 목적격 보어로 쓰여 사람이나 사물의 상태 · 성질 표현

2 부사

- 역할: 동사, 형용사, 다른 부사 혹은 문장 전체를 수식
- 형태: 주로 ① ____________

*빈도부사: 어떤 일이 얼마나 자주 일어나는지 나타내는 말로, be동사나 조동사의 ② _________, 일반동사의 ③ _________에 옴

never	〈	seldom	〈	④_________	〈	⑤_________	〈	usually	〈	always
(결코 ~않다)		(거의 ~않는)		(가끔)		(자주)		(대개, 보통)		(항상)

-thing, -body, -one으로 끝나는 대명사는 형용사가 뒤에서 수식한다는 것 기억하기!
문장 내 빈도부사가 올 수 있는 위치 알아두기!

3 비교 표현

원급 비교	〈⑥_________+형용사/부사의 원급+as〉 〈not+as[so]+형용사/부사의 원급+as〉	'~만큼 …한[하게]' '~만큼 …하지 않은[않게]'
비교급	〈비교급+⑦_________〉	'~보다 더 …한[하게]'
최상급	〈the+최상급〉 〈one of the+최상급+⑧_________〉	'가장 ~한[하게]' '가장 ~한 … 중의 하나'

형용사/부사의 비교급, 최상급 형태 알아두기(특히, 불규칙 변화인 경우)!
〈one of the+최상급〉 뒤에 복수명사가 오는지 확인하기!

문제로 개념 다지기

밑줄 친 부분이 어법상 맞으면 O, 틀리면 X 표시하고 바르게 고치시오.

1 Serena bought an apartment nice last month.
2 Why do you eat so fastly?
3 They sometimes had meetings together.
4 Seoul is the bigger than Ulsan.
5 My father always is in his study.
6 He is one of the oldest member of our book club.
7 Rabbits are the most cutest animals in the world.
8 Kate is as more polite as her sister.

전치사

It is warm here **in** May. [시간의 전치사]
What is that **on** your desk? [장소의 전치사]

전치사란?

명사(구)나 대명사 앞에 쓰여서 시간, 장소, 방향 등을 나타내는 말입니다.

시간의 전치사 in / on / at

■ 전치사는 명사(구)나 대명사 앞에 쓰여서 시간, 장소, 방향 등을 나타내는 말이다.
■ 시간을 나타내는 전치사에는 in, on, at 등이 있다.

in	연도, 월, 계절, 오전, 오후 등 비교적 긴 시간을 나타낼 때 **in** 2018, **in** May, **in** winter, **in** the morning
on	날짜, 요일, 특정한 날을 나타낼 때 **on** July 4, **on** Friday, **on** New Year's Day
at	구체적인 시각, 하루의 때, 특정한 시점을 나타낼 때 **at** seven thirty, **at** midnight, **at** that time

A 다음 밑줄 친 부분을 어법에 맞게 고쳐 쓰시오.

1 Let's meet in noon.
2 I was born on 2005.
3 The movie starts on 3:40.
4 I will go to Europe at August.
5 What are you going to do at Sunday?
6 People eat turkey in Thanksgiving Day.

B 다음 빈칸에 in, on, at 중 알맞은 전치사를 쓰시오.

1 It snowed a lot __________ January.
2 We live __________ the 21st century.
3 Come to my office __________ five thirty.
4 My friend got married __________ May 5.
5 I sometimes have a snack __________ midnight.
6 Did you meet your boyfriend __________ your birthday?

C 다음 우리말과 같은 뜻이 되도록 문장을 완성하시오.

1 우리는 그때 서로를 몰랐다.
We didn't know each other __________ __________ __________.

2 그는 저녁에 TV를 본다.
He watches TV __________ __________ __________.

3 토요일 오후에 만나는 게 어때요?
How about meeting __________ __________ __________?

시간의 전치사 around / before / after / for / during / until / by

■ 시간을 나타내는 전치사에는 around, before, after, for, during, until, by 등도 있다.

around	~경에, ~ 무렵에	**around** noon, **around** lunchtime, **around** sunset
before	~ 전에	**before** breakfast, **before** 8:30, **before** dark
after	~ 후에	**after** the meeting, **after** nine o'clock, **after** lunch
for	~ 동안	**for** a week, **for** three hours, **for** two years
during	~ 동안	**during** summer vacation, **during** the weekend, **during** class
until	~까지 (지속)	**until** next Monday, **until** tomorrow, **until** 5 p.m.
by	~까지는 (완료)	**by** this weekend, **by** twelve o'clock, **by** tomorrow morning

★ 내신만점 TIP 시간의 전치사 for 뒤에는 숫자를 포함하는 구체적인 기간, during 뒤에는 특정한 기간을 나타내는 명사(구)가 온다는 것을 기억하자.

A 다음 우리말과 같은 뜻이 되도록 빈칸에 알맞은 전치사를 쓰시오.

1 나는 자정 무렵에 잠자리에 들었다.
I went to bed ________ midnight.

2 Stephan은 내일 아침까지 여기에 머물러야 한다.
Stephan should stay here ________ tomorrow morning.

3 우리 방과 후에 도서관에 갈래?
Shall we go to the library ________ school?

4 그들은 영화를 보는 동안 큰 소리로 떠들었다.
They talked loudly ________ the movie.

5 그 버스가 정오까지는 도착할 것이다.
The bus will arrive ________ noon.

6 그는 몇 주 동안 동남아시아를 여행했다.
He traveled in Southeast Asia ________ a few weeks.

B 다음 우리말과 같은 뜻이 되도록 문장을 완성하시오.

1 너는 쇼핑하기 전에 목록을 작성해야 한다.
You should make a list ________ ________.

2 Brian은 2시간 동안 요리를 하는 중이었다.
Brian was cooking ________ ________ ________.

3 당신은 월요일 2시경에 나를 만나러 와도 좋아요.
You can come and see me ________ ________ on Monday.

4 나는 보고서를 다음 수요일까지 끝내야 한다.
I have to finish my report ________ ________ ________.

Point 03 장소의 전치사 in / on / at

■ 장소를 나타내는 전치사에는 in, on, at 등이 있다.

in	도시, 국가 등 비교적 넓은 장소를 나타낼 때나 건물과 사물의 내부를 나타낼 때 **in** Chicago, **in** Japan, **in** a building, **in** a box
on	접촉해 있는 상태를 나타낼 때 **on** the table, **on** the ground, **on** the skin
at	비교적 좁은 장소나 한 지점을 나타낼 때 **at** home, **at** the airport, **at** my uncle's

A 다음 밑줄 친 부분을 어법에 맞게 고쳐 쓰시오.

1 He is studying on school now.
2 Hang your picture at the wall.
3 Look at those stars on the sky.
4 There is a nice café in the corner.
5 One of my best friends studies at London.
6 The German couple lives in the 3rd floor.

B 다음 빈칸에 in, on, at 중 알맞은 전치사를 쓰시오.

1 Your key is __________ the table.
2 Joan will stay __________ her grandmother's.
3 There's no bed __________ my room.
4 Put those things __________ your pocket.
5 Emily is standing __________ the carpet.
6 I ate some delicious cake __________ the party.

C 다음 우리말과 같은 뜻이 되도록 ( ) 안의 말을 이용하여 문장을 완성하시오.

1 나는 그를 버스 정류장에서 봤다. (see)
I __________ __________ __________ the bus stop.

2 우리는 바닥에 누워서 잠깐 쉬었다. (floor)
We lay __________ __________ __________ and took a break.

3 인터넷은 세계에서 가장 큰 도서관이다. (world)
The Internet is the biggest library __________ __________ __________.

Point 04 장소의 전치사 near / over / under / to / behind

■ 장소를 나타내는 전치사에는 near, over, under, to, behind 등도 있다.

near	~ 근처에	**near** the station, **near** here, **near** my house
over	~ 위에 (표면에 접촉해 있지 않은 상태)	**over** my head, **over** the horizon, **over** the roof
under	~ 아래에	**under** the table, **under** the sea, **under** a bridge
to	~로 (목적지)	**to** the department store, **to** the west, **to** the left
behind	~ 뒤에	**behind** the car, **behind** the building, **behind** the tree

A **다음 우리말과 같은 뜻이 되도록 〈보기〉에서 알맞은 전치사를 골라 문장을 완성하시오.**

〈보기〉 near over under to behind

1 Michael은 침대 밑에 숨었다.
Michael hid ________ the bed.

2 그는 그녀의 머리 위로 공을 던졌다.
He threw the ball ________ her head.

3 오른쪽으로 돌아라, 그러면 너는 그것을 볼 수 있을 것이다.
Turn ________ the right, and you'll see it.

4 나는 내 가방을 그 의자 뒤에 두었다.
I put my bag ________ the chair.

5 너희 집 근처에 제과점이 있니?
Is there a bakery ________ your house?

6 나는 누군가에게 호수공원으로 가는 길을 물었다.
I asked someone the way ________ Lake Park.

B **다음 우리말과 같은 뜻이 되도록 문장을 완성하시오.**

1 놀이터 근처에 가게 하나가 있다.
________ ________ ________ ________ ________ the playground.

2 문 위쪽의 팻말에는 '환영'이라고 쓰여있었다.
The sign ________ ________ ________ said "Welcome."

3 헬리콥터들이 도시 위를 날고 있었다.
Helicopters ________ ________ ________ the city.

4 그들은 그 우산 아래에서 서로 이야기했다.
They talked to each other ________ ________ ________.

구 전치사 in front of / next to / across from

■ 구 전치사는 둘 이상의 단어로 이루어진 전치사로, in front of, next to, across from 등이 있다.

in front of	~ 앞에	There's a café **in front of** the theater.
next to	~ 옆에 (= beside)	I was standing **next to** my favorite singer.
across from	~ 맞은편에 (= opposite)	Let's meet at the bookstore **across from** the Art Center.

A 다음 두 문장이 같은 뜻이 되도록 문장을 완성하시오.

1 Beth is standing behind Tony.
→ Tony is standing ______________ Beth.

2 Can you see the girl sitting beside George?
→ Can you see the girl sitting ______________ George?

3 I'm at the fast-food restaurant opposite my school.
→ I'm at the fast-food restaurant ______________ my school.

B 다음 우리말과 같은 뜻이 되도록 문장을 완성하시오.

1 네 책은 내 가방 옆에 있다.
Your book is ________ ________ ________ ________.

2 나는 주유소 맞은편에 있는 슈퍼마켓을 보았다.
I saw a supermarket ________ ________ the gas station.

3 그가 쇼핑몰 앞에서 너를 기다리고 있다.
He is waiting for you ________ ________ ________ the shopping mall.

C 다음 우리말과 같은 뜻이 되도록 ( ) 안의 말을 배열하여 문장을 완성하시오.

1 제가 창문 옆에 앉을 수 있나요? (I, to, the window, next, can, sit)

____

2 그는 내 문 앞에 상자 하나를 두고 갔다. (a box, my door, front, he, in, left, of)

____

3 박물관 맞은편에 도서관이 있다. (a library, the museum, is, across, there, from)

____

Point 06 구 전치사 between A and B/from A to B

▪ 구 전치사에는 between A and B, from A to B도 있다.

between A and B	A와 B 사이에	Judy sat **between** Anne **and** me.
from A to B	A부터 B까지	The shop is open **from** 9 a.m. **to** 6 p.m.

A 다음 우리말과 같은 뜻이 되도록 빈칸에 알맞은 전치사를 쓰시오.

1 A부터 B까지 선을 그어라.
Draw a line __________ A __________ B.

2 지난주에 한국과 일본 사이에 회의가 있었다.
There was a meeting __________ Korea __________ Japan last week.

3 우리 아버지는 오전 10시부터 오후 7시까지 일하신다.
My father works __________ 10 a.m. __________ 7 p.m.

4 나는 수학과 체육 사이에 과학 수업이 있다.
I have science class __________ math __________ PE.

5 그 식당의 직원들은 3시부터 5시까지 휴식을 취한다.
The restaurant's workers take a break __________ three __________ five.

6 여기서 서울 타워까지 운전해서 얼마나 걸리나요?
How long does it take to drive __________ here __________ Seoul Tower?

B 다음 우리말과 같은 뜻이 되도록 ( ) 안의 말을 이용하여 문장을 완성하시오.

1 저녁 6시에서 7시 사이에 돌아올게요. (6 p.m., 7 p.m.)
I will be back __________ __________ __________ __________

2 봄은 3월부터 5월까지 계속된다. (March, May)
Spring lasts __________ __________ __________ __________.

3 1과 10 사이에서 숫자 하나를 고르세요. (one, ten)
Choose a number __________ __________ __________ __________.

4 이건 너와 나 사이의 비밀이야. (you, me)
This is a secret __________ __________ __________ __________.

5 공항에서 그 도시까지는 약 30km입니다. (the airport, the city)
It's about 30 km __________ __________ __________ __________ __________
__________.

[15-17] 다음 밑줄 친 부분이 어법상 틀린 것을 고르시오.

15

① It often rains in fall.
② I have no classes at Sunday.
③ My father came home at midnight.
④ We should get there by one o'clock.
⑤ It's between the bank and the laundry shop.

16

① I'll be there around 8 p.m.
② My office is beside to City Hall.
③ The kids sat under the tree.
④ He lived there from 2009 to 2015.
⑤ The boy is crying in front of the door.

17

① Maria only slept in an hour last night.
② Let's go shopping on Friday.
③ There was a fire in the building.
④ They plan to meet at 7:30 p.m.
⑤ She worked out during lunchtime.

18

다음 우리말을 영어로 바르게 옮긴 것은?

① 테이블 앞에 상자가 있다.
There is a box behind the table.
② 나는 정오 무렵에 점심을 먹는다.
I eat lunch after noon.
③ 그는 극장 맞은편에 서 있다.
He is standing next to the theater.
④ 그 나라는 태국과 베트남 사이에 있다.
The country is from Thailand to Vietnam.
⑤ 나는 다음 주까지 두바이에 머무를 예정이다.
I'm going to stay in Dubai until next week.

19

(A), (B), (C)의 괄호 안에서 알맞은 것끼리 바르게 짝지어진 것은?

(A) I held an umbrella [over / with] her head.
(B) He traveled from Seattle [to / in] Boston.
(C) My friend was waiting for me [on / at] the bus stop.

	(A)		(B)		(C)
①	over	……	in	……	on
②	over	……	to	……	on
③	over	……	to	……	at
④	with	……	to	……	at
⑤	with	……	in	……	at

고난도

20

다음 중 어법상 옳은 것을 모두 고르면? (3개)

① There is a boat under the bridge.
② She studied fashion on New York.
③ He arrived here on October 22.
④ We do the dishes after dinner.
⑤ I was at a summer camp during two weeks.

서술형 따라잡기

01
다음 우리말과 같은 뜻이 되도록 〈보기〉에서 알맞은 전치사를 골라 문장을 완성하시오.

〈보기〉 across from　around　during

(1) 나는 정오 무렵에 잠에서 깼다.
I woke up ______________ noon.

(2) 우리 집은 라디오 방송국 맞은편에 있다.
My house is ______________ the radio station.

(3) 공연 중에는 정숙하세요.
Please keep quiet ______________ the performance.

02
주어진 말을 이용하여 우리말과 뜻이 같도록 문장을 완성하시오.

너는 다음 월요일까지 그 책을 다 읽을 수 있니?
(finish, the book)

→ ________ ________ ________ ________
________ ________ ________ next Monday?

03
주어진 말을 알맞게 배열하여 우리말과 뜻이 같도록 문장을 완성하시오.

(1) 그 아기들은 몸무게가 3kg에서 5kg 사이이다.
(between, weigh, 3 kg, 5 kg, and, the babies)
→ ______________________________

(2) 모퉁이에 장난감 가게가 있다.
(on, there, the corner, a toy shop, is)
→ ______________________________

04
다음 그림을 보고, 문장을 완성하시오.

(1) The bakery is ________ the flower shop ________ the bookstore.

(2) There is a bicycle ________ ________ ________ the bakery.

05
다음 표를 보고, 질문에 답하시오.

Dan's Plan	
12:00 p.m.	go to the library
1:00 p.m. – 3:00 p.m.	play tennis
4:00 p.m. – 6:00 p.m.	meet some friends

(1) Q: When will Dan go to the library?
A: He'll go there ________ noon.

(2) Q: How long will Dan play tennis?
A: He'll play tennis ________ ________ ________.

(3) Q: When will Dan be with his friends?
A: He'll be with them ________ four o'clock ________ six o'clock.

고난도

06
다음 현장학습 안내문을 읽고, 틀린 부분을 모두 찾아 바르게 고쳐 쓰시오. (3군데)

School Field Trip!

We will go to the National Museum at May 21. You will be able to enjoy many great works of art during three hours. We will go there together by bus. So let's meet in front in the school at nine o'clock.

S E L F N O T E

핵심 포인트 정리하기

1 시간의 전치사

in (비교적 긴 시간) / on (특정한 날) / ①________ (특정한 시점): '~에'
②________: '~경에', '~ 무렵에' / before: '~ 전에' / after: '~ 후에'
for, during: '~ 동안' / ③________ (지속): '~까지' / ④________ (완료): '~까지는'

2 장소의 전치사

in (비교적 넓은 곳) / ⑤________ (접촉해 있는 상태) / at (비교적 좁은 곳): '~에'
near: '~ 근처에' / ⑥________ (표면에 접촉해 있지 않은 상태): '~ 위에'
under: '~ 아래에' / to(목적지): '~로' / behind: '~ 뒤에'

3 구 전치사

in front of: '~ 앞에' / next to: '~ 옆에' / ⑦________________: '~ 맞은편에'
⑧________________: 'A와 B 사이에' / from A to B: 'A부터 B까지'

in, on, at의 쓰임을 구분하여 알아두기!
<for + 숫자 포함 구체적인 기간>, <during + 특정한 기간을 나타내는 명사>라는 것 잊지 말기!

문제로 개념 다지기

다음 우리말을 영어로 옮길 때, 밑줄 친 부분이 어법상 맞으면 O, 틀리면 X 표시하고 바르게 고치시오.

1 너는 이틀 동안 내 전화를 받지 않았다.
You didn't answer my calls <u>during</u> two days.

2 한국에서 새 학기는 보통 3월에 시작한다 .
A new semester usually begins <u>on</u> March in Korea.

3 나는 다음 주까지 에세이를 제출해야 한다.
I should hand in my essay <u>until</u> next week.

4 그는 그 호텔에 온종일 머물렀다.
He stayed <u>at</u> the hotel all day.

5 새들이 지붕 위로 날아갔다.
Birds flew <u>over</u> the roof.

6 고양이 한 마리가 우리 집 앞에 앉아 있었다.
A cat was sitting <u>across from</u> my house.

7 8월은 7월과 9월 사이에 있다.
August is <u>from July to September</u>.

MEMO

MEMO

MEMO

BURGER
MEMO

MEMO

지은이

NE능률 영어교육연구소

NE능률 영어교육연구소는 혁신적이며 효율적인 영어 교재를 개발하고 영어 학습의 질을 한 단계 높이고자 노력하는 NE능률의 연구조직입니다.

문제로 마스터하는 중학영문법 〈LEVEL 1〉

펴 낸 이 주민홍
펴 낸 곳 서울특별시 마포구 월드컵북로 396(상암동) 누리꿈스퀘어 비즈니스타워 10층
㈜NE능률 (우편번호 03925)
펴 낸 날 2018년 7월 5일 개정판 제1쇄 발행
2024년 9월 15일 제21쇄
전 화 02 2014 7114
팩 스 02 3142 0356
홈페이지 www.neungyule.com
등록번호 제1-68호
I S B N 979-11-253-2365-5 53740
정 가 11,000원

NE 능률

고객센터

교재 내용 문의 : contact.nebooks.co.kr (별도의 가입 절차 없이 작성 가능)
제품 구매, 교환, 불량, 반품 문의 : 02-2014-7114
☎ 전화문의는 본사 업무시간 중에만 가능합니다.

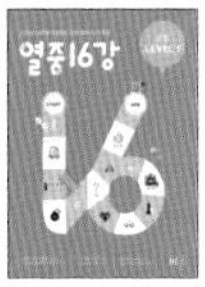

NE능률 교재 MAP

문법
구문
서술형

아래 교재 MAP을 참고하여 본인의 현재 혹은 목표 수준에 따라 교재를 선택하세요.
NE능률 교재들과 함께 영어실력을 쑥쑥~ 올려보세요!
MP3 등 교재 부가 학습 서비스 및 자세한 교재 정보는 www.nebooks.co.kr 에서 확인하세요.

초1-2

초3
그래머버디 1
초등영어 문법이 된다 Starter 1

초3-4
그래머버디 2
초등영어 문법이 된다 Starter 2
초등 Grammar Inside 1
초등 Grammar Inside 2

초4-5
그래머버디 3
Grammar Bean 1
Grammar Bean 2
초등영어 문법이 된다 1
초등 Grammar Inside 3
초등 Grammar Inside 4

초5-6
Grammar Bean 3
Grammar Bean 4
초등영어 문법이 된다 2
초등 Grammar Inside 5
초등 Grammar Inside 6

초6-예비중
능률중학영어 예비중
Grammar Inside Starter
원리를 더한 영문법 STARTER

중1
능률중학영어 중1
Grammar Zone 입문편
Grammar Zone 워크북 입문편
1316 Grammar 1
문제로 마스터하는 중학영문법 1
Grammar Inside 1
열중 16강 문법 1
쓰기로 마스터하는 중학서술형 1학년
중학 천문장 1

중1-2
능률중학영어 중2
1316 Grammar 2
문제로 마스터하는 중학영문법 2
Grammar Inside 2
열중 16강 문법 2
원리를 더한 영문법 1
중학영문법 총정리 모의고사 1
중학 천문장 2

중2-3
Grammar Zone 기초편
Grammar Zone 워크북 기초편
1316 Grammar 3
원리를 더한 영문법 2
중학영문법 총정리 모의고사 2
쓰기로 마스터하는 중학서술형 2학년
중학 천문장 3

중3
능률중학영어 중3
문제로 마스터하는 중학영문법 3
Grammar Inside 3
열중 16강 문법 3
중학영문법 총정리 모의고사 3
쓰기로 마스터하는 중학서술형 3학년

예비고-고1
문제로 마스터하는 고등영문법
올클 수능 어법 start
천문장 입문

고1
Grammar Zone 기본편 1
Grammar Zone 워크북 기본편 1
Grammar Zone 기본편 2
Grammar Zone 워크북 기본편 2
필히 통하는 고등 영문법 기본편
필히 통하는 고등 서술형 기본편
천문장 기본

고1-2
필히 통하는 고등 영문법 실력편
필히 통하는 고등 서술형 실전편
TEPS BY STEP G+R Basic

고2-3
Grammar Zone 종합편
Grammar Zone 워크북 종합편
올클 수능 어법 완성
천문장 완성

고3

수능 이상/
토플 80-89·
텝스 600-699점
TEPS BY STEP G+R 1

수능 이상/
토플 90-99·
텝스 700-799점
TEPS BY STEP G+R 2

수능 이상/
토플 100·
텝스 800점 이상
TEPS BY STEP G+R 3

중학 핵심 문법을
문제로 확실히 끝내는

LEVEL 1

문제로 마스터하는 중학영문법

정답 및 해설

NE 능률

LEVEL 1

문제로 마스터하는 중학영문법

정답 및 해설

Chapter 01 인칭대명사와 be동사

POINT 01 인칭대명사와 be동사의 현재형 p.10

A 1 am 2 is 3 are 4 are 5 are

B 1 She's 2 It's 3 They're 4 I'm 5 You're

C 1 are 2 is 3 It's

POINT 02 be동사의 과거형 p.11

A 1 was 2 was 3 were 4 were 5 was

B 1 are 2 were 3 was 4 is 5 were

C 1 is 2 is 3 were 4 You were 5 He was

POINT 03 be동사의 부정문 p.12

A 1 isn't 2 aren't 3 weren't 4 wasn't
5 It's not[It isn't] 6 We're not[We aren't]

B 1 We are not[We're not, We aren't] in the same class.
2 I am not[I'm not] a baseball player.
3 My mother is not[My mother's not, My mother isn't] in the office.
4 Mark was not[Mark wasn't] with his girlfriend.
5 Some people are not[Some people aren't] afraid of ghosts.
6 They were not[They weren't] in New York last month.

POINT 04 be동사의 의문문 p.13

A 1 Was she in the hospital?
2 Is John at the museum?
3 Is it very interesting?
4 Were you a police officer?
5 Are they cheerleaders for our team?

B 1 Are you 2 she is 3 Was he 4 we were

POINT 05 There is[are] p.14

A 1 are 2 was 3 There were not 4 Is, there is

B 1 There is not[isn't] a book in my bag.
2 There was a big sport event.
3 Are there hamburgers on the table?

C 1 There aren't any coins in her purse.
2 Is there a computer in his room?
3 There were two birds on the roof.

POINT 06 인칭대명사의 격 변화 –주격/소유격/목적격/소유대명사 p.15

A 1 his 2 her 3 my 4 It 5 Our 6 him 7 theirs

B 1 Their, me 2 My, hers 3 She, Laura's
4 mine, them 5 you, yours

내신대비 TEST p.16

01 ③ 02 ① 03 ④ 04 ⑤ 05 ② 06 ③
07 ③ 08 ③ 09 ③ 10 ① 11 ⑤ 12 ④
13 ② 14 ④ 15 ② 16 ② 17 ④ 18 ②
19 ③ 20 ②

서술형 따라잡기 p.19

01 (1) are, them (2) yours, Teddy's
02 (1) He was not (2) It is, Its
03 (1) Were Julie and David in the same class?
(2) Don't touch the camera. It is[It's] mine.
04 yours, it isn't[it's not], My
05 (1) is, His (2) Are, I'm not, I'm
(3) are, They are
06 (1) The blanket is not[isn't] his.
(2) Was your son a lawyer?

01 it을 주어로 하는 be동사의 현재형 의문문의 부정 대답은 No, it isn't.이다.

02 명사를 포함하는 소유대명사가 필요하다. (my guitar = mine)

03 Sophia는 3인칭 단수이고, last year로 보아 과거의 일이므로 was를 써야 한다.

04 ⑤의 are는 '(~에) 있다'의 의미이고, ①, ②, ③, ④의 be동사는 모두 '~이다'의 의미이다.

05 대답하는 사람의 입장에서 Cindy와 Jack을 받는 주격 대명

사는 they이며, A에 대한 대답으로 긍정의 경우 Yes, they are., 부정의 경우 No, they aren't.가 와야 한다.

06 대답하는 사람의 입장에서 you와 your sister를 받는 주격 대명사는 we이며, A에 대한 대답으로 긍정의 경우 Yes, we are., 부정의 경우 No, we aren't.가 와야 한다.

07 〈There is[are]+명사〉의 현재형 의문문이고 a smart TV는 단수명사이므로, A에 대한 대답으로 긍정의 경우 Yes, there is., 부정의 경우 No, there isn't.가 와야 한다.

08 첫 번째 빈칸에는 that boy를 받는 3인칭 단수 주격 대명사 he가 와야 하고, 두 번째 빈칸에는 명사 son을 수식하는 소유격 my가 와야 한다.

09 첫 번째 빈칸에는 주어 it에 대한 be동사 현재형의 부정형인 isn't가 와야 하고, 두 번째 빈칸에는 '그의 것'이라는 의미의 소유대명사 his가 와야 한다.

10 〈There is[are]+명사〉에서 be동사 뒤의 명사가 cookies인 복수명사이므로 첫 번째 빈칸에는 are가 와야 하고, 두 번째 빈칸에는 전치사 for의 목적어로 '너희(들)'이라는 의미의 목적격 you가 와야 한다.

11 ⑤ 현재 Andrew 선생님이 교무실에 계시냐는 질문에 과거에 계셨다는 대답은 자연스럽지 않다.

12 those bags는 3인칭 복수이므로 be동사의 부정형으로 were not이 와야 하고, '우리의 것'이라는 의미를 나타내는 소유대명사 ours가 와야 한다.

13 '~이 있다'라는 의미를 나타내는 〈There is[are]+명사〉에서 be동사 뒤의 명사가 a pine tree인 단수명사이므로 There is가 와야 하고, '그녀의'라는 의미를 나타내는 소유격 her가 와야 한다.

14 ④ You에 적합한 be동사 과거형의 부정형은 weren't이다.

15 ② '그들의 것'이라는 의미의 소유대명사 theirs가 와야 한다.

16 ②의 her는 소유격이고, ①, ③, ④, ⑤는 목적격이다.

17 ④의 his는 소유대명사이고, ①, ②, ③, ⑤는 소유격이다.

18 B의 응답에서 주어가 각각 I와 we이므로 빈칸에는 Are you가 와야 한다.

19 (A) 주어가 you이므로 Were가 알맞다.
(B) 동사 helps의 목적어로 목적격 them이 적절하다.
(C) 주어가 3인칭 복수인 Jason and his cousin이므로 be동사는 are가 와야 한다.

20 (c) Dan and I는 1인칭 복수이므로 be동사는 are가 와야 한다.
(d) country를 수식하는 소유격 your가 와야 한다.

서술형 따라잡기

01 (1) '~이 있다'라는 의미를 나타내는 〈There is[are]+명사〉에서 be동사 뒤의 명사가 many animals인 복수명사이므로 첫 번째 빈칸에는 현재형인 are을 쓴다. 두 번째 빈칸에는 동사 like의 목적어로 앞 문장의 many animals를 받는 3인칭 복수 목적격인 them이 와야 한다.
(2) 문맥상 you와 Teddy는 각각 '너의 것', 'Teddy의 것'이라는 의미의 소유대명사 yours와 Teddy's가 되어야 한다.

02 (1) 주어는 3인칭 단수 He이고 과거 일에 대해 말하고 있으므로 be동사의 과거형인 was를 쓴다. be동사의 부정형은 동사 뒤에 not을 쓴다.
(2) 앞의 a book을 대신하는 주격 대명사 It과 '(~에) 있다'라는 의미인 be동사의 3인칭 단수형 is를 쓴다. '그것의'의 의미로 cover를 수식하는 소유격 Its를 쓴다.

03 (1) 주어가 3인칭 복수인 Julie and David이므로 be동사로 Were가 와야 한다.
(2) Its와 me는 각각 앞의 the camera를 대신하는 주격 대명사 It과 '나의 것'이라는 의미의 소유대명사 mine이 되어야 한다.

04 Amy의 대답으로 보아, Sam의 질문에는 이 모자가 Amy의 것인지 물어보는 말이 와야 알맞다. Amy의 대답에는 it isn't[it's not]와 cap을 수식하는 소유격 My가 와야 한다.

05 (1) 주어가 3인칭 단수이므로 첫 번째 빈칸에는 is를 쓴다. 두 번째 빈칸에는 nickname을 수식하는 소유격 His가 와야 한다.
(2) 주어가 2인칭 단수이므로 첫 번째 빈칸에는 Are를 쓴다. Alice는 영국 출신이므로, 부정 대답으로 No, I'm not.이 와야 한다. '나는 ~이다'라는 의미로는 I am의 축약형인 I'm을 쓴다.
(3) 주어가 3인칭 복수이므로 첫 번째 빈칸에는 are를 쓴다. Junho와 Alice를 받는 주격 대명사는 They이고 이때 be동사는 are를 쓴다.

06 (1) 주어인 The blanket은 3인칭 단수이므로 동사는 is를, '그의 것'이라는 의미의 소유대명사는 his를 쓴다. be동사의 부정형은 be동사 뒤에 not을 쓴다.
(2) 주어인 '너의 아들'은 3인칭 단수이고, 과거의 일에 대해 물어보고 있으므로 동사는 was를 쓴다. '너의'는 소유격 your로 표현한다. be동사의 의문문은 〈be동사+주어 ~?〉의 어순이 되어야 알맞다.

SELF NOTE p.20

A 핵심 포인트 정리하기

① mine ② his ③ her ④ us ⑤ theirs ⑥ was
⑦ were ⑧ be동사, not ⑨ Is[Are], there

B 문제로 개념 다지기

1 O 2 X, Is
3 X, We are not[We're not, We aren't]
4 O 5 X, they are 6 O

Chapter 02 일반동사

POINT 01 일반동사의 현재형 I - 1인칭/2인칭 주어 p.22

A 1 make 2 speak 3 watch 4 practice 5 work

B 1 I need your advice.
2 We feel happy on Christmas.
3 Julia and you like each other.
4 I have plans this evening.

POINT 02 일반동사의 현재형 II - 3인칭 주어 p.23

A 1 eats 2 likes 3 call 4 walks 5 gets
6 works 7 drink

B 1 looks 2 begins 3 needs 4 closes 5 ride
6 sends 7 climb

POINT 03 일반동사의 3인칭 단수형 만드는 방법 p.24

A 1 flies 2 teaches 3 has 4 wants 5 cries
6 does 7 uses 8 plays 9 washes 10 reads

B 1 goes 2 enjoys 3 runs 4 envies 5 makes

POINT 04 일반동사의 과거형 I - 규칙 변화 p.25

A 1 studied 2 worked 3 stopped 4 arrived
5 asked 6 visited 7 moved

B 1 dropped 2 opened 3 trusted 4 showed
5 planned 6 tried 7 stayed

POINT 05 일반동사의 과거형 II - 불규칙 변화 1 p.26

A 1 met 2 came 3 felt 4 found 5 went 6 ate
7 gave 8 said 9 saw

B 1 caught 2 heard 3 thought 4 built 5 left

POINT 06 일반동사의 과거형 III - 불규칙 변화 2 p.27

A 1 made 2 lost 3 had 4 sang 5 carried
6 enjoyed 7 spent 8 bought, sent

B 1 hurt 2 took 3 put 4 shut 5 hit 6 cut
7 cost 8 read

POINT 07 일반동사의 부정문 I - don't/doesn't p.28

A 1 don't 2 doesn't 3 doesn't keep
4 doesn't get 5 don't know

B 1 Alex doesn't have a car.
2 I don't practice the violin in the morning.
3 My dog doesn't look healthy.
4 Nick and Lily don't have lunch together at school.

C 1 doesn't work 2 don't go 3 doesn't spend

POINT 08 일반동사의 부정문 II - didn't p.29

A 1 I didn't turn off the light.
2 Susie didn't pass the exam.
3 They didn't understand the questions.
4 You didn't want a tablet PC for a gift.
5 Jake didn't tell me about the rumor.
6 We didn't buy a birthday cake for Judy.

B 1 I didn't meet 2 They didn't have
3 Ross didn't write 4 He saw, he didn't say
5 Sophia fell, she didn't cry

POINT 09 일반동사의 의문문 I - Do/Does p.30

A 1 Do I look smart?
2 Does he eat garlic?
3 Do you live in Beijing?
4 Do they study French?
5 Does Kate have three brothers?

6 Do we take a test every month?

B 1 Does Andy love 2 Do you like
3 Do they know 4 Does she have
5 Does this bus go, it does
6 Do you walk, I don't

POINT 10 일반동사의 의문문 II – Did p.31

A 1 Did he catch the ball?
2 Did Lily lose her passport?
3 Did you go to the museum?
4 Did they help the old man?
5 Did your classmates come here?

B 1 Did 2 Does 3 Do 4 Did 5 Do

C 1 Did he leave 2 Did you have, we did, had
3 Did, like, they did, thanked

내신대비 TEST p.32

01 ③ 02 ⑤ 03 ④ 04 ② 05 ① 06 ②
07 ④ 08 ④ 09 ⑤ 10 ① 11 ④ 12 ②, ⑤
13 ④ 14 ③ 15 ⑤ 16 ③ 17 ⑤ 18 ⑤
19 ③ 20 ③

서술형 따라잡기 p.35

01 (1) didn't[did not] watch the movie
(2) takes a walk

02 (1) Do Sharon and Brad eat meat? / Sharon and Brad do not[don't] eat meat.
(2) Did Joseph hit 20 home runs last season? / Joseph did not[didn't] hit 20 home runs last season.

03 (1) studied at the library
(2) did not[didn't] study at the library

04 Does he cook

05 (1) didn't visit her grandmother
(2) ate pizza with her friends
(3) did her homework

06 bring → brought / don't like → doesn't like

01 3인칭 단수동사인 drives가 쓰였으므로, 주어는 3인칭 단수인 She가 적절하다.

02 주어가 1인칭, 2인칭이거나 3인칭 복수형일 경우 부정문에서 don't를 사용하므로 빈칸에는 They가 적절하다.

03 주어가 2인칭(you)일 때 일반동사의 현재형 의문문은 Do로 시작한다.

04 주어가 3인칭(she)일 때 일반동사의 과거형 의문문에 대한 대답은 Yes, she did. 또는 No, she didn't.이다.

05 주어가 3인칭 단수(Matt)일 때 일반동사의 현재형 의문문에 대한 대답은 Yes, he does. 또는 No, he doesn't.이다.

06 Do you ~?에 대한 대답으로 Yes, I do.나 No, I don't.가 오는데, B의 빈칸 뒤에 온 내용으로 보아 긍정의 대답이 적절하다.

07 ④ 주어가 1인칭 복수(We)인 일반동사의 부정문은 〈주어+don't+동사원형 ~〉의 형태이다.

08 ④ 주어가 3인칭 단수(He)이고 현재시제이므로 finish를 finishes로 써야 한다.

09 첫 번째 빈칸에는 3인칭 단수 주어(Frank)의 현재형 의문문에 사용되는 Does가, 두 번째 빈칸에는 3인칭 단수 주어(She)의 부정문에 사용되는 does가 와야 한다.

10 첫 번째 문장은 yesterday로 보아 과거시제이므로 didn't가, 두 번째 문장은 시제가 과거인 일반동사의 의문문에 대한 부정의 대답이므로 didn't가 와야 한다.

11 주어가 3인칭 단수(He)인 현재시제의 부정문은 〈주어+doesn't+동사원형 ~〉의 형태이다.

12 yesterday로 보아 시제는 과거이므로 동사의 과거형을 써야 한다. ②와 ⑤가 각각 buy와 give의 올바른 과거형이다. ① look의 과거형은 looked, ③ cost의 과거형은 cost, ④ pay의 과거형은 paid이다.

13 3인칭 단수(Julie)를 주어로 하는 일반동사의 현재형 의문문에 대한 긍정의 대답이므로 첫 번째 빈칸에는 does가, 두 번째 빈칸에는 study의 3인칭 단수 형태인 studies가 와야 한다.

14 B의 대답으로 보아 A에는 시제가 과거인 일반동사의 의문문이 와야 하므로 첫 번째 빈칸에는 Did, 두 번째 빈칸에는 break를 쓴다.

15 ⑤ 주어가 3인칭 복수(your parents)인 의문문이므로 Does 대신 Do 혹은 Did가 와야 한다.

16 일반동사 keep의 과거형은 kept이다.

17 ⑤의 does는 '하다'라는 의미의 일반동사이고, 나머지는 일반동사의 부정문이나 의문문을 만들 때 사용되는 조동사이다.

18 ①, ②, ③, ④에는 일반동사의 과거시제 부정문과 의문문을 만드는 did가 와야 한다. ⑤에는 주어가 1인칭 단수(I)일 때 일반동사의 현재형 부정문을 만드는 do가 와야 한다.

19 (a)는 3인칭 단수(he)를 주어로 하는 일반동사의 현재형 의문문이므로 Does를 써야 한다. (b)는 1인칭 복수(We)를 주어로 하는 일반동사의 현재형 부정문이므로 don't를 써야 한다.

20 일반동사 worry의 과거형은 worried이다.

서술형 따라잡기

01 (1) 주어진 우리말 뜻으로 보아 과거시제인 일반동사의 부정문이므로 동사원형 앞에 didn't[did not]를 쓴다.
(2) 현재시제이고 주어(Julie)는 3인칭 단수이므로 일반동사 take의 3인칭 단수형인 takes를 쓴다.

02 (1) 주어가 3인칭 복수(Sharon and Brad)인 일반동사의 현재형 의문문은 Do로 시작한다. 부정문은 동사원형 앞에 don't를 쓴다.
(2) 일반동사의 과거형 의문문은 Did로 시작한다. 부정문은 동사원형 앞에 didn't를 쓴다.

03 (1) 과거를 나타내는 부사 yesterday가 있으므로 study의 과거시제인 studied를 써야 한다.
(2) 과거를 나타내는 부사 last weekend가 있으므로 과거형 부정문을 나타내는 didn't[did not]가 와야 한다.

04 B의 대답으로 보아 주어가 3인칭 단수(he)인 현재형 의문문이므로 〈Does+주어+동사원형〉의 형태인 Does he cook를 쓴다.

05 (1) Suji는 월요일에 할머니를 찾아뵙지 않았으므로 didn't를 이용하여 과거형 부정문으로 표현한다.
(2) Suji는 수요일에 친구들과 피자를 먹었으므로 동사 eat의 과거형인 ate를 쓴다.
(3) Suji는 금요일에 숙제를 했으므로 동사 do의 과거형인 did를 쓴다.

06 두 번째 문장에서 a month ago가 과거시제를 나타내므로 bring의 과거형인 brought를 써야 한다. 마지막 문장에서 주어가 3인칭 단수(he)이며 현재시제인 경우 부정문은 〈doesn't+동사원형〉으로 나타내므로 doesn't like를 써야 한다.

SELF NOTE p.36

A 핵심 포인트 정리하기
① -s, -es ② -ed, -d ③ don't, doesn't ④ didn't
⑤ Do, Does ⑥ Did

B 문제로 개념 다지기
1 do not 2 enjoys 3 went 4 Did 5 plays
6 drank 7 doesn't 8 have

Chapter 03 명사와 관사

POINT 01 셀 수 있는 명사 I – 규칙 변화 1 p.38

A 1 cats 2 tomatoes 3 boxes 4 flowers
5 stars 6 presents 7 friends 8 watches
9 shirts 10 plans 11 classes 12 ideas
13 foxes 14 cards 15 pianos 16 ships
17 addresses 18 heroes

B 1 arms 2 maps 3 cookies 4 sandwiches
5 houses 6 egg, potatoes 7 questions
8 bananas 9 boats 10 songs
11 shirts, jackets

POINT 02 셀 수 있는 명사 II – 규칙 변화 2 p.39

A 1 countries 2 combs 3 factories 4 shelves
5 mirrors 6 bodies 7 pictures 8 wallets
9 hobbies 10 parties 11 keys 12 mouths
13 wolves 14 windows 15 diaries 16 families
17 puppies 18 brushes

B 1 mistakes 2 buses 3 boxes 4 toys
5 roofs 6 babies 7 knives 8 cities, buildings
9 stories 10 leaves 11 holidays

POINT 03 셀 수 있는 명사 III – 불규칙 변화 p.40

A 1 teeth 2 feet 3 families 4 cliffs 5 clubs
6 sheep 7 men 8 bugs 9 children 10 cities

B 1 mice 2 deer 3 fish 4 women
5 chickens, geese 6 oxen

POINT 04 셀 수 없는 명사 p.41

A 1 France 2 Sugar 3 music 4 luck 5 ink
6 is 7 information 8 honey 9 coffee
10 questions, health

B 1 news 2 water 3 spoons 4 money 5 time
6 America

POINT 05 명사 – 수량 표현 I p.42

A 1 slices of pizza 2 loaves of bread
3 pieces of cake 4 cartons of milk
5 pairs of scissors

B 1 pair of pants 2 bottles of wine
3 bowls of rice 4 glasses of apple juice
5 pieces of cheese

C 1 piece 2 slices 3 pair 4 bottles 5 cups

POINT 06 명사 – 수량 표현 II p.43

A 1 Water 2 many 3 smoke 4 children
5 days 6 is butter 7 sandwiches 8 a little
9 milk 10 much

B 1 Few students 2 much courage
3 a few keys 4 are many toys, boxes
5 glasses, milk, a little cheese

POINT 07 관사 I – 부정관사 a/an p.44

A 1 an 2 a 3 X 4 an 5 an 6 a 7 a 8 an
9 an 10 a

B 1 once a day 2 an interesting story
3 bought a magazine 4 is a university student
5 a piece of paper

POINT 08 관사 II – 정관사 the p.45

A 1 a 2 The 3 an 4 the 5 the, the 6 a, The
7 the 8 The 9 a, the 10 a, the

B 1 the Internet 2 the living room
3 a good musician 4 The bag
5 The moon, the earth

POINT 09 관사의 생략 I p.46

A 1 a 2 a 3 X 4 X 5 X 6 X 7 X 8 an
9 a 10 X, a

B 1 I had lunch with Jane.
2 Did you come here by taxi?
3 Bill went to bed at ten last night.
4 Christians go to church on Sunday.
5 Paula plays badminton every Wednesday.

POINT 10 관사의 생략 II p.47

A 1 bus, a bus 2 a car, the car 3 salt, the salt
4 the novel, a novel
5 a restaurant, the restaurant

B 1 the 2 the 3 the 4 a 5 the 6 X 7 the
8 X 9 a 10 a, The 11 X 12 The

내신대비 TEST p.48

01 ⑤	02 ⑤	03 ②	04 ④	05 ④	06 ②
07 ⑤	08 ②	09 ③	10 ④	11 ③	12 ③
13 ④	14 ⑤	15 ⑤	16 ③	17 ④	18 ③
19 ⑤	20 ④				

서술형 따라잡기 p.51

01 mice
02 (1) many → much
(2) monkey → monkeys / photoes → photos
03 geese, oxen, deer, donkey
04 ate two bowls of rice
05 (1) three slices[pieces] of pizza, two glasses of milk
(2) two pieces of cake, a[one] bottle of juice
06 an, X, X

01 부정관사 a는 셀 수 있는 명사의 단수형 앞에 사용한다.
02 a few 뒤에는 셀 수 있는 명사의 복수형이 온다.
03 much 뒤에는 셀 수 없는 명사가 온다.
04 ④ child의 복수형은 children이다.

05 수량을 표현할 때 scissors는 a pair of를, juice는 a glass of를 단위로 사용하고, 복수형은 단위를 나타내는 명사에 -(e)s를 붙여서 나타낸다.

06 첫 번째 문장의 TV는 서로 알고 있는 대상을 지칭하므로 첫 번째 빈칸에는 the가 와야 한다. 두 번째 문장에서는 TV가 본래의 용도로 쓰였으므로 두 번째 빈칸에는 관사가 필요 없다.

07 첫 번째 빈칸 뒤에 셀 수 있는 명사 sheep이 왔으므로 many나 a few를 쓸 수 있다. 두 번째 빈칸 뒤에 운동경기명(tennis)이 왔으므로 관사를 쓰지 않는다.

08 ② air는 셀 수 없는 명사이므로 부정관사와 함께 쓰지 않는다.

09 ③ coffee는 셀 수 없는 명사이므로 부정관사와 함께 쓰지 않는다.

10 수식어(in the vase)의 꾸밈을 받는 flower 앞에는 정관사 The를 쓰고, water는 셀 수 없는 명사이므로 little 혹은 a little과 같은 수량 표현을 쓴다.

11 수식어(on your left)의 꾸밈을 받는 woman과, 태양(sun)과 같이 하나뿐인 존재 앞에는 정관사 The를 쓴다.

12 advice와 cake는 수량을 표현할 때 a piece of를 사용한다.

13 information과 snow 모두 셀 수 없는 명사이므로 관사가 필요 없다.

14 주어진 단어를 배열하면 We bought two pieces of furniture.이고 네 번째 오는 단어는 pieces이다. 셀 수 없는 명사 furniture는 수량을 표현할 때 a piece of를 사용하며 복수형은 pieces of로 나타낸다.

15 ⑤ '안경'을 뜻하는 glasses는 항상 복수형으로 쓰며, a pair of를 써서 수량을 표현한다.

16 ③ hour는 셀 수 있는 명사이므로 복수형 hours가 되어야 한다.

17 ④ a few 뒤에는 셀 수 있는 명사의 복수형이 오므로 weeks가 되어야 한다.

18 〈보기〉와 ③의 a는 막연한 하나를 가리킨다. ①과 ④는 '~마다'의 의미이고, ②와 ⑤는 '하나'라는 의미로 쓰였다.

19 ⑤ 일반적으로 식사(breakfast)를 나타내는 말 앞에는 관사를 쓰지 않는다.

20 (a) of France가 capital을 뒤에서 수식하고 있으므로 capital 앞에는 정관사 the가 와야 한다.
(c) woman의 복수형은 women이다.

서술형 따라잡기

01 집에서 모두 네 마리의 쥐를 발견한 것이므로, mouse의 복수형인 mice를 쓴다.

02 (1) 셀 수 없는 명사 work 앞에는 many가 아닌 much를 쓴다.
(2) 첫 번째 문장에서 a few 뒤에는 복수명사가 오므로 monkeys로 쓴다. 두 번째 문장에서 photo의 복수형은 photos이다.

03 goose의 복수형은 geese, ox의 복수형은 oxen이다. deer는 단수형과 복수형의 형태가 같으며, donkey는 앞에 관사 a가 왔으므로 형태를 변화시키지 않는다.

04 rice는 a bowl of를 사용해 수량을 표현한다. 복수형은 그릇을 나타내는 명사인 bowl에 -s를 붙여서 나타낸다.

05 (1) pizza는 a slice[piece] of를, milk는 a glass of를 사용하여 수량을 표현한다. 이때 복수형은 slice[piece]와 glass에 -(e)s를 붙여서 나타낸다.
(2) cake는 a piece of를, juice는 a bottle of를 사용하여 수량을 표현한다. 이때 복수형은 piece에 -s를 붙여 나타낸다.

06 • hour는 셀 수 있는 명사이며 첫 발음이 모음이므로 앞에 부정관사 an을 쓴다.
• 침대가 잠자러 가는 곳이라는 본래의 용도로 쓰였으므로 bed 앞에 관사를 쓰지 않는다.
• 학교가 공부하러 가는 곳이라는 본래의 용도로 쓰였으므로 school 앞에 관사를 쓰지 않는다.

SELF NOTE p.52

A 핵심 포인트 정리하기

① books ② potatoes ③ deer ④ mice ⑤ men ⑥ piece ⑦ 있는 ⑧ 없는 ⑨ an ⑩ the

B 문제로 개념 다지기

1 X, pieces of cake 2 X, sheep 3 O 4 O 5 X, The 6 X, an hour

Chapter 04 대명사

POINT 01 지시대명사 – this/that p.54

A 1 this 2 that 3 these 4 those 5 those

B 1 Is this backpack yours?
2 Those children are happy.
3 These are jackets for women.
4 That is Julie's boyfriend.
5 That tree is so big.
6 Do you keep these promises?
7 My mother made those muffins.

POINT 02 부정대명사 I – one p.55

A 1 one 2 it 3 one 4 one 5 ones

B 1 ones 2 one 3 them 4 it

C 1 One should make decisions carefully.
2 I like the pink ones.
3 I bought one for her

POINT 03 부정대명사 II – some/any p.56

A 1 any 2 some 3 some 4 some 5 any
6 any 7 any 8 some 9 any 10 any, some

B 1 Do you have any plans tonight?
2 Do you want some ice cream?
3 bought some snacks for me
4 doesn't have any good songs
5 Do you have any problems

POINT 04 비인칭 주어 it p.57

A 1 It's 5:30. 2 It's Thursday. 3 It is cloudy.
4 It's May 8. 5 It is about five kilometers.
6 It takes half an hour.

B 1 It is dark outside 2 It is my birthday
3 It is ten to five 4 It takes an hour
5 It is ten kilometers 6 It was rainy, it is sunny

POINT 05 재귀대명사 p.58

A 1 herself 2 itself 3 myself 4 ourselves
5 themselves 6 ourselves 7 themselves

B 1 myself 2 yourself 3 herself 4 themselves
5 ourselves 6 himself 7 ourselves

POINT 06 재귀대명사의 용법 – 재귀/강조 p.59

A 1 myself, X 2 (ourselves) 3 themselves, X
4 (itself)

B 1 Susan은 직접 설거지를 했다. 〈강조 용법〉
2 내 남동생은 혼잣말을 했다. 〈재귀 용법〉
3 엄마는 이 케이크를 직접 만드셨다. 〈강조 용법〉
4 그 학생은 학급 친구들에게 그녀 자신을 소개했다. 〈재귀 용법〉
5 그 예술가는 직접 그 그림들에 대해 설명했다. 〈강조 용법〉

내신대비 TEST p.60

01 ③	02 ③	03 ①	04 ④	05 ④	06 ③
07 ②	08 ③	09 ①	10 ②	11 ①	12 ④
13 ⑤	14 ④	15 ⑤	16 ③	17 ⑤	18 ③
19 ①	20 ④				

서술형 따라잡기 p.63

01 (1) Are those your pets
(2) These are, tablet PCs, the old ones
02 (1) One (2) It
03 (1) It (2) it (3) one
04 (1) He cares about himself.
(2) There were some pencils on the desk.
05 (1) Did Mike move the box himself?
[Did Mike himself move the box?]
(2) They looked at themselves in the mirror.
06 (1) any (2) some (3) That

01 앞에 언급된 것과 같은 종류의 불특정한 사물을 가리킬 때 부정대명사 one을 쓴다.

02 긍정의 평서문에서 '약간'의 의미를 갖는 부정대명사 some이 적절하다.

03 특정한 사물 the movie를 받는 대명사는 it이다.

04 ④의 this는 지시대명사이고 나머지는 모두 명사를 앞에서 수식하는 지시형용사이다.

05 '약간(의)', '어떤'의 의미로 의문문에서는 any를, 긍정의 평서문에서는 some을 사용한다.

06 첫 번째 빈칸에는 앞에 나온 purse와 같은 종류의 불특정한 것을 나타내는 one이, 두 번째 빈칸에는 this purse라는 특정 사물을 받는 It이 적절하다.

07 첫 번째 빈칸에는 '약간(의)'의 의미로 긍정의 평서문에 쓰이는 some이, 두 번째 빈칸에는 주어 I를 강조하는 재귀대명사 myself가 적절하다.

08 ③ 부정문에서는 some이 아닌 any를 쓴다.

09 〈보기〉와 ②, ③, ④, ⑤의 It은 비인칭 주어인 반면, ①의 It은 특정한 것을 지칭하는 인칭대명사이다.

10 〈보기〉와 ①, ③, ④, ⑤는 강조 용법의 재귀대명사인 반면, ②의 herself는 동사의 목적어로 쓰인 재귀 용법의 재귀대명사이다.

11 (c) 앞에 나온 단수명사인 tie와 같은 종류의 불특정한 것을 나타내는 one이 와야 한다.
(e) 문장의 주어가 3인칭 복수이므로 take care of의 목적어로 재귀대명사 themselves가 와야 한다.

12 '~이 자랑스럽다'라는 의미인 be proud of의 목적어로 '우리 자신'이라는 의미의 재귀대명사 ourselves가 온다.

13 ⑤ 부정문에서는 any를 쓴다.

14 날씨와 날을 나타내는 비인칭 주어 It이 들어가야 한다.

15 각각 동사 enjoyed와 know의 목적어 역할을 하는 재귀대명사가 필요하다. 문장의 주어가 3인칭 복수명사이므로 빈칸에는 themselves가 와야 한다.

16 '약간(의)', '어떤'의 의미로 부정문과 의문문에서는 any를 쓴다.

17 ①, ②, ③, ④는 재귀 용법의 재귀대명사인 반면, ⑤의 themselves는 주어를 강조하는 강조 용법의 재귀대명사로 생략이 가능하다.

18 ③ '약간(의)', '어떤'의 의미로 긍정의 평서문에서는 some을 쓴다.

19 ① 주어가 She이므로 주어를 강조하는 강조 용법의 재귀대명사로 herself가 와야 한다.

20 (A) 시간을 나타내는 비인칭 주어 It이 알맞다.
(B) 긍정의 평서문에서 '약간(의)', '어떤'의 의미로 쓰이는 some이 알맞다.
(C) 재귀대명사 herself가 쓰인 것으로 보아 주어 자리에는 3인칭 단수명사인 The child가 알맞다.

서술형 따라잡기

01 (1) 지시대명사 that의 복수형으로 those를 쓴다.
(2) 지시대명사 This의 복수형으로 These를 쓴다. 부정대명사 one의 복수형은 ones이다.

02 (1) 일반인을 가리킬 때 부정대명사 One을 쓴다.
(2) 특정한 사물 a nice bag을 받는 대명사는 It이다.

03 (1) 날씨를 나타내는 비인칭 주어 It을 써야 한다.
(2) 특정한 사물인 my black jacket을 받는 대명사 it을 써야 한다.
(3) 앞에 나온 jacket과 같은 종류의 불특정한 것을 나타내는 부정대명사 one을 써야 한다.

04 (1) 전치사 about의 목적어로 재귀대명사 himself가 와야 한다.
(2) '~가 있다'는 〈There + be동사 + 명사〉의 형태로 표현한다. '약간의'라는 의미의 some은 형용사로 명사 앞에 쓰인다.

05 (1) 주어인 Mike를 강조하는 재귀대명사 himself를 이용한다.
(2) 동사 look at의 목적어 역할을 하는 재귀대명사를 쓴다. 재귀대명사의 3인칭 복수형은 themselves이다.

06 (1) 의문문에서는 부정대명사로 any를 쓴다.
(2) 긍정의 평서문에서는 부정대명사로 some을 쓴다.
(3) pink one은 단수이므로 이를 수식하는 지시형용사로는 That을 써야 한다.

SELF NOTE

p.64

A 핵심 포인트 정리하기
① this ② those ③ ones ④ some ⑤ any
⑥ ourselves ⑦ yourself ⑧ themselves

B 문제로 개념 다지기
1 X, that 2 O 3 X, ones 4 O
5 X, themselves 6 O

Chapter 05 시제

POINT 01 현재시제 p.66

A 1 are 2 plays 3 is 4 opens 5 are 6 has
7 goes 8 gets 9 takes 10 eat

B 1 is 2 studies hard 3 look tired
4 is the capital 5 Water boils
6 are tall, handsome

POINT 02 과거시제 p.67

A 1 snowed 2 came 3 wrote 4 painted
5 read

B 1 am, was 2 sat 3 put 4 was, gave
5 drives, drove

C 1 had 2 baked 3 sent 4 lied

POINT 03 진행형 만드는 법 p.68

A 1 sleeping 2 saying 3 making 4 bringing
5 having 6 meeting 7 buying 8 taking
9 winning 10 sitting 11 driving 12 staying
13 opening 14 dying 15 running 16 flying

B 1 doing 2 drinking 3 burning 4 arriving
5 sending 6 waiting 7 eating 8 looking
9 washing 10 entering 11 standing

POINT 04 현재진행형과 과거진행형 p.69

A 1 I was flying to Hawaii.
2 She is learning French.
3 He was holding a big box.
4 The monkey is climbing the tree.
5 You were smiling at me.
6 We are making Christmas cards.
7 They are talking on the phone.
8 Ted was driving to the gas station.
9 Susie and Dean were having dinner.
10 Gary was singing a song for me.

B 1 was choosing 2 were jumping 3 was crying
4 are taking a nap 5 is using the Internet
6 is solving math problems

POINT 05 진행형의 부정문 p.70

A 1 I'm not[I am not] going shopping.
2 She is not[She isn't / She's not] packing her bag.
3 Andrew was not[wasn't] driving his car.
4 They were not[weren't] wearing uniforms.

B 1 I'm not[I am not] waiting for her speech.
2 Kate and Alex were lying to each other.
3 The dog isn't[is not] playing with a ball.
4 You weren't[were not] wasting my time.

C 1 isn't hiding 2 wasn't reading 3 wasn't doing

POINT 06 진행형의 의문문 p.71

A 1 Is he exercising?
2 Were they speaking Chinese?
3 Is she winking at you?
4 Was Tony fixing his computer?
5 Were you sleeping at the library?
6 Are they running on the playground?
7 Was the boy eating potato chips?

B 1 I'm not 2 No, I wasn't 3 Yes, they are

C 1 Was he lying 2 Are they cutting
3 Were you looking for

내신대비 TEST p.72

01 ③ 02 ① 03 ④ 04 ② 05 ② 06 ③
07 ③ 08 ② 09 ⑤ 10 ⑤ 11 ③ 12 ②
13 ④ 14 ②, ⑤ 15 ⑤ 16 ④ 17 ④ 18 ③
19 ① 20 ③

서술형 따라잡기 p.75

01 (1) is (2) brought (3) cleans
02 My friends were not dancing on stage.
03 (1) He is paying 400 dollars a month for this apartment. / Was he paying 400 dollars a month for this apartment?

(2) Are they eating strawberries for dessert? / They were not[weren't] eating strawberries for dessert.

04 (1) is sitting (2) is lying (3) are running

05 (1) No, she wasn't, was drawing a picture

(2) No, she isn't, is making some food

06 were, called, went out

01 yesterday로 보아 과거를 나타내는 시제를 써야 하므로 wore가 알맞다.

02 문장의 전후 관계로 보아 현재진행형으로 〈be동사의 현재형+v-ing〉의 형태가 와야 한다.

03 last night로 보아 과거를 나타내는 시제를 써야 하고, 주어가 복수형이므로 were talking이 알맞다.

04 ② -e로 끝나는 동사는 e를 빼고 -ing을 붙여 진행형을 만들어야 하므로 moving이 알맞다.

05 know는 상태를 나타내는 동사이므로 진행형으로 쓰지 않는다.

06 want는 상태를 나타내는 동사이므로 진행형으로 쓰지 않는다.

07 이메일을 확인하고 있냐는 A의 질문에 B는 컴퓨터 게임을 하고 있다고 말하고 있으므로 ③이 적절하다.

08 어제 이 시간에 비가 많이 내리고 있었냐는 A의 질문에, B는 비가 매우 많이 내리고 있었다고 말하고 있으므로 ②가 적절하다.

09 과거진행형을 만들기 위해 be동사의 과거형 were가 필요하다.

10 현재 진행 중인 일을 묻고 답하는 대화로 첫 번째 빈칸에는 doing이, 두 번째 빈칸에는 watching이 와야 한다.

11 sending과 they aren't로 보아 A의 질문은 현재진행형이 되어야 하므로 첫 번째 빈칸에는 Are가, 10 minutes ago로 보아 두 번째 빈칸에는 과거시제인 sent가 와야 한다.

12 주어진 단어들을 배열하면 'The children were not waving at us.'이므로 네 번째에 올 단어는 waving이다.

13 ④ 불변의 사실을 나타낼 때는 현재시제를 사용하므로 was가 is로 바뀌어야 한다.

14 ① 과거진행형 의문문은 〈be동사의 과거형+주어+v-ing ~?〉의 형태이고, 주어가 2인칭(you)이므로 Was가 아닌 Were를 써야 한다.

③ last month로 보아 과거에 일어난 일을 이야기하고 있으므로 buy의 과거형인 bought를 써야 한다.

④ 과거진행형 부정문은 〈be동사의 과거형+not+v-ing〉의 형태이므로, was not using을 써야 한다.

15 ⑤ 역사적 사실은 과거시제로 쓴다.

16 ④ have는 소유를 나타내는 동사이므로 진행형으로 쓰지 않는다.

17 ④ 과거의 특정 시점에 진행 중이던 일을 나타내므로 과거진행형의 의문문은 〈be동사의 과거형+주어+v-ing〉의 형태로 쓴다.

18 주어가 3인칭 복수(Ian and Sue)이고, 과거진행형의 부정문으로 써야 하므로 〈were not+v-ing〉의 형태가 되어야 한다.

19 (c) every morning으로 보아 일상적인 습관을 나타내고 있고, 주어가 3인칭 단수일 때 현재시제는 takes가 알맞다.

(d) now로 보아 현재 진행 중인 일을 나타내므로 am recording이 알맞다.

20 (A) 불변의 사실이므로 현재시제 is를 쓴다.

(B) 과거의 동작을 나타내므로 과거시제 found를 쓴다.

(C) 소유를 나타내는 동사는 진행형으로 쓰지 않으므로 had를 쓴다.

서술형 따라잡기

01 (1) tonight이 있으므로 현재시제로 쓴다.

(2) yesterday가 있으므로 과거시제로 쓴다.

(3) every day와 these days로 보아 현재를 중심으로 하는 일상적인 습관을 나타내고 있으므로 현재시제인 cleans를 쓴다.

02 과거진행형의 부정문은 〈be동사의 과거형+not+v-ing〉의 형태로 쓴다.

03 (1) 현재진행형의 평서문은 〈be동사의 현재형+v-ing〉, 과거진행형의 의문문은 〈be동사의 과거형+주어+v-ing ~?〉의 형태로 쓴다.

(2) 현재진행형의 의문문은 〈be동사의 현재형+주어+v-ing ~?〉, 과거진행형의 부정문은 〈be동사의 과거형+not+v-ing〉의 형태로 쓴다.

04 (1) 여자는 벤치에 앉아 있으므로 is sitting을 쓴다.

(2) 남자는 풀밭 위에 누워 있으므로 is lying을 쓴다.

(3) 아이들이 강을 따라 달리고 있으므로 are running을 쓴다.

05 (1) 한 시간 전에 Amy는 그림을 그리고 있었으므로 No, she

wasn't.로 답하고, draw a picture를 과거진행형을 사용해 쓴다.

(2) Julie는 지금 음식을 만들고 있으므로 No, she isn't.로 답하고, make some food를 현재진행형을 사용해 쓴다.

06 • yesterday가 있으므로 과거시제로 쓴다.
• 과거에 이미 끝난 동작(전화했던 것)에 대해 이야기하는 것이므로 과거시제를 쓴다.
• 과거에 이미 끝난 동작(쇼핑하러 간 일)에 대해 이야기하고 있으므로 과거시제를 쓴다.

SELF NOTE p.76

A 핵심 포인트 정리하기
① v-ing ② be동사의 과거형 ③ be동사, not, v-ing
④ be동사, v-ing ⑤ not

B 문제로 개념 다지기
1 goes 2 lost 3 invented 4 is 5 wants
6 were not 7 Were

Chapter 06 조동사

POINT 01 will p.78

A 1 will visit 2 won't[will not] give 3 will be
4 not ask

B 1 I won't[I'll not, I will not] wear a raincoat.
2 Will they join us?
3 He will[He'll] be in the kitchen.
4 She will[She'll] invite a lot of people.

C 1 won't sing 2 will begin 3 Will, be, I'll be

POINT 02 be going to p.79

A 1 is going to make 2 is going to show
3 is going to arrive 4 are going to visit
5 is going to go

B 1 am going to wash the dishes
2 Are you going to have dinner
3 is going to be nice
4 are not[aren't] going to watch

C 1 Are you going to help me?
2 She isn't going to change her hairstyle.
3 I'm going to meet my friend in Japan.

POINT 03 can p.80

A 1 I can 2 Yes, you can 3 No, you can't
4 No, he can't

B 1 Can you open 2 can use
3 cannot[can't] climb 4 cannot[can't] go outside
5 Can you send a text message

POINT 04 can과 be able to p.81

A 1 Are you able to do 2 is not[isn't] able to play
3 am able to make 4 were able to hear
5 was not[wasn't] able to use
6 are able to deliver

B 1 are able to 2 Are you able to
3 was not[wasn't] able to 4 was able to
5 will be able to

C 1 I'm able to tell 2 Is Joe able to run
3 weren't able to lift

POINT 05 may p.82

A 1 May I have some ice cream?
2 May I use your laptop?
3 That may not be true.
4 She may be sick.

B 1 may not sit 2 may be 3 May I try on
4 may not know 5 May I take a picture

POINT 06 must p.83

A 1 ⓑ 2 ⓐ 3 ⓒ 4 ⓑ 5 ⓒ 6 ⓐ

B 1 We must take a taxi.
2 You must not drive a car.
3 I must finish the race.
4 You must not be late again.
5 That film must be interesting.

6 He cannot be at the hospital now.

POINT 07 have to p.84

A 1 have to go to bed 2 have to stop
3 have to call 4 have to clean 5 has to go

B 1 has to work 2 Does, have to go
3 has to meet 4 didn't have to wear
5 Do, have to finish 6 had to walk

POINT 08 should p.85

A 1 Should, take 2 should apologize
3 should wear 4 shouldn't believe

B 1 He cannot[can't] be tired
2 We don't have to tell the truth
3 You must not bring food
4 should listen to this song

내신대비 TEST p.86

01 ④	02 ③	03 ②	04 ③	05 ①	06 ④
07 ②	08 ②	09 ⑤	10 ⑤	11 ①	12 ⑤
13 ③	14 ③	15 ①	16 ④	17 ④	18 ②
19 ④	20 ④				

서술형 따라잡기 p.89

01 (1) must be hungry (2) cannot[can't] be
02 (1) He is not[isn't] going to say hello to her. / Is he going to say hello to her?
(2) She didn't have to come back home by ten. / Did she have to come back home by ten?
03 Were you able to get a good seat?
04 (1) must stay silent during the show
(2) must not take pictures during the show
05 (1) can drive (2) is not able to play
06 (1) must be kind
(2) doesn't have to go to school

01 신호등이 빨간 불이어서 길을 건너면 안 된다는 내용이므로 빈칸에는 금지를 나타내는 must not이 와야 한다.

02 오늘 오후에 비가 올 예정이니 우산을 가져가라는 내용이므로 빈칸에는 미래를 나타내는 will이 가장 적절하다.

03 어제 온종일 운동을 한 것으로 보아 Eric이 분명 피곤할 것이라고 추측하는 내용이므로, 빈칸에는 강한 추측을 나타내는 must가 와야 한다.

04 허가의 의미를 지니는 can은 may로 바꾸어 쓸 수 있다.

05 is going to는 미래의 일을 나타내는 will로 바꾸어 쓸 수 있다.

06 ④ '~해야 한다'의 의미를 나타내는 조동사 should를 쓴다.

07 '~임이 틀림없다'라는 의미의 강한 추측을 나타내는 조동사 must를 쓴다.

08 〈Will you ~?〉에 대한 부정의 대답으로 No, I won't.가 와야 한다.

09 빈칸 뒤에서 '다음 주 토요일이 어때?'라고 묻는 것으로 보아 빈칸에는 '내일은 볼 수 없다'는 부정의 대답이 와야 한다.

10 ⑤ should는 '~해야 한다'의 의미를 지니는 조동사이고 과거의 의미를 지니지 않으므로 B에서 had to를 이용해 답하는 것은 어색하다.

11 ②,③,④,⑤의 must는 '~해야 한다'라는 의무의 의미인 반면, ①의 must는 '~임이 틀림없다'라는 강한 추측의 의미이다.

12 ⑤ '~임이 틀림없다'라는 의미의 강한 추측을 나타낼 때는 must를 쓴다.

13 have to의 의문문은 〈Do/Does+주어+have to ~?〉이므로 A의 빈칸에는 have가 와야 하고 이에 대한 부정의 대답으로 B의 빈칸에는 doesn't가 와야 한다.

14 늦게 일어나서 제시간에 도착할 수 없었다는 의미이므로 첫 번째 빈칸에는 wasn't가, 그래서 모든 사람들에게 사과를 해야 했다는 의미이므로 두 번째 빈칸에는 had to가 와야 한다.

15 문맥상 '~할 수 없다'라는 의미의 can't가 와야 한다.

16 ④ have to의 부정형인 don't have to는 '~할 필요가 없다'라는 의미이고, must not은 '~하면 안 된다'라는 의미이다.

17 ④ 조동사는 주어의 인칭이나 수에 관계없이 형태가 변하지 않으므로 mays는 may가 되어야 한다.

18 ② 조동사 can의 과거형은 could 또는 were able to로 써야 한다.

19 (c) 조동사 can을 이용해 카메라를 수리할 수 있는지 묻는 질문에, (b) be able to를 이용한 답변이 이어지고, (d) should를 이용해 그렇다면 무엇을 해야 하는지 묻는 질문에, (a) have to로 답하는 문장이 이어지는 것이 알맞다.

20 (a) 조동사 can 뒤에는 동사원형이 와야 한다.
(c) 의무를 나타내는 조동사 must는 과거형이 없으므로 must cleaned는 had to clean의 형태가 되어야 한다.

서술형 따라잡기

01 (1) 문맥상 '~임이 틀림없다'라는 의미의 강한 추측을 나타내는 must를 이용해 써야 한다.
(2) 문맥상 '~일 리가 없다'라는 의미의 강한 부정적 추측을 나타내는 cannot[can't]를 이용해 써야 한다.

02 (1) 예정을 나타내는 be going to의 부정형은 〈be동사+not+going to〉, 의문문은 〈be동사+주어+going to ~?〉로 쓴다.
(2) have to의 과거시제 부정문은 didn't have to를 쓰며, 과거시제 의문문은 〈Did+주어+have to ~?〉로 나타낸다.

03 가능을 나타내는 be able to의 과거시제 의문문은 〈Was/Were+주어+able to+동사원형 ~?〉의 형태로 쓴다.

04 해야 하는 일은 must, 해서는 안 되는 일은 must not을 이용해 표현한다.

05 (1) 할 수 있는 일은 조동사 can 또는 be able to를 이용해 표현한다.
(2) 할 수 없는 일은 cannot 또는 〈be동사+not+able to+동사원형〉을 이용해 표현한다.

06 (1) 문맥상 '친절한 게 틀림없다'라는 의미의 강한 추측을 나타내는 must be kind를 써야 한다.
(2) 문맥상 '학교에 갈 필요가 없다'라는 의미의 doesn't have to go to school을 써야 한다.

SELF NOTE p.90

A 핵심 포인트 정리하기
① 동사원형 ② ~할 것이다 ③ be able to ④ may
⑤ must not ⑥ have to

B 문제로 개념 다지기
1 (1) must (2) don't have to (3) was not able to
2 (1) X, May I introduce (2) O (3) X, should be
(4) X, Do I have to wear (5) X, will not go

Chapter 07 의문문

POINT 01 who / what으로 시작하는 의문문 p.92

A 1 Who is he? 2 Who drew this?
3 What did you buy? 4 What did they eat?
5 Who is the author? 6 What can she write?

B 1 What did, make 2 Who is 3 Who is coming
4 What subject is 5 Who won 6 What will, do

POINT 02 which로 시작하는 의문문 p.93

A 1 Which do you like better
2 Which seat do you want
3 Which search engine do you use

B 1 What 2 Which 3 Who 4 Which

C 1 Who gave you 2 Which do you like
3 Which sport do you watch

POINT 03 when / where로 시작하는 의문문 p.94

A 1 When is 2 Where are they
3 When did you buy 4 Where did you see
5 When[What time] does

B 1 Where 2 Where 3 When 4 When
5 Where

C 1 Where does she live 2 Where were you
3 When did Mark call 4 What time did you meet

POINT 04 why로 시작하는 의문문 p.95

A 1 Why did he change 2 Who took this picture
3 Where did you get 4 Why do you need
5 Why were you angry

B 1 Why don't 2 Why, Because
3 Why, Because 4 When

C 1 Why, stop 2 Why, have to do
3 Why don't, save 4 Why do you like
5 Why don't we go

POINT 05 how로 시작하는 의문문 p.96

A 1 How was your date 2 How did she make

3 How was your trip 4 How did you become
5 How did people invent

B 1 How 2 Who 3 How 4 Why 5 How
6 Where

C 1 How did you meet 2 How is the weather
3 How did he know 4 How do you study

POINT 06 〈how+형용사/부사〉로 시작하는 의문문 p.97

A 1 How old 2 How long 3 How much
4 How many 5 How often

B 1 How long 2 How tall is 3 How many years
4 How much water 5 How many times

내신대비 TEST p.98

01 ④	02 ②	03 ③	04 ①	05 ②	06 ②
07 ④	08 ①	09 ②	10 ②	11 ④	12 ①
13 ④	14 ③	15 ②	16 ⑤	17 ②	18 ⑤
19 ③	20 ③				

서술형 따라잡기 p.101

01 (1) Who bought (2) When did you go
02 When, Who, How
03 (1) Why were you late
(2) How many people are there
04 (1) What is, David (2) How old
(3) Where is, He is
05 What → How / how you got → how did you get
06 (1) How often do you go to yoga class
(2) Why did you see a doctor

01 스마트폰이 있는 장소를 물어보는 질문이므로 Where가 와야 한다.
02 오른손에 무엇이 있는지를 물어보는 질문이므로 What이 와야 한다.
03 소풍이 어떠했는지를 물어보는 질문이므로 How가 와야 한다.
04 ①의 what은 '무엇'이라는 뜻의 의문사인 반면, ②,③,④,⑤의 what은 명사 앞에 쓰여 '무슨', '어떤'이라는 뜻을 나타내는 의문형용사이다.
05 어디로 여행을 갔는지를 묻고 있으므로 ②가 적절하다.
06 B에서 도봉산을 등산했다고 했으므로 무엇을 했었는지를 묻는 ②가 적절하다.
07 얼마나 오래 걸리는지를 물을 때에는 〈How long ~?〉을 쓴다.
08 '무엇'이라는 의미의 의문사로, 명사 앞에도 쓰일 수 있는 What이 와야 한다.
09 '어떤', '얼마나 ~한'의 의미를 지니는 의문사 How가 와야 한다.
10 첫 번째 빈칸에는 문맥상 '누가 ~에 가고 있니?'가 자연스러우므로 의문사 Who가, 두 번째 빈칸에는 '우리 ~하지 않을래?'라는 의미의 권유 표현이 될 수 있도록 Why가 와야 한다.
11 첫 번째 빈칸에는 셀 수 있는 명사 앞에 올 수 있는 many가, 두 번째 빈칸에는 선택을 묻는 의문문에서 사용하는 Which가 와야 한다.
12 〈Why don't we ~?〉는 '우리 ~하지 않을래?'라는 의미를 지니는 권유의 표현이므로 이에 대한 긍정의 대답인 ①이 가장 적절하다.
13 빈도를 나타내는 답변으로 보아 첫 번째 빈칸에는 의문사 How often, 이유를 나타내는 답변으로 보아 두 번째 빈칸에는 의문사 Why가 와야 한다.
14 (a)에는 빈도를 묻는 (How) often, (b)에는 셀 수 없는 명사 앞에 쓰여 양을 묻는 (How) much, (c)와 (e)에는 셀 수 있는 명사 앞에 쓰여 수를 묻는 (How) many, (d)에는 길이나 기간을 묻는 (How) long이 올 수 있다. 키나 높이를 묻는 (How) tall은 어느 빈칸에도 어울리지 않는다.
15 ② 직장에 어떻게 가냐고 묻는 질문에 그것을 좋아한다는 답변은 어울리지 않는다.
16 ⑤ 수영하러 가자고 권유하는 표현에 네가 바쁘지 않기 때문이라는 답변은 어울리지 않는다.
17 ② '얼마나 많이 ~'라는 의미로 양을 물을 때는 How much를 쓴다.
18 ⑤ 무엇을 도울지를 묻고 있으므로 What을 써야 한다. 나머지는 의문사 Why를 쓴다.
19 (d) 의문사가 문장에서 주어 역할을 하는 경우 3인칭 단수 취급하므로 wants가 와야 한다.
(e) 의문사가 있는 일반동사의 과거시제 의문문은 〈의문사+did+주어+동사원형 ~?〉의 형태이므로 happen이 와야 한다.
20 후식으로 '무엇'을 주문했는지 묻는 질문 (c)에 대한 답으로 (b)

가 이어지고, 왜 체리 파이를 주문하지 않았는지 묻는 질문 (d)에 그 이유를 답하는 (a)가 이어지는 것이 가장 자연스럽다.

서술형 따라잡기

01 (1) 의문사가 주어일 때는 〈의문사+동사 ~?〉의 어순으로 쓴다.
(2) 의문사가 있는 일반동사의 과거시제 의문문은 〈의문사+did+주어+동사원형 ~?〉의 형태로 쓴다.

02 첫 번째 빈칸에는 '언제' 갔는지 물을 때 사용하는 의문사 When, 두 번째 빈칸에는 '누가' 콘서트를 열었는지 물을 때 사용하는 의문사 Who가 필요하며, 아주 좋았다고 답하는 것으로 보아 마지막 빈칸에는 어땠는지를 물을 때 사용하는 의문사 How가 와야 한다.

03 (1) 의문사가 있는 be동사의 의문문은 〈의문사+be동사+주어 ~?〉의 형태로 쓴다.
(2) 수를 물을 때는 〈How many+명사+동사+주어 ~?〉의 형태로 쓴다.

04 (1) 이름이 무엇인지 묻는 의문문으로 〈What+be동사+주어 ~?〉를 쓴다.
(2) 나이를 묻는 의문문으로 〈How old+be동사+주어 ~?〉를 쓴다.
(3) 국적을 묻는 의문문으로 〈Where+be동사+주어+from?〉을 쓴다.

05 거리를 물을 때에는 〈How far ~?〉 의문문을 이용한다. 의문사가 있는 일반동사의 과거시제 의문문은 〈의문사+did+주어+동사원형 ~?〉의 형태로 쓴다.

06 (1) 빈도를 나타내는 답변으로 보아 '얼마나 자주'라는 의미의 How often을 이용한 의문문을 써야 한다.
(2) 이유를 나타내는 답변이 이어지는 것으로 보아, 의문사 Why를 이용한 의문문이 와야 한다.

SELF NOTE

p.102

A 핵심 포인트 정리하기
① 의문사 ② who ③ what ④ which ⑤ when
⑥ where ⑦ Because ⑧ how often
⑨ how much

B 문제로 개념 다지기
1 X, Why were 2 X, What 3 O 4 X, is
5 X, How much

Chapter 08 문장의 종류

POINT 01 부가 의문문의 형태

p.104

A 1 doesn't he 2 can't they 3 did she
4 do you 5 weren't you

B 1 does he 2 can't he 3 didn't you
4 didn't she 5 won't they

C 1 is it 2 didn't you 3 is she 4 can't she

POINT 02 부가 의문문의 응답

p.105

A 1 wasn't it, No, it wasn't
2 didn't he, Yes, he did
3 isn't it, Yes, it is

B 1 No, I didn't 2 shall we
3 will you 4 didn't she, Yes, she did
5 can you, No, I can't

POINT 03 부정 의문문의 형태

p.106

A 1 Isn't this yours?
2 Wasn't it expensive?
3 Isn't he a designer?
4 Don't you feel thirsty?
5 Can't they deliver it?
6 Didn't he take notes?
7 Doesn't she play tennis well?
8 Won't she move to New York?
9 Weren't you interested in animals?

B 1 Won't you eat some fish?
2 Weren't you with him?
3 Can't he come to Korea?
4 Don't you trust me?
5 Didn't she close the window?
6 Didn't he go to school yesterday?

POINT 04 부정 의문문의 응답

p.107

A 1 Isn't, No, he isn't 2 Didn't, No, he didn't
3 Won't, Yes, she will 4 Doesn't, No, he doesn't

B 1 Yes, it is 2 Yes, it is 3 No, he didn't
4 No, she can't

POINT 05 선택 의문문의 형태 p.108

A 1 Is he American or British?
2 Is she your girlfriend or your sister?
3 Are you going to Tokyo or Beijing?
4 Did you order potato chips or cheese sticks?
5 Does he prefer horror movies or action movies?

B 1 Will you, or 2 Which, or 3 Which, or
4 Which do you, or 5 Does she, or

POINT 06 선택 의문문의 응답 p.109

A 1 They[Whales] are 2 I bought 3 I'll go
4 They are going to open

B 1 Does, or, It starts
2 Did you eat[have], I ate[had]
3 Which do you, I want a necklace

POINT 07 what으로 시작하는 감탄문 p.110

A 1 What hot soup this is!
2 What big hands he has!
3 What a beautiful day it is!
4 What nice people they are!
5 What a witty man Jack is!
6 What a pretty T-shirt it is!
7 What a long message she sent!

B 1 What a clever dog it is!
2 What a good friend you are!
3 What a dirty room this is!
4 What a shy boy you are!
5 What spicy food you cooked!
6 What a charming voice Jude has!
7 What a great man he is!

POINT 08 how로 시작하는 감탄문 p.111

A 1 What a huge 2 the story is 3 How peaceful
4 small these shoes 5 a cute dress

B 1 How cheap it is!
2 How friendly you are!
3 How deep this lake is!
4 How short her hair is!
5 How difficult this problem was!
6 How exciting the game was!
7 How comfortable the sofa is!

C 1 How funny 2 How heavy
3 What useful 4 What a wonderful

POINT 09 명령문 I p.112

A 1 Be nice to people. 2 Wear a seat belt.
3 Don't be in a hurry. 4 Don't tell him the truth.

B 1 turn on 2 Don't go out 3 Don't listen to
4 Get up

C 1 Open the door, please.[Please open the door.]
2 Don't worry about me.
3 Don't make the same mistake again.
4 Don't park your car here.

POINT 10 명령문 II p.113

A 1 Let's not 2 have 3 or 4 and 5 Let's

B 1 Read this book, and you'll learn many things.
2 Study hard, or you won't pass the exam.
3 Visit the website, and you will get a coupon.

C 1 Let's find 2 or you'll forget 3 Let's not go
4 and you'll get

내신대비 TEST p.114

01 ③	02 ④	03 ①	04 ⑤	05 ①	06 ③
07 ③	08 ①	09 ④	10 ①	11 ①	12 ②
13 ②	14 ③	15 ④	16 ②	17 ④	18 ③
19 ④	20 ④				

서술형 따라잡기 p.117

01 (1) What cute girls they are!
(2) Let's go to the shopping center today.
02 (1) Exercise every day, and (2) Don't lie, or

03 (1) Bob doesn't run fast, does he?
(2) How clever the dolphin is!
04 Don't throw trash
05 (1) Yes, he can (2) No, he doesn't
06 (1) you cannot[can't] get up early
(2) you can focus on your work

01 시제가 과거이고 일반동사가 쓰인 긍정문이 앞에 나오면, 부정의 부가 의문문인 didn't you를 쓴다.

02 how로 시작하는 감탄문은 〈How+형용사/부사(+주어+동사)!〉의 형태이다.

03 선택 의문문이므로 or가 와야 한다.

04 ⑤의 빈칸 뒤에 〈형용사+명사+주어+동사〉가 이어지므로 What이, 나머지는 모두 뒤에 〈형용사+주어+동사〉가 이어지므로 How가 와야 한다.

05 how로 시작하는 감탄문은 〈How+형용사/부사(+주어+동사)!〉의 형태로 쓴다.

06 〈Why don't we ~?〉는 '우리 ~하지 않을래?'로 권유의 의미를 갖는다. 따라서 빈칸에는 Let's가 와야 한다.

07 빈칸 뒤에 도움이 필요하냐는 말이 이어지고 있는 것으로 보아, 중국어를 할 수 있다는 긍정의 답변이 오는 것이 적절하다. A에서 조동사 can을 이용해 질문을 했으므로 Yes, I can.이 와야 한다.

08 뒤에 그녀의 영화를 좋아한다는 말이 이어지는 것으로 보아, 빈칸에는 그녀는 훌륭한 여배우라는 긍정의 답변이 오는 것이 적절하다. be동사를 이용한 부정 의문문에 대한 긍정의 대답으로는 Yes, she is.를 쓴다.

09 A는 부가 의문문이므로 첫 번째 빈칸에는 조동사 will의 부정형인 won't가 와야 한다. B에서 Yes로 답하고 있으므로, 두 번째 빈칸에는 will이 와야 한다.

10 첫 번째 빈칸에는 뒤에 〈형용사+주어+동사〉가 이어지므로 감탄문을 만드는 How가 와야 한다. 두 번째 빈칸에는 '조용히 해라'라는 의미의 긍정 명령문이 와야 하므로, be동사의 동사원형인 Be를 쓴다.

11 첫 번째 빈칸에는 감탄문을 만드는 What이, 두 번째 빈칸에는 의문사 What이 와야 한다.

12 첫 번째 빈칸에는 명령문 뒤에서 '그러지 않으면'의 의미를 갖는 or가, 두 번째 빈칸에는 선택 의문문에서 '혹은'이라는 의미로 쓰이는 or가 와야 한다.

13 how로 시작하는 감탄문은 〈How+형용사/부사(+주어+동사)!〉의 형태로 쓴다.

14 시제가 현재이고 일반동사가 쓰인 부정문이 앞에 나오면, 긍정의 부가 의문문인 does he를 쓴다.

15 ④ 맥락상 B의 답변에서 명령문 Study hard 뒤에 '그러면'의 의미를 갖는 and가 와야 한다.

16 ② 명령문의 부가 의문문은 보통 〈~, will you?〉를 쓴다.

17 (A) 뒤에 〈부사+주어+동사〉가 이어지므로 감탄문을 만드는 How가 와야 한다.
(B) 명령문 뒤에서 '그렇지 않으면'의 의미를 갖는 or가 와야 한다.
(C) 선택 의문문이므로 or가 와야 한다.

18 ③ Let's not 다음에는 동사원형이 온다.

19 ④ 조동사 will의 부가 의문문으로 won't you가 와야 한다.

20 (a) 뒤에 〈형용사+주어+동사〉가 이어지고 있으므로, What이 아닌 How가 와야 한다.
(d) 권유의 부정 명령문은 〈Let's not+동사원형〉의 형태로 쓴다.

서술형 따라잡기

01 (1) what으로 시작하는 감탄문은 〈What+a/an+형용사+명사(+주어+동사)!〉의 형태로 쓴다. 명사가 복수형일 경우에는 관사를 생략한다.
(2) 권유의 명령문은 명령문 앞에 Let's를 붙인다.

02 (1) 의미상 '…해라, 그러면 ~할 것이다'라는 뜻의 〈명령문+and ~〉로 바꾸어 쓸 수 있다.
(2) 의미상 '…하지 마라, 그러지 않으면 ~할 것이다'라는 뜻의 〈부정 명령문+or ~〉로 바꾸어 쓸 수 있다.

03 (1) 일반동사가 쓰인 부정문 뒤에 긍정의 부가 의문문인 does he를 붙여 표현한다.
(2) how로 시작하는 감탄문은 〈How+형용사/부사(+주어+동사)!〉의 형태로 쓴다.

04 부정 명령문은 〈Don't+동사원형〉의 형태로 쓴다.

05 (1) 부정 의문문에 대한 긍정의 대답으로 Yes, he can.을 쓴다.
(2) 시제가 현재이고, 3인칭 단수 주어(Mike)가 쓰인 부가 의문문에 대한 부정의 대답으로 No, he doesn't.를 쓴다.

06 (1) '…하지 마라, 그러지 않으면 ~할 것이다'라는 뜻의 〈부정 명

령문+or ~〉가 와야 한다.

(2) 의미상 '…해라, 그러면 ~할 것이다'라는 뜻의 〈명령문+and ~〉가 와야 한다.

SELF NOTE p.118

A 핵심 포인트 정리하기

① 부정의 부가 의문문 ② 긍정의 부가 의문문 ③ Yes ④ No ⑤ not ⑥ or ⑦ a/an ⑧ How ⑨ 동사원형 ⑩ Don't ⑪ Let's ⑫ Let's not ⑬ and

B 문제로 개념 다지기

1 O 2 X, Be kind 3 X, Let's see 4 O 5 X, or 6 X, Let's not go 7 X, Yes, it is

Chapter 09 문장의 형태

POINT 01 1형식 / 2형식 문장 p.120

A 1 Alex는 노래를 잘한다., 1
2 Marie는 과학자가 되었다., 2
3 보성은 녹차로 유명하다., 2
4 그 가게에 있는 드레스는 예쁘다., 2
5 탁자 위에 있는 전화기가 울렸다., 1

B 1 The sun sets in the west.
2 They walked along the beach.
3 Chris is a high school student.
4 His jokes are very funny.
5 My parents live in Boston.

POINT 02 감각동사+형용사 p.121

A 1 happy 2 sick 3 strange 4 delicious 5 awful

B 1 felt 2 sounded 3 terrible 4 tastes 5 great

C 1 taste sour 2 looks kind 3 feels soft 4 smells sweet

POINT 03 3형식 / 4형식 문장 p.122

A 1 She writes novels for teenagers.
2 I teach children math.
3 I want a cheeseburger
4 I saw Kevin a few days ago.
5 They asked me a lot of questions.

B 1 She bought a new bag
2 Rachel made us a pie
3 tell me the way
4 He knows, famous people
5 gave me a teddy bear

POINT 04 4형식 문장 → 3형식 문장으로의 전환 I p.123

A 1 two glasses of water to us
2 an umbrella to David 3 the story to you
4 her room to them 5 his bicycle to me
6 a text message to me

B 1 showed my picture to 2 gave, to Linda
3 teaches history to 4 the comic book to me
5 your running shoes to him

POINT 05 4형식 문장 → 3형식 문장으로의 전환 II p.124

A 1 of 2 for 3 to you 4 for 5 to 6 to

B 1 some orange juice for you
2 a box of doughnuts for us
3 my dog a doghouse
4 Mom dinner

POINT 06 5형식 문장의 목적격 보어 I p.125

A 1 interesting 2 a great tennis player 3 clean 4 an angel 5 happy

B 1 I kept the window open.
2 The news made her angry.
3 He calls his daughter "sweetie."

C 1 made me sad 2 found, easy 3 keep you healthy

POINT 07 5형식 문장의 목적격 보어 II p.126

A 1 to take care of 2 to come 3 to stop

4 to call　5 to be

B 1 I didn't tell him to leave.
2 I want you to read this book.
3 He wants me to be confident.
4 I expected you to come back on Saturday.
5 He asked Helen to lend him some money.
6 The teacher allowed me to stay in the classroom.

POINT 08 5형식 문장의 목적격 보어 III p.127

A 1 eat　2 to be　3 shake[shaking]　4 stay
5 knock[knocking]

B 1 make people laugh　2 let me wear
3 watched, float[floating]　4 allowed him to sing
5 felt, touch[touching]　6 helped, to become
7 expect her to study

내신대비 TEST p.128

01 ③	02 ①	03 ②	04 ⑤	05 ②	06 ⑤
07 ④	08 ①	09 ②	10 ①	11 ④	12 ①
13 ③	14 ③	15 ④	16 ⑤	17 ⑤	
18 ④, ⑤	19 ①	20 ②			

서술형 따라잡기 p.131

01 (1) Sam the ball　(2) some bread for them
02 (1) saw Martin following me
(2) helped me (to) wash the dishes
03 (1) ordered Ned to stay silent
(2) heard her shouting[shout] at people
04 (1) smells delicious　(2) told us the big news
(3) made her happy
05 (1) some cookies for Jeremy
(2) a book to Sophia
06 (1) to read an English book
(2) clean the bathroom
(3) take care of her sister

01 동사 buy는 4형식 문장에서 3형식 문장으로 전환할 때 간접목적어 앞에 전치사 for를 쓴다.

02 5형식 문장에서 지각동사 watch는 목적격 보어로 동사원형이나 현재분사를 취한다.

03 5형식 문장에서 동사 expect는 목적격 보어로 to부정사를 취한다.

04 ⑤ 동사 make는 4형식 문장에서 3형식 문장으로 전환할 때 간접목적어 앞에 전치사 for를 쓴다. 나머지는 모두 간접목적어 앞에 전치사 to를 쓴다.

05 감각동사 look은 보어로 형용사를 취한다.

06 빈칸에는 감각동사와 같이 보어로 형용사를 취하는 동사가 와야 한다.

07 동사 make가 쓰인 5형식 문장에는 목적격 보어 자리에 명사(구)나 형용사(구)가 올 수 있으며, make가 사역동사로 쓰일 경우에는 목적격 보어 자리에 동사원형이 온다.

08 '~을 허락하다'의 의미를 지닌 사역동사 let이나 have는 목적격 보어로 동사원형을 쓰고, 동사 allow는 목적격 보어로 to부정사를 쓴다.

09 동사 keep은 목적어 your kids를 보충 설명해 주는 목적격 보어로 형용사를 취하며, 동사 want는 목적격 보어로 to부정사를 취한다.

10 2형식 문장의 보어 자리에는 형용사 cold가 와야 하며, 사역동사 let은 목적격 보어로 동사원형 use를 취한다.

11 지각동사 see는 목적격 보어로 동사원형이나 현재분사를 취한다. 동사 send는 4형식 문장에서 3형식 문장으로 전환할 때 간접목적어 앞에 전치사 to를 쓴다.

12 동사 lend는 4형식 문장에서 3형식 문장으로 전환할 때 간접목적어 앞에 전치사 to를 쓰며, 5형식 문장에서 동사 ask는 목적격 보어로 to부정사를 쓴다.

13 5형식 문장에서 make의 목적격 보어 자리에는 형용사(famous)가 올 수 있고, make가 사역동사로 쓰일 경우 목적격 보어 자리에는 동사원형(wear)이 온다.

14 ③ 동사 buy는 4형식 문장에서 3형식 문장으로 전환할 때 간접목적어 앞에 전치사 for를 쓴다.

15 ④는 〈수여동사+간접목적어+직접목적어〉 형태의 4형식 문장인 반면, 나머지는 모두 〈동사+목적어+목적격 보어〉 형태의 5형식 문장이다.

16 ⑤ 동사 teach는 〈teach+간접목적어(you)+직접목적어(Spanish)〉 혹은 〈teach+직접목적어(Spanish)+to+간접목적어(you)〉의 형태로 써야 한다.

17 ⑤ 지각동사 hear는 목적격 보어로 동사원형이나 현재분사를

취한다.

18 ④ 사역동사 have는 목적격 보어로 동사원형 make를 취한다.

⑤ 5형식 문장에서 동사 think는 목적격 보어로 형용사 useful을 취한다.

19 (A) 감각동사 taste는 보어로 형용사를 취한다.

(B) 동사 ask는 4형식 문장에서 3형식 문장으로 전환할 때 간접목적어 앞에 전치사 of를 쓴다.

(C) 지각동사 see는 목적격 보어로 동사원형이나 현재분사를 취한다.

20 (a) 2형식 문장에서 감각동사 look 뒤에 명사가 올 때는 전치사 like가 함께 쓰인다.

(c) 3형식 문장에서 동사 make는 〈make+직접목적어(a cookie)+for+간접목적어(my brothers)〉의 형태로 써야 한다.

(d) 3형식 문장에서 동사 give는 〈give+직접목적어(the English menu)+to+간접목적어(me)〉의 형태로 써야 한다.

서술형 따라잡기

01 (1) 〈pass+직접목적어+to+간접목적어〉의 3형식 문장은 〈pass+간접목적어+직접목적어〉로 바꾸어 쓸 수 있다.

(2) 동사 get은 4형식 문장에서 3형식 문장으로 전환할 때 간접목적어 앞에 전치사 for를 쓴다.

02 (1) 주어진 문장은 〈지각동사(see)+목적어+목적격 보어(현재분사)〉의 형태로 쓸 수 있다.

(2) 주어진 문장은 〈사역동사(help)+목적어+목적격 보어(동사원형/to부정사)〉의 형태로 쓸 수 있다.

03 (1) 동사 order는 목적격 보어로 to부정사를 취한다.

(2) 지각동사 hear는 목적격 보어로 동사원형이나 현재분사를 취한다.

04 (1) 감각동사 smell은 보어로 형용사를 취한다.

(2) 4형식 문장에서 동사 tell은 〈동사+간접목적어(us)+직접목적어(the big news)〉의 형태로 쓴다.

(3) 동사 make는 〈동사+목적어(her)+목적격 보어(happy)〉의 형태로 쓴다.

05 (1) 동사 buy는 4형식 문장에서 3형식 문장으로 전환할 때 간접목적어 앞에 전치사 for를 쓴다.

(2) 동사 lend는 4형식 문장에서 3형식 문장으로 전환할 때 간접목적어 앞에 전치사 to를 쓴다.

06 (1) 동사 want는 목적격 보어로 to부정사를 취한다.

(2) 사역동사 have는 목적격 보어로 동사원형을 취한다.

(3) 사역동사 make는 목적격 보어로 동사원형을 취한다.

SELF NOTE p.132

A 핵심 포인트 정리하기

① 형용사 ② 목적어 ③ 목적격 보어 ④ 전치사
⑤ to ⑥ for ⑦ of ⑧ to부정사
⑨ 원형부정사[동사원형]

B 문제로 개념 다지기

1 X, strange 2 O 3 X, to Fred 4 X, warm
5 O 6 O 7 X, carry

Chapter 10 to부정사와 동명사

POINT 01 to부정사의 명사적 용법 I – 주어 역할 p.134

A 1 It is dangerous to travel alone.
2 It is exciting to go on a picnic.
3 It is easy to ride the subway.
4 It is relaxing to jog along the river.

B 1 It is important to keep 2 To become a nurse is
3 It is, to open 4 To watch, is unnecessary
5 It was difficult to understand
6 It is amazing to see

POINT 02 to부정사의 명사적 용법 II – 보어/목적어 역할 p.135

A 1 그는 새 자전거를 살 필요가 있었다.
2 내 계획은 이번 달에 영어 소설 한 권을 읽는 것이다.
3 Ann은 어떤 것도 말하기를 거부했다.
4 그의 목표는 사진작가가 되는 것이다.

B 1 is to repair cars
2 don't want to be late
3 hope to come here again
4 is to play the cello
5 decided not to have a bagel
6 wanted to eat bibimbap

POINT 03 to부정사의 명사적 용법 III – 의문사+to부정사 p.136

A 1 what to do 2 when to go 3 how to drive

B 1 when to come 2 who(m) to invite
3 where to go 4 what to buy 5 how to use

C 1 Ted는 나에게 런던에서 어디에 머물지 말했다.
2 너는 기타를 어떻게 치는지 아니?

POINT 04 to부정사의 형용사적 용법 – 명사/대명사 수식 p.137

A 1 to eat 2 something to show 3 to love
4 nothing important to say 5 to talk 6 to do

B 1 doesn't have a suit to wear
2 anything interesting to do
3 time to say goodbye
4 have several things to buy
5 has some homework to finish
6 many places to visit
7 There is nothing to eat

POINT 05 to부정사의 부사적 용법 I – 목적 p.138

A 1 to swim with them 2 to learn Italian
3 to pack her things 4 to stay awake
5 to share his ideas 6 to tell you

B 1 그는 나를 도와주기 위해 일찍 왔다.
2 나는 새 휴대전화를 사기 위해 돈을 모았다.
3 그녀는 약간의 과일을 사기 위해 시장에 갔다.
4 나는 영어책을 읽기 위해 사전을 이용해야 했다.
5 이 동아리에 가입하시려면 이름을 써 주세요.

POINT 06 to부정사의 부사적 용법 II – 감정의 원인/결과 p.139

A 1 to read 2 to get 3 too, to run
4 enough to lift

B 1 sad to hear 2 too busy to have
3 grew up to be[become]
4 old enough to watch
5 happy to go on a date

POINT 07 동명사의 역할 I – 주어/보어 역할 p.140

A 1 Playing 2 taking 3 Reading 4 swimming
5 Meeting 6 Living 7 Driving

B 1 is taking pictures
2 Swimming in a deep river is
3 Writing English essays is difficult
4 Drinking soda is not good
5 Riding roller coasters scares
6 is getting up late in the morning

POINT 08 동명사의 역할 II – 목적어 역할 p.141

A 1 helping 2 driving 3 going 4 to make

B 1 working for a shoe company
2 missing the train

C 1 I'm good at singing
2 Don't stop challenging
3 We should avoid using
4 finished washing the dishes
5 She didn't mind turning off

내신대비 TEST p.142

01 ②	02 ④	03 ①	04 ②	05 ②	06 ④
07 ③	08 ⑤	09 ④	10 ④	11 ②	12 ①
13 ③	14 ①	15 ③	16 ③	17 ②	18 ⑤
19 ⑤	20 ②				

서술형 따라잡기 p.145

01 (1) too expensive to buy
(2) It is, to climb mountains

02 (1) playing the violin
(2) to ride a bike[bicycle]

03 have anything to eat, to buy some snacks

04 (1) He was surprised to hear the noise.
(2) Do you mind opening the window?

05 (1) old enough to go hiking
(2) too young to take a diving class

06 (1) what to do
(2) someone helpful to guide me

01 to부정사가 주어 역할을 하는 경우, 주어 자리에 가주어 It을 쓰고 to부정사를 문장 뒤로 보낼 수 있다.

02 동사 avoid는 동명사를 목적어로 취한다.

03 '어떻게 만드는지'의 의미로 how to make를 써야 한다.

04 〈보기〉와 ②의 동명사는 동사의 목적어로 쓰였다. ①의 동명사는 주어, ③, ④는 보어, ⑤는 전치사의 목적어로 쓰였다.

05 동사 plan은 to부정사를 목적어로 취하고, to부정사가 주어 역할을 하는 경우에는 주어 자리에 가주어 It을 쓰고 to부정사를 문장 뒤로 보낸다.

06 〈too+형용사/부사+to부정사〉는 '너무 ~하여 …할 수 없다'라는 의미이다.

07 동사 want는 to부정사를 목적어로, give up은 동명사를 목적어로 취한다.

08 B가 남산 공원에 가는 방법을 설명하고 있으므로 '어떻게 ~할지'의 〈how+to부정사〉가 와야 한다.

09 〈-thing으로 끝나는 대명사+형용사+to부정사〉의 어순으로 쓴다.

10 ④ '…할 만큼 충분히 ~하다'라는 의미로 〈형용사/부사+enough+to부정사〉의 형태가 와야 한다.

11 동사 enjoy는 동명사를 목적어로 취한다.

12 동사 refuse는 to부정사를 목적어로 취한다.

13 ③은 부사적 용법(결과)의 to부정사이고, 나머지는 모두 형용사적 용법이다.

14 ①은 명사적 용법(목적어)의 to부정사이고, 나머지는 모두 부사적 용법이다.

15 동사 quit은 동명사를 목적어로 취한다.

16 ③ '자라서 (결과적으로) ~이 되다'라는 의미로 부사적 용법(결과)의 to부정사가 와야 한다.

17 ② 지각동사는 to부정사를 목적격 보어로 취할 수 없다.

18 주어진 말을 배열하면 'I can't decide what to cook for dinner.'이므로 네 번째에 오는 단어는 what이다.

19 (A) 동사 mind는 동명사를 목적어로 취한다.
(B) 동명사와 to부정사 모두 '~하는 것'이라는 의미로 문장에서 주어로 쓰일 수 있다.
(C) to부정사가 주어 역할을 하는 경우, 주어 자리에 가주어 It을 쓰고 to부정사를 문장 뒤로 보낼 수 있다.

20 (b) 진주어 to lose weight를 대신하여 주어 자리에 가주어 It이 와야 한다.
(d) 전치사 in의 목적어로 동명사가 와야 한다.

서술형 따라잡기

01 (1) '너무 ~하여 …할 수 없다'라는 의미는 〈too+형용사/부사+to부정사〉의 형태로 쓴다.
(2) 주어로 쓰인 동명사구는 to부정사구로 바꾸어 쓸 수 있다. 이때 주어 자리에 가주어 It을 쓰고 진주어인 to부정사구는 문장 뒤로 보낼 수 있다.

02 (1) 전치사 at 뒤에는 목적어 역할을 하는 동명사가 와야 한다.
(2) 주어로 쓰인 to부정사 대신 가주어 It을 주어 자리에 쓰고, 진주어는 문장 뒤로 보낼 수 있다.

03 to부정사가 -thing으로 끝나는 대명사를 수식할 경우에는 대명사 뒤에 위치한다. to부정사로 '~하려'라는 의미의 목적을 나타낼 수 있다.

04 (1) 형용사(surprised) 뒤에 감정의 원인을 나타내는 부사적 용법의 to부정사가 와야 한다.
(2) 동사 mind는 동명사를 목적어로 취한다.

05 (1) Emma는 산을 등반하기에 충분히 나이가 들었음을 〈형용사/부사+enough+to부정사〉를 이용해 나타낸다.
(2) Andy는 너무 어려서 다이빙 수업을 들을 수 없음을 〈too+형용사/부사+to부정사〉를 이용해 나타낸다.

06 (1) '무엇을 할지'는 what to do로 나타낸다.
(2) 〈-one으로 끝나는 대명사+형용사+to부정사〉의 어순으로 써야 한다.

SELF NOTE

p.146

A 핵심 포인트 정리하기
① to, 동사원형 ② 목적어 ③ 형용사 ④ 목적
⑤ too+형용사/부사+to부정사 ⑥ 동사원형, -ing

B 문제로 개념 다지기
1 X, to introduce 2 X, to meet 3 X, asking
4 O 5 X, deep enough to swim 6 X, seeing
7 X, to dance

Chapter 11 접속사

POINT 01 등위 접속사 and p.148

A 1 gentle and smart
2 Frank and Sarah
3 and long, blond hair

B 1 beautiful 2 ate 3 (to) play 4 (will) sing

C 1 We read books and took pictures.
2 He can speak both Chinese and Japanese.
3 She saved money to buy a laptop and to travel to India.

POINT 02 등위 접속사 but p.149

A 1 but 2 and 3 but

B 1 but I didn't get a good seat
2 but he is not popular
3 but I don't like it

C 1 She was sad, but she didn't cry.
2 I failed the test, but I'll try again.
3 Susan was nice to Mike, but she didn't like him.

POINT 03 등위 접속사 or p.150

A 1 or (with) Jack
2 but Natalie didn't (go on a picnic)
3 and (to) Namdaemun Market

B 1 or 2 either, or 3 or

C 1 Is today the 25th or the 26th?
2 That girl's name is either Justine or Julia.
3 He is going to make money or go on a trip.

POINT 04 등위 접속사 so p.151

A 1 so I added water 2 so he opened the window
3 so I can introduce them

B 1 and 2 but 3 so 4 but 5 or

C 1 I stayed up late last night, so I feel tired now.
2 I called her name, but she didn't look at me.
3 I ordered ice cream and cheesecake.
4 You can make an exchange or get a refund.

POINT 05 종속 접속사 when / while p.152

A 1 When I get there, I'll call you. [I'll call you when I get there.]
2 When Alice heard a strange sound, she felt scared. [Alice felt scared when she heard a strange sound.]
3 When David crossed the street, he saw the accident. [David saw the accident when he crossed the street.]

B 1 when I was 2 While we were eating dinner
3 When I arrived 4 wears, when she reads
5 While he is walking

POINT 06 종속 접속사 before / after p.153

A 1 before 2 after 3 When 4 before 5 While

B 1 arrived before the sun set
2 fell asleep after he had dinner
3 I borrow the book after you read it
4 should go to the dentist before it is too late
5 gave me his number when I met him yesterday

POINT 07 종속 접속사 because / if p.154

A 1 before 2 Because 3 after 4 If

B 1 because, wasn't interesting 2 if you leave
3 because he didn't feel 4 If you are hungry
5 If I get 6 because I don't have

POINT 08 종속 접속사 that p.155

A 1 It is surprising that you like Tony.
2 It is a problem that he often loses things.
3 It is a secret that I broke the window.
4 It is amazing that she became a comedian.
5 It is true that she never eats nuts.

B 1 That they stole something
2 That I didn't invite her
3 that the song is good
4 that I didn't bring my cell phone
5 that she is a basketball player

내신대비 TEST p.156

01 ① 02 ⑤ 03 ② 04 ④ 05 ② 06 ④
07 ③ 08 ③ 09 ⑤ 10 ③ 11 ④ 12 ⑤
13 ② 14 ④ 15 ⑤ 16 ④ 17 ⑤ 18 ③
19 ④ 20 ④

서술형 따라잡기 p.159

01 (1) if you feel sick (2) that our team will win
02 (1) stayed in bed because
(2) had lunch before I came here
03 (1) but you didn't reply
(2) or I'll buy some at the bakery
(3) and I won the gold medal
04 (1) before (2) either, or (3) after
05 (1) If she is late, I will[I'll] be angry.
(2) He has both a book and a camera.
06 or → and / will come → comes

01 의미상 '~와'의 의미인 등위 접속사 and가 와야 한다.

02 '만약 ~하다면'의 의미인 조건을 나타내는 종속 접속사 If가 와야 한다.

03 앞 문장의 내용과 반대되는 내용을 이어주는 등위 접속사 but이 와야 한다.

04 시간의 순서상 불을 지핀 것이 텐트를 친 후의 일이므로 '~한 후에'의 의미인 종속 접속사 After가 와야 한다.

05 ② '~할 때'의 의미인 종속 접속사 when이 와야 한다.

06 '~한 후에'의 의미인 종속 접속사 after를 쓰고, 때의 접속사가 이끄는 부사절에서는 미래시제 대신 현재시제를 쓴다.

07 ③ 'A이거나 B'라는 의미로 ⟨either A or B⟩를 쓴다.

08 첫 번째 빈칸에는 '~ 때문에'의 의미인 이유를 나타내는 종속 접속사 Because가, 두 번째 빈칸에는 '만약 ~하다면'의 의미인 조건을 나타내는 종속 접속사 If가 와야 한다.

09 첫 번째 빈칸에는 목적어절을 이끄는 종속 접속사 that이, 두 번째 빈칸에는 '또는'의 의미인 등위 접속사 or가 와야 한다.

10 첫 번째 빈칸에는 '~한 후에'의 의미인 종속 접속사 after가, 두 번째 빈칸에는 '그리고'의 의미인 등위 접속사 and가 와야 한다.

11 ④에는 시간의 순서상 '~한 후에'의 의미인 종속 접속사 after가 오고, 나머지는 명사절을 이끄는 접속사 that이 와야 한다.

12 ⑤ Jason과 Ann 둘 다를 초대하겠냐는 질문에, Yes라고 말하며 Jason만 초대하겠다고 답하는 것은 어색하다.

13 ① 'A와 B 둘 다'라는 의미로 ⟨both A and B⟩가 와야 한다.
③ 문맥상 '~하기 전에'라는 의미인 종속 접속사 before가 와야 한다.
④ 'A이거나 B'라는 의미로 ⟨either A or B⟩를 쓴다.
⑤ '또는'의 의미인 등위 접속사 or가 와야 한다.

14 첫 번째 빈칸에는 '~할 때'의 의미인 종속 접속사 When이, 두 번째 빈칸에는 '언제'를 나타내는 의문사 When이 와야 한다.

15 첫 번째 빈칸에는 가주어 It에 대한 진주어인 명사절을 이끄는 접속사 that이, 두 번째 빈칸에는 문장의 목적어절을 이끄는 접속사 that이 와야 한다.

16 ④ 'A이거나 B'라는 의미로 ⟨either A or B⟩를 쓰거나, 'A와 B 둘 다'라는 의미로 ⟨both A and B⟩를 쓴다.

17 ⑤ and는 문법적으로 대등한 단어, 구, 절을 연결하는 등위 접속사이므로 having을 have의 과거시제인 had로 고쳐야 한다.

18 (A) 가주어 It에 대한 진주어인 명사절을 이끄는 접속사 that이 와야 한다.
(B) 뒤에 코트를 입어야 하는 이유가 이어지고 있으므로 종속 접속사 because가 와야 한다.
(C) 등위 접속사 or는 문법적으로 대등한 구를 연결하므로 동사원형 watch가 와야 한다.

19 (b) 접속사 if가 이끄는 조건의 부사절에서는 미래시제 대신 현재시제를 쓴다.
(c) 때의 부사절에서는 미래시제 대신 현재시제를 쓴다.
(d) 뒤에 강에서 수영을 하지 않은 이유가 이어지고 있으므로 종속 접속사 because가 와야 한다.

20 ④의 that은 가주어 It에 대한 진주어인 명사절을 이끄는 접속사이므로 생략할 수 없는 반면, ①, ②, ③, ⑤의 that은 목적어 역할을 하는 명사절을 이끄는 접속사이므로 생략이 가능하다.

서술형 따라잡기

01 (1) '만약 ~하다면'의 의미로 종속 접속사 if를 쓴다.
(2) 목적어 역할을 하는 명사절을 이끄는 접속사 that을 이용한다.

02 (1) 이유를 나타내는 종속 접속사 because가 I had a cold 앞에 와서 '감기에 걸렸기 때문에 침대에 누워있었다.'라는 의미

가 되도록 배열한다.

(2) '나는 여기에 오기 전에 점심을 먹었다.'라는 의미가 되어야 하므로 종속 접속사 before가 I came here 앞에 오도록 배열한다.

03 (1) 문자 메시지를 보냈다는 내용은 답변을 받지 못했다는 내용과 어울리며, 두 문장은 서로 반대되는 내용이므로 등위 접속사 but으로 연결한다.

(2) 쿠키를 구울 것이라는 내용은 빵집에서 살 것이라는 내용과 어울리며, 둘 중 하나를 선택하는 경우이므로 등위 접속사 or로 연결한다.

(3) 마라톤을 뛰었다는 내용과 금메달을 땄다는 내용이 서로 어울리며, 두 문장은 '그리고'라는 뜻의 등위 접속사 and를 이용해 연결한다.

04 (1) 발레 수업은 개를 산책시키기 전에 받으므로 종속 접속사 before를 쓴다.

(2) 3시부터는 바이올린을 연습하거나 책을 읽으므로 〈either A or B〉를 써야 한다.

(3) TV 시청 후에 일기를 쓰므로 종속 접속사 after를 쓴다.

05 (1) 조건을 나타내는 종속 접속사 If를 이용한다. If가 이끄는 조건절에서는 현재시제가 미래시제를 대신한다.

(2) 'A와 B 둘 다'의 의미일 때는 〈both A and B〉를 쓴다.

06 조깅을 하러 갔다는 내용과 카페에서 간식을 먹었다는 내용을 '그리고'라는 뜻의 등위 접속사 and로 연결해야 한다. If가 이끄는 조건절에서는 미래시제 대신 현재시제를 쓰므로 will come을 comes로 고쳐야 한다.

SELF NOTE p.160

A 핵심 포인트 정리하기

① but ② both A and B ③ either A or B
④ when ⑤ ~하기 전에 ⑥ if ⑦ It

B 문제로 개념 다지기

1 X, watched 2 X, or 3 X, (to) drink 4 X, that
5 O 6 O 7 X, snows

Chapter 12 형용사와 부사

POINT 01 형용사의 역할 p.162

A 1 nice 2 delicious 3 a good 4 beautiful
5 careful 6 nothing new
7 something interesting 8 dangerous

B 1 I left the window open.
2 She found this puzzle easy.
3 His mistake made me angry.
4 I want to be someone important.
5 Did you buy everything necessary for dinner?

POINT 02 부사의 역할 / 형태 I p.163

A 1 specially 2 sadly 3 differently 4 kindly
5 usually 6 loudly 7 nicely 8 necessarily
9 quietly 10 easily 11 wisely 12 carefully
13 strongly 14 terribly 15 clearly
16 heavily 17 importantly 18 angrily

B 1 kind 2 strangely 3 slowly 4 easily
5 happily 6 quietly 7 simple 8 great
9 Luckily 10 safe

POINT 03 부사의 형태 II p.164

A 1 high 2 late 3 nearly[almost] 4 hardly
5 fast

B 1 기차가 약간 늦게 도착했다.
2 만약 당신이 일찍 끝내면 집에 가도 좋아요.
3 시험에 어려운 문제들이 몇 개 있었다.
4 그는 19세기 초에 태어났다.
5 나는 정말 열심히 일해서 성공하게 되었다.

POINT 04 빈도부사 p.165

A 1 ② 2 ① 3 ①

B 1 always 2 often 3 sometimes
4 never 5 usually

C 1 seldom goes to school
2 should always be careful
3 often calls his girlfriend

POINT 05 원급 비교 p.166

A 1 as comfortable as 2 as light as
3 not as[so] expensive as 4 as much as
5 as interesting as 6 not as[so] hot as

B 1 as tall as 2 not as[so] thick as 3 as wide as

POINT 06 비교급과 최상급 만드는 방법 p.167

A 1 heavier, heaviest
2 more important, most important
3 louder, loudest
4 more careful, most careful
5 busier, busiest
6 smaller, smallest
7 worse, worst
8 prettier, prettiest
9 cuter, cutest
10 more terrible, most terrible

B 1 better 2 hottest 3 more 4 easier
5 most expensive 6 fastest

POINT 07 비교급 p.168

A 1 thinner than 2 bigger than 3 faster than
4 more difficult than 5 prettier than
6 younger than 7 more important than
8 more exciting than 9 cheaper than
10 better than

B 1 more slowly 2 earlier than
3 more money than 4 much heavier than
5 more serious than
6 a lot more expensive than

POINT 08 최상급 p.169

A 1 the best 2 the happiest 3 the hottest
4 the longest 5 the most comfortable
6 the tallest 7 the youngest 8 the highest
9 the most dangerous

B 1 the worst mistake 2 the most famous
3 the most impressive 4 the most popular
5 the richest people 6 one of the oldest houses

내신대비 TEST p.170

01 ③ 02 ① 03 ② 04 ④ 05 ④ 06 ⑤
07 ② 08 ② 09 ⑤ 10 ③ 11 ② 12 ⑤
13 ④ 14 ③ 15 ② 16 ① 17 ③ 18 ④
19 ③ 20 ①

서술형 따라잡기 p.173

01 (1) shorter than (2) the tallest
02 (1) usually plays the guitar
(2) sometimes takes pictures
(3) often reads books
03 (1) bigger than (2) the most diligent
04 (1) I will never forget you.
(2) She is one of the smartest people
05 (1) older than (2) as fast as (3) the lightest
06 hardly, thinner, the worst

01 감각동사 look 뒤에는 보어로 형용사가 온다. ③ lovely는 '사랑스러운'을 뜻하는 형용사이고, 나머지는 모두 부사이다.

02 원급 비교는 〈as+형용사/부사의 원급+as〉의 형태로 쓴다.

03 '~보다 더 …한'의 의미인 〈비교급+than〉이 와야 한다. 형용사 cold의 비교급은 colder이다.

04 ④는 명사와 형용사의 관계이고, 나머지는 모두 형용사와 부사의 관계이다.

05 비교급을 강조하는 부사는 much, even, still, a lot, far 등이다. very는 비교급을 강조할 수 없다.

06 원급 비교는 〈as+형용사/부사의 원급+as〉의 형태로 쓴다.

07 앞에 more가 있으므로 비교급 wiser는 빈칸에 쓸 수 없다.

08 ② ugly의 비교급은 uglier, 최상급은 ugliest이다.

09 첫 번째 빈칸 앞에 the가 쓰인 것으로 보아 최상급 largest가, 두 번째 빈칸 뒤에 than이 쓰인 것으로 보아 비교급 longer가 와야 한다.

10 첫 번째 빈칸에서 -thing으로 끝나는 대명사의 경우 형용사가 뒤에서 수식하므로 something hot이 오고, 두 번째 빈칸에는 found의 목적격 보어로 형용사를 써야 하므로 impressive가 와야 한다.

11 선택 의문문에서 둘 중 어느 것이 더 좋은지를 묻고 답하고 있으므로 비교급 better가 와야 한다.

12 '가장 ~한 … 중의 하나'의 의미는 ⟨one of the+최상급+복수명사⟩를 쓴다.

13 ④ '~만큼 …한'이라는 의미의 ⟨as+형용사/부사의 원급+as⟩의 as가 와야 한다. 나머지는 '~보다 더 …한'이라는 의미인 ⟨비교급+than⟩의 than이 와야 한다.

14 '나는 Joe만큼 독일어를 잘 말하지 못한다.'라는 의미는 'Joe가 나보다 독일어를 더 잘 말한다.'라는 의미이므로 ③이 같은 의미의 문장이다.

15 ② 목적격 보어 자리에는 형용사 happy가 와야 한다.

16 ① ⟨as+형용사/부사의 원급+as⟩의 구문이므로 less가 아닌 원급 little이 와야 한다.

17 ③ hardly는 '거의 ~않다'라는 의미의 부사이다.

18 ④ '늦은'이라는 의미로, 보어로 쓰일 수 있는 형용사가 와야 한다. lately는 '최근에'라는 의미의 부사이다.

19 (A) 목적격 보어 자리에는 형용사 horrible이 와야 한다.
(B) '거의'라는 의미의 부사가 와야 한다.
(C) '잘'이라는 의미의 부사가 와야 한다.

20 (c) very는 비교급을 강조할 수 없다.
(e) 원급 비교는 ⟨as+형용사/부사의 원급+as⟩의 형태로 쓴다.

서술형 따라잡기

01 (1) Jenny가 Phillip보다 키가 작으므로, 형용사 short를 이용해 ⟨비교급+than⟩의 형태로 쓴다.
(2) Jack이 세 학생 중에서 가장 키가 크므로, 형용사 tall을 이용해 ⟨the+최상급⟩의 형태로 쓴다.

02 (1) 일주일 중 기타를 6일 연주하므로 plays the guitar를 usually와 함께 쓴다. 빈도부사는 일반동사 앞에 쓴다.
(2) 일주일 중 사진을 하루 찍으므로 takes pictures를 sometimes와 함께 쓴다.
(3) 일주일 중 책을 4일 읽으므로 reads books를 often과 함께 쓴다.

03 (1) '서울은 뉴욕만큼 크지 않다.'라는 의미는 '뉴욕이 서울보다 더 크다'라는 의미이므로 비교급인 bigger than이 와야 한다.
(2) 'Tony가 반의 다른 모든 소년들보다 더 부지런하다.'라는 의미는 'Tony가 반에서 가장 부지런한 소년이다.'라는 의미이므로 최상급 표현인 the most diligent가 와야 한다.

04 (1) 빈도부사 never는 조동사 뒤, 일반동사 앞에 온다.
(2) '가장 ~한 … 중의 하나'는 ⟨one of the+최상급+복수명사⟩로 쓴다.

05 (1) Luis가 Becky보다 나이가 더 많으므로 비교급인 older than을 쓴다.
(2) Thomas와 Max는 속도에서 같은 점수를 받았으므로 원급 비교인 as fast as를 쓴다.
(3) Becky는 네 마리의 개들 중에서 무게가 가장 적게 나가므로 최상급인 the lightest를 쓴다.

06 첫 번째 빈칸에는 문맥상 '거의 ~않다'라는 의미의 부사 hardly가 적절하다. 두 번째 빈칸에는 뒤의 than으로 보아 전보다 '훨씬 말라 보였다'라는 의미가 되어야 하므로 thin의 비교급을 쓴다. 세 번째 빈칸에는 아팠던 이번 여름이 인생에서 '최악의' 방학 중 하나였다는 말이 들어가는 것이 자연스러우므로 bad의 최상급인 the worst를 쓴다.

SELF NOTE p.174

A 핵심 포인트 정리하기
① 형용사+ly ② 뒤 ③ 앞 ④ sometimes ⑤ often ⑥ as ⑦ than ⑧ 복수명사

B 문제로 개념 다지기
1 X, a nice apartment 2 X, so fast 3 O
4 X, bigger 5 X, is always
6 X, one of the oldest members
7 X, the cutest 8 X, as polite as

Chapter 13 전치사

POINT 01 시간의 전치사 in/on/at p.176

A 1 at 2 in 3 at 4 in 5 on 6 on
B 1 in 2 in 3 at 4 on 5 at 6 on
C 1 at that time 2 in the evening
3 on Saturday afternoon

POINT 02 시간의 전치사 around/before/after/for/during/until/by p.177

A 1 around 2 until 3 after 4 during 5 by 6 for

B 1 before shopping 2 for two hours
3 around two 4 by next Wednesday

POINT 03 장소의 전치사 in/on/at p.178

A 1 at[in] 2 on 3 in 4 on 5 in 6 on

B 1 on 2 at 3 in 4 in 5 on 6 at

C 1 saw him at 2 on the floor 3 in the world

POINT 04 장소의 전치사 near/over/under/to/behind p.179

A 1 under 2 over 3 to 4 behind 5 near 6 to

B 1 There is a shop[store] near 2 over the door
3 were flying over 4 under the umbrella

POINT 05 구 전치사 in front of/next to/across from p.180

A 1 in front of 2 next to 3 across from

B 1 next to my bag 2 across from 3 in front of

C 1 Can I sit next to the window?
2 He left a box in front of my door.
3 There is a library across from the museum.

POINT 06 구 전치사 between A and B / from A to B p.181

A 1 from, to 2 between, and 3 from, to
4 between, and 5 from, to 6 from, to

B 1 between 6 p.m. and 7 p.m.
2 from March to May 3 between one and ten
4 between you and me
5 from the airport to the city

내신대비 TEST p.182

01 ③	02 ⑤	03 ①	04 ③	05 ④	06 ③
07 ④	08 ④	09 ②	10 ①	11 ⑤	12 ④
13 ①	14 ③	15 ②	16 ②	17 ①	18 ⑤
19 ③	20 ①, ③, ④				

서술형 따라잡기 p.185

01 (1) around (2) across from (3) during
02 Can you finish reading the book by
03 (1) The babies weigh between 3 kg and 5 kg.
(2) There is a toy shop on the corner.
04 (1) between, and (2) in front of
05 (1) at (2) for two hours (3) from, to
06 at May 21 → on May 21 / during → for /
in front in → in front of

01 오전(morning)과 함께 쓰는 전치사 in이 와야 한다.

02 크리스마스 날이라는 특정한 날을 나타내므로 전치사 on이 와야 한다.

03 night라는 하루의 때를 나타내므로 전치사 at이 와야 한다.

04 첫 번째 문장은 '~ 앞에'를 뜻하는 구 전치사 in front of가, 두 번째 문장은 'A부터 B까지'를 뜻하는 구 전치사 from A to B가 와야 한다.

05 첫 번째 빈칸에는 '~ 전에'를 뜻하는 전치사 before가, 두 번째 빈칸에는 비교적 넓은 장소를 나타낼 때 쓰는 전치사 in이 와야 한다.

06 ③의 빈칸에는 '~에서'라는 의미로 비교적 좁은 장소를 나타내는 전치사 at이, 나머지는 모두 접촉한 상태를 나타내는 전치사 on이 와야 한다.

07 ④의 빈칸에는 near(~ 근처에), in front of(~ 앞에), behind(~ 뒤에) 등 장소를 나타내는 전치사를 쓸 수 있는 반면, 나머지에는 '~로(목적지)'를 뜻하는 전치사 to가 와야 한다.

08 ④의 to는 동사 decide의 목적어로 쓰인 to부정사인 반면, 나머지는 모두 전치사 to로 쓰였다.

09 첫 번째 빈칸에는 특정한 날을 나타내는 전치사 on이, 두 번째 빈칸에는 '책꽂이 위에'로 장소를 나타내는 전치사 on이 와야 한다.

10 첫 번째 빈칸에는 '~로'로 방향을 나타내는 전치사 to가, 두 번째 빈칸에는 '~ 옆에'를 의미하는 구 전치사 next to의 to가 와야 한다.

11 ⑤의 전치사 by는 '~까지는'이라는 의미로 동작의 완료를 나타내는 반면, after는 '~ 후에'라는 의미의 전치사이다.

12 '~ 옆에'를 의미하는 전치사 next to가 와야 한다.

13 '~까지(지속)'를 의미하는 전치사 until이 와야 한다.

14 ③ because는 이유를 나타내는 접속사로 문장이 아닌 (대)명사(구) 앞에 올 수 없다.

15 ② 요일 앞에는 전치사 on을 쓴다.

16 ② beside는 그 자체가 '~ 옆에'를 의미하는 전치사이므로 to와 함께 쓸 수 없다. 따라서 beside를 next로 고쳐야 한다.

17 ① '~ 동안'이라는 의미로 숫자를 포함하는 구체적인 기간 앞에는 for를 써야 한다.

18 ① '~ 앞에'를 의미하는 구 전치사 in front of를 써야 한다.
② '~ 무렵에'를 의미하는 전치사 around를 써야 한다.
③ '~ 맞은편에'를 의미하는 구 전치사 across from을 써야 한다.
④ 'A와 B 사이에'를 의미하는 구 전치사 between A and B를 써야 한다.

19 (A) '~ 위에'라는 의미로 표면에 접촉해 있지 않은 상태를 나타내는 전치사 over를 쓴다.
(B) 'A부터 B까지'를 의미하는 구 전치사 from A to B를 쓴다.
(C) '~에서'라는 의미로 한 지점을 나타내는 전치사 at을 쓴다.

20 ② New York과 같은 도시명 앞에는 전치사 in을 쓴다.
⑤ '~ 동안'이라는 의미로 숫자를 포함하는 구체적인 기간 앞에는 전치사 for를 쓴다.

서술형 따라잡기

01 (1) '~ 무렵에'를 의미하는 전치사 around를 쓴다.
(2) '~ 맞은편에'를 의미하는 구 전치사 across from을 쓴다.
(3) '~ 동안'이라는 의미로 특정한 기간을 나타내는 명사(구) 앞에는 전치사 during을 쓴다.

02 '~까지는 (완료)'의 의미로 전치사 by를 쓴다.

03 (1) 'A와 B 사이에'라는 의미로 구 전치사 between A and B를 쓴다.
(2) 표면에 접촉해 있는 상태를 나타내는 전치사 on을 쓴다.

04 (1) 'A와 B 사이에'라는 의미로 구 전치사 between A and B를 쓴다.
(2) '~ 앞에'라는 의미로 구 전치사 in front of를 쓴다.

05 (1) Dan은 '정오에' 도서관에 갈 예정이므로 구체적인 시각을 나타내는 전치사 at을 쓴다.
(2) Dan은 1시부터 3시까지 '두 시간 동안' 테니스를 칠 예정이므로 전치사 for를 쓴다.
(3) Dan은 '4시부터 6시까지' 친구들과 있을 예정이므로 구 전치사 from A to B를 쓴다.

06 특정한 날짜 앞에는 전치사 on을, '~ 동안'이라는 의미로 숫자를 포함하는 구체적인 기간을 나타낼 때는 전치사 for를 쓴다. '학교 앞에서'라는 의미로는 구 전치사 in front of를 써야 한다.

SELF NOTE

p.186

A 핵심 포인트 정리하기

① at ② around ③ until ④ by ⑤ on ⑥ over
⑦ across from ⑧ between A and B

B 문제로 개념 다지기

1 X, for 2 X, in 3 X, by 4 O 5 O
6 X, in front of
7 X, between July and September

총괄평가 1회

01 ④ 02 ③ 03 ④ 04 ⑤ 05 in front of 06 ③ 07 ⑤ 08 three pairs of socks 09 ⑤ 10 ④ 11 ① 12 ② 13 She does not[doesn't] know Henry's parents. 14 Were they watching the fireworks in the park? 15 Did he have a good time at the concert? 16 ③ 17 ② 18 I will never visit 19 we are not going to go 20 ③ 21 ② 22 ④ 23 being late 24 How tall is, Where does, live 25 ②, ⑤ 26 eating, to become, eating, to drink

01 문장의 주어는 he이고, 시제는 과거이며 부정의 대답이므로 wasn't가 와야 한다.

02 이어지는 답변에서 회사에 가는 '방법'을 말하고 있으므로 '어떻게'의 뜻으로 방법을 물어볼 때 쓰는 How가 와야 한다.

03 last weekend로 보아 과거의 일이므로 catch의 과거형 caught가 와야 한다.

04 '~만큼 …하지 않은[않게]'는 〈not as[so]+형용사/부사의 원급+as〉를 써서 나타내므로 빈칸에는 as가 와야 한다.

05 내가 Stephen의 뒤에 서 있다는 것은, Stephen이 내 앞에 서 있다는 것이므로 in front of를 쓴다.

06 '~임이 틀림없다'라는 강한 추측을 나타내는 조동사 must가 와야 한다.

07 일반동사의 과거형 긍정문이 사용된 문장의 부가의문문이므로 didn't you가 알맞다.

08 '양말 한 켤레'는 a pair of socks이므로 '양말 세 켤레'는 pair를 복수로 하여 three pairs of socks로 쓴다.

09 능력이나 가능을 나타내는 조동사 can은 be able to로 바꾸어 쓸 수 있다. 주어가 you이고 의문문이므로 Are you able to가 알맞다.

10 〈보기〉와 ④는 각각 앞의 대명사 anything과 명사 a pen을 수식하는 형용사적 용법의 to부정사이다. ①은 목적을 나타내는 부사적 용법, ②는 진주어로 쓰인 명사적 용법, ③은 목적어로 쓰인 명사적 용법, ⑤는 감정의 원인을 나타내는 부사적 용법으로 쓰인 to부정사이다.

11 첫 번째 빈칸에는 〈both A and B(A와 B 둘 다)〉의 and가 와야 하고, 두 번째 빈칸에는 '…해라, 그러면 ~할 것이다'라는 의미를 갖는 〈명령문+and ~〉의 and가 와야 한다.

12 ② foot의 복수형은 feet이다.

13 주어가 3인칭 단수이고 현재시제일 때 부정문은 〈does not [doesn't]+동사원형〉으로 나타낸다.

14 과거진행형의 의문문은 〈Was[Were]+주어+v-ing ~?〉로 나타낸다.

15 일반동사의 과거형 의문문은 〈Did+주어+동사원형 ~?〉으로 나타낸다.

16 감탄문은 〈What+a/an+형용사+명사(+주어+동사)!〉 또는 〈How+형용사/부사(+주어+동사)!〉로 나타낸다.

17 ② make는 목적격 보어로 동사원형을 취하므로 cry를 써야 한다.

18 빈도부사 never는 조동사 will 뒤, 일반동사 visit 앞에 쓴다.

19 '~할 예정이다'라는 뜻의 〈be going to+동사원형〉의 부정은 〈be동사+not+going to+동사원형〉의 순으로 쓴다.

20 finish는 동명사를 목적어로 취하는 동사이다.

21 첫 번째 빈칸에는 뒤에 복수형 명사가 있으므로 지시형용사 These 또는 Those가 와야 하고, 두 번째 빈칸에는 앞에 나온 apples와 같은 종류의 불특정한 것을 가리키는 부정대명사 ones가 와야 한다.

22 첫 번째 빈칸에는 뒤에 than이 있으므로 easy의 비교급인 easier가 와야 하고, 두 번째 빈칸에는 easy의 최상급인 the easiest가 와야 한다.

23 전치사 about 뒤에 동사가 올 때는 동명사 형태로 와야 하므로 being late를 쓴다.

24 키를 물을 때는 〈How tall+be동사+주어?〉를 쓴다. 두 번째 질문에서는 장소를 나타내는 의문사 where를 써서 사는 곳을 묻는다. 주어가 3인칭 단수이고 일반동사 현재형의 의문문이므로 〈Where+does+주어+동사원형?〉의 어순으로 쓴다.

25 ② 'A부터 B까지'의 의미로 구 전치사 from A to B를 쓴다. ⑤ '가장 ~한 …중의 하나'는 〈one of the+최상급+복수명사〉로 countries가 되어야 한다.

26 enjoy는 동명사를 목적어로 취하는 동사이므로 뒤에 eating을 쓴다. decide는 to부정사를 목적어로 취하는 동사이므로 뒤에 to become을 쓴다. consider는 동명사를 목적어로 취하는 동사이므로 뒤에 eating을 쓴다. plan은 to부정사를 목적어로 취하는 동사이므로 뒤에 to drink를 쓴다.

총괄평가 2회

01 ⑤ 02 ② 03 ③ 04 ④ 05 the 06 X
07 a 08 ⑤ 09 ③ 10 cooks, washes
11 She is going to pick me up at the airport.
12 Paul has to finish his homework by 6:00.
13 ④ 14 ① 15 Who sent 16 ②
17 What time, How often 18 ③ 19 ③
20 happily → happy 21 ② 22 ③ 23 ②
24 People don't like her because she is rude. [Because she is rude, people don't like her.]
25 ① 26 ① 27 (1) heavier than (2) lighter than (3) the heaviest

01 앞에 나온 sneakers와 같은 종류의 불특정한 것을 가리키는 부정대명사 ones가 와야 한다.

02 조건을 나타내는 부사절에서는 현재시제로 미래를 나타내고 주어가 3인칭 단수이므로 comes가 와야 한다.

03 문장의 진주어가 되는 명사절을 이끄는 접속사 that이 와야 한다. 여기서 It은 가주어이다.

04 3형식 문장에서 간접목적어(me) 앞에 전치사 to를 쓸 수 있는 동사는 give이다. 나머지 동사는 모두 간접목적어 앞에 전치사 for를 쓴다.

05 ⟨play+the+악기명⟩이므로 정관사 the를 쓴다.

06 교통수단을 나타내는 명사와 by를 함께 쓸 때는 명사 앞에 관사를 쓰지 않는다.

07 '한 달에 한 번'은 once a month로 나타내므로 부정관사 a를 쓴다.

08 첫 번째 빈칸에는 과거를 나타내는 last month가 있으므로 과거형인 didn't walk가 와야 하고, 두 번째 빈칸에는 '요즈음'이라는 의미의 these days가 있고 주어가 3인칭 단수인 he이므로 현재형 walks가 와야 한다.

09 첫 번째 빈칸에는 '너의 것'이라는 의미의 소유대명사 yours가 와야 하고, 두 번째 빈칸에는 뒤에 명사 new bike가 있으므로 '나의'라는 의미의 소유격 my가 와야 한다.

10 일상적인 행동을 나타내므로 현재시제를 써야 한다. 주어가 모두 3인칭 단수인 my mother와 my father이므로, 동사는 모두 3인칭 단수 현재형의 형태로 쓴다.

11 주어가 3인칭 단수인 She이므로 ⟨is going to+동사원형⟩으로 쓴다.

12 주어가 3인칭 단수인 Paul이므로 ⟨has to+동사원형⟩으로 쓴다.

13 권유의 표현인 ⟨Let's ~.⟩는 '우리 ~하지 않을래?'라는 의미의 ⟨Why don't we ~?⟩로 바꾸어 쓸 수 있다.

14 money가 셀 수 없는 명사이므로 첫 번째 빈칸에는 '거의 없는'의 뜻을 나타내는 little이 와야 하고, coins가 셀 수 있는 명사이므로 두 번째 빈칸에는 '약간의'의 뜻을 나타내는 a few가 와야 한다.

15 의문사가 주어일 때는 ⟨의문사+동사 ~?⟩의 어순이 되어야 하므로 Who sent를 쓴다.

16 ⟨보기⟩와 ②의 must는 '~임이 틀림없다'라는 강한 추측을 나타내는 반면, 나머지는 모두 '~해야 한다'라는 의무를 나타낸다.

17 이어지는 답변에서 시각을 말하고 있으므로 첫 번째 빈칸에는 '몇 시에'를 묻는 What time을 쓴다. 이어지는 답변에서 once or twice a week라는 빈도를 말하고 있으므로 두 번째 빈칸에는 '얼마나 자주'를 묻는 How often을 쓴다.

18 첫 번째 빈칸에는 'A이거나 B'를 나타내는 ⟨either A or B⟩의 or가 와야 하고, 두 번째 빈칸에는 '…해라, 그러지 않으면 ~할 것이다'라는 의미를 나타내는 ⟨명령문+or ~⟩의 or가 와야 한다.

19 첫 번째 빈칸에는 진주어 to eat 이하를 대신하는 가주어 It이 와야 하고, 두 번째 빈칸에는 시간을 나타낼 때 쓰는 비인칭 주어 It이 와야 한다.

20 '~하게 보이다'는 ⟨look+형용사⟩이므로 부사 happily는 형용사 happy가 되어야 한다.

21 감탄문은 ⟨What+a/an+형용사+명사(+주어+동사)!⟩ 또는 ⟨How+형용사/부사(+주어+동사)!⟩로 나타낸다. 복수명사 dolls가 있으므로 빈칸에는 What beautiful dolls가 와야 한다.

22 plan은 to부정사를 목적어로 취하는 동사이므로 뒤에 동명사 working이 올 수 없다.

23 ②의 cutting은 현재진행형 ⟨be동사+v-ing⟩로 쓰인 현재분사이고 나머지는 모두 동명사이다.

24 '그녀는 무례하기 때문에 사람들은 그녀를 싫어한다.'라는 의미가 되도록 she is rude 앞에 이유를 나타내는 접속사 because를 쓴다. 이유를 나타내는 부사절은 문장의 앞이나 뒤에 올 수 있다. (문장의 앞에 올 때는 부사절 뒤에 쉼표를 쓴다.)

25 지각동사(hear)는 목적격 보어로 동사원형 또는 현재분사를 쓰므로 knocks는 knock 또는 knocking이 되어야 한다.

26 (c) '어떻게 ~할지'는 〈how+to부정사〉의 형태로 쓴다.
(d) 형용사와 to부정사가 함께 -thing으로 끝나는 대명사를 수식할 때는 〈대명사(something)+형용사(important)+to부정사(to tell you)〉의 어순으로 쓴다.

27 (1) Jake는 55kg이고 Tom은 52kg이므로 형용사 heavy의 비교급을 써서 heavier than으로 나타낸다.
(2) Tom은 52kg이고 Steve는 60kg이므로 형용사 light의 비교급을 써서 lighter than으로 나타낸다.
(3) Steve가 세 학생 중 가장 체중이 많이 나가므로 형용사 heavy의 최상급을 써서 the heaviest로 나타낸다.

총괄평가 3회

01 ① **02** ⑤ **03** ④ **04** ③ **05** Yes, it is **06** ④ **07** ④ **08** ⑤ **09** these stamps to me **10** ③ **11** ② **12** I found it boring **13** ⑤ **14** three times a day **15** ④ **16** ② **17** ① **18** ④
19 one of the most popular songs
20 homework do → homework to do / will finish → finish **21** ③ **22** ③ **23** (1) but I don't have enough money (2) and I checked my email (3) or I will have mushroom pizza

01 '너는 ~하고 있니?'라며 현재진행형을 사용해 묻는 질문에 대한 부정의 답이므로, I'm not이 와야 한다.

02 과거를 나타내는 yesterday가 있으므로 leave의 과거형인 left가 와야 한다.

03 우유와 오렌지 주스 둘 중 '어느 것'을 더 좋아하는지 묻고 있는 선택 의문문이므로 의문사 Which가 와야 한다.

04 expect는 목적격 보어로 to부정사를 취하므로 to send가 와야 한다.

05 부정 의문문에 긍정의 의미로 답할 때는 Yes로 답하므로, Yes, it is를 쓴다.

06 조동사 will의 부정형 won't가 쓰인 문장의 부가 의문문이므로 will he?가 되어야 한다.

07 〈보기〉의 문장은 'Peter는 Sarah만큼 키가 크지 않다.'라는 뜻이므로 ④ 'Peter는 Sarah보다 키가 작다.'와 같은 의미이다.

08 허가를 구하는 May I는 Can I로 바꾸어 쓸 수 있다.

09 〈show+간접목적어(me)+직접목적어(these stamps)〉의 4형식 문장을 같은 뜻의 3형식 문장으로 바꿀 때 간접목적어 앞에 전치사 to를 써야 하므로 show these stamps to me가 알맞다.

10 '~일 리가 없다'라는 강한 부정적 추측이므로 조동사 cannot[can't]가 와야 한다.

11 '약간'의 의미로 긍정의 평서문에 쓰이는 부정대명사는 some이다.

12 '나는 그것이 지루하다는 것을 알게 되었다'라는 의미의 5형식 문장으로, 〈주어(I)+동사(found)+목적어(it)+목적격 보어(boring)〉의 어순으로 쓴다.

13 〈보기〉와 ⑤의 to부정사는 감정의 원인을 나타내는 부사적 용법의 to부정사이다. ①은 주어로 쓰인 명사적 용법, ②는 대명사를 수식하는 형용사적 용법, ③은 보어로 쓰인 명사적 용법, ④는 목적어로 쓰인 명사적 용법의 to부정사이다.

14 '하루에 세 번'은 three times a day로 쓴다.

15 첫 번째 빈칸에는 주어가 It이고 과거를 나타내는 yesterday가 있으므로 be동사의 과거형 was가 와야 하고, 두 번째 빈칸에는 주어가 it이고 현재를 나타내는 now가 있으므로 be동사의 현재형 is가 와야 한다.

16 refuse는 to부정사를 목적어로 취하는 동사이므로 첫 번째 빈칸에는 to come이 와야 하고, avoid는 동명사를 목적어로 취하는 동사이므로 두 번째 빈칸에는 talking이 와야 한다.

17 비교급을 강조할 때는 비교급 앞에 much, a lot, even, still, far 등을 쓴다. very는 비교급 앞에 올 수 없다.

18 ④ 일상적인 행동을 나타내므로 현재시제를 써야 하고, 주어가 3인칭 단수인 He이므로 gets up이 되어야 한다.

19 '가장 ~한 … 중의 하나'는 〈one of the+최상급+복수명사〉로 나타낸다.

20 '할 숙제'라는 의미로 homework 뒤에 형용사적 용법의 to부정사 to do를 써야 한다. 조건을 나타내는 부사절에서는 현재시제로 미래를 나타내므로 will finish는 finish가 되어야 한다.

21 이어지는 답변에서 '지하철을 탔다'라는 공항에 간 방법을 말

하고 있으므로, 첫 번째 빈칸에는 방법을 묻는 의문사 How가 와야 하고, 두 번째 빈칸에는 '스키를 타는 법'을 나타내는 〈how+to부정사〉의 how가 와야 한다.

22 (c) want는 to부정사를 목적어로 취하는 동사이므로 playing은 to play가 되어야 한다.
(d) 앞에 나온 my camera와 같은 종류의 불특정한 것을 나타내는 부정대명사 one을 써야 한다.

23 (1) '사진 앨범을 사고 싶지만 충분한 돈이 없다.'라는 의미가 되도록 '그러나'의 의미를 가진 접속사 but과 I don't have enough money를 쓴다.
(2) '컴퓨터를 켜서 내 이메일을 확인했다.'라는 의미가 되도록 '그리고'의 의미를 가진 접속사 and와 I checked my email을 쓴다.
(3) '크림 파스타를 먹거나 버섯 피자를 먹을 것이다.'라는 의미가 되도록 '또는'의 의미를 가진 접속사 or와 I will have mushroom pizza를 쓴다

MEMO

MEMO

MEMO

MEMO

MEMO

문제로
마스터하는
중학영문법